THE

LONG JOURNEY HOME

THE
LONG JOURNEY HOME

RE-VISIONING THE MYTH OF
DEMETER AND PERSEPHONE
FOR OUR TIME

EDITED BY

Christine Downing

SHAMBHALA

Boston & London

1994

Shambhala Publications, Inc.
Horticultural Hall
300 Massachusetts Avenue
Boston, Massachusetts 02115

9 8 7 6 5 4 3 2 1

First Edition
Designed by Dede Cummings/IPA
Printed in the United States of America on acid-free paper ∞

Distributed in the United States by Random House, Inc.,
and in Canada by Random House of Canada Ltd

Library of Congress Cataloging-in-Publication Data

The Long journey home: re-visioning the myth of Demeter and
Persephone for our time/[edited by] Christine Downing. —1st ed.
p.   cm.
Includes bibliographical references.
ISBN 0-87773-937-4 (pbk.: alk. paper)
1. Demeter (Greek deity)   2. Persephone (Greek deity)
3. Mythology, Greek—Psychological aspects.   4. Mothers and
daughters.   5. Women—Psychology.   I. Downing, Christine, 1931–
BL820.C5L66   1994   93-39134
292.1'3—dc20   CIP

Dedicated to Carol P. Christ,
who blessed
my first written reflections
on Persephone
in a way that has nurtured
all my subsequent writing

CONTENTS

PART THREE: CONTEMPORARY WOMEN'S RETELLINGS

ACKNOWLEDGMENTS

I WOULD LIKE to thank Charles Ascher and Jonathan Young
of Pacifica Graduate Institute for the invitation to lecture on paths
to the power of myth, which first suggested to me the appropriate-
ness of gathering together recent reinterpretations and re-visionings of the myth of Demeter and Persephone.

The enthusiasm of Karen Brown, William Doty, and David L.
Miller for this project helped me decide to go forward with it.
River Malcolm's sense of its importance has sustained me
throughout the months devoted to its completion.

I would also like to thank the many contributors to this volume
who agreed to let me use their work and most especially those
who wrote essays specifically for inclusion here: Carol Christ,
Naomi Goldenberg, Gloria Orenstein, Annis Pratt, and Laura
Simms.

I feel a special debt and want publicly to express an apology to
some writers who had graciously agreed to the inclusion of essays
that my publisher's sense of the appropriate length for this volume
forced me to exclude: Phyllis Chesler, Genia Pauli-Haddon, Mara
Lynn Keller, and Betty DeShong Meador. Some indication of
their understanding of the myth and the rituals associated with it
is given in the introductions to the various subsections of this
book. The list of further readings at the end of the volume pro-

vides the bibliographic material that will enable readers to find these materials. This list also includes materials by Jane Harrison, C. G. Jung, and Carl Kerenyi that I had planned to include and had received permission to use but reluctantly agreed to leave out.

David Cohen came to my rescue when I was most devastated by the prospect of amputating my book by reminding me that I shouldn't have expected to put together a book about Persephone and Demeter without having to spend a few days in the underworld.

Once again Elaine Rother has helped me immeasurably: she has typed and retyped, made innumerable telephone calls, and prepared the many different versions of the manuscripts for mailing; she has celebrated with me when things have gone well and commiserated when they have not. I cannot imagine how, now that I have retired from San Diego State University and will soon move to the Northwest, I will manage to put a book together without her help. I also want to thank Kim Berling for her careful photocopying of the previously published material included in the volume and of many other relevant materials not included.

I want to thank Jonathan Green for encouraging me to submit a book proposal to Shambhala Publications and Emily Hilburn Sell for her editorial supervision of the project.

I dedicated my first book, *The Goddess: Mythological Images of the Feminine,* to my mother and my daughter. This book, too, emerges out of my sense of how much I owe to both and how deeply I love them.

THE
LONG JOURNEY HOME

INTRODUCTION

I HAVE LONG BEEN fascinated by the sacred myths and rituals of initiation through which women and men of the ancient world were helped to discover and become themselves. I have long believed that remembering and reimagining these traditions might help us do likewise. Like James Hillman, I believe that although myths don't tell us how, they help us to question, imagine, go deeper.[1] Myths help us to enter the complexity of our situations more deeply, with more love of the perplexities themselves and of those caught up in them.

The myth of Demeter and Persephone stirs the imagination of almost all who hear it. Greek rituals associated with it recognized its relevance to the cycle of vegetal life, to the human fear of death and hope for immortality, to the deep bonds that exist among women, particularly mothers and daughters. Some of these rituals were open only to women, others also included men. The myth appears to have particular resonance for women, and many seem to feel that in some sense it is *the* myth for them, as the Oedipus myth may be *the* myth for men. Yet we find amazingly different meanings in it.

My own involvement with Greek mythology and particularly with Greek goddesses was initiated almost fifteen years ago by a dream that led me to remember how my myth-loving mother had welcomed me, her first child, a daughter born on the first day of spring, as *her* Persephone. Continued reflection on this memory and its significance for me as an adult woman led to my book *The Goddess*, in which, looking at the myth from the perspective of Persephone, I contrasted my view with that of the Homeric "Hymn to Demeter," which (as the title suggests) adopts Demeter's view, identifying with her grief over the loss of her daughter and her assumption that time spent in the underworld can only be understood negatively. I, by contrast, spoke of the importance of Persephone's being taken out of the role of daughter and taking her own place as goddess of the underworld. I focused on how Persephone initiates us into a recognition of the underworld as a sacred realm and thus into a different relation to periods during our lifetime when we are abducted from our preoccupation with worldly tasks and with others and into a different relation to death.

In the intervening years, I have become fascinated with how this myth has compelled the attention of many other women, and with how differently each of us reads it. This has given me a renewed appreciation of the power of a myth to engender new mythmaking (which is what demonstrates that a myth is still functioning as a myth) and has taught me to value other dimensions of this myth, other ways in which it is pertinent to the lives of contemporary women, and to pay more attention to its social and cosmological aspects as well as its psychological and metaphysical ones.

Some women have found in this myth resources for the imaginal re-creation of a prepatriarchal matristic, that is, woman centered, world. Many, concentrating on the myth's account of Demeter's love of Persephone, have seen it primarily in terms of how it valorizes the beauty and power of the mother-daughter bond. Others have focused on Hades' abduction of Persephone and read the myth as primarily a story about paternal violation; about rape, incest, abuse; about male intrusion into women's mysteries; about the rise of patriarchy and the suppression of goddess religion.

Yet this same myth has also been interpreted as one that might help move us beyond the fantasy of a conflict-free world ruled by an all-giving and all-powerful mother, beyond the illusion of female innocence and perfect love. It has been seen as representing a necessary initiation for women that frees them from being defined by the roles of mother or daughter and as teaching the necessity of coming to terms with loss and limitation and with experiences that provoke rage and grief.

Most feminists have focused on ways of understanding the myth that reveal its particular relevance to women's lives, but many have recognized that the myth is not just about women's psychology but also about gender issues, not just about mothers and daughters but also about the relations between women and men. Some have gone further and suggested that the myth may be profoundly important to the self-understanding of men as well as of women. They note that the Eleusinian mysteries, the most important rites associated with these two goddesses, were open to all, men and women, and that all initiates regardless of gender temporarily adopted names with feminine endings, as though the transformed understanding of human relationships and of death that the mysteries provided required entrance into a female perspective.

An even more inclusive interpretation is suggested by some ecofeminists who, moving beyond seeing the myth primarily through a psychological lens, emphasize its relevance to their concerns about the earth's renewal.

Exposure to these many different perspectives underlies my own reengagement with this myth, which I truly felt I had fully honored long ago. I have come to see the story of Demeter and Persephone as providing us with resources for the articulation of a vision sorely needed by all of us, a vision that may move us beyond an identification with peculiarly female or male perspectives but is nonetheless unquestionably informed by some of the things women have learned from the matristic past, from our dreams, from one another, and from our bodies. I see myself and most of the other women drawn to this myth as not interested only in learning what it meant *then,* in the world of classical Greece or in an imagined prepatriarchal world, but in reimagining it; that is, in using the myth to help us imagine forward to a possible postpatriarchal world.

This imagining forward involves a careful listening to and honoring of the many different explications spawned by the ancient myth. I believe the differences among our interpretations make manifest the diversity that exists within contemporary feminism, a diversity that I celebrate, for feminism as I understand it means conversation, not agreement. The various interpretations contradict, complement, complicate, and ultimately enrich one another. Just as no one version of a myth is the "real" one, just as a myth *is* its many variants, so no one interpretation is the "right" one; the myth *means* these many different understandings of it. Thus this book gathers together a rich cornucopia of these rereadings of the Demeter/Persephone myth; together they *are* the myth as it lives among us today.

To appreciate fully the diversity represented by these contemporary re-visionings requires an engagement with the ancient sources on which these rereadings are based and also with the traditional nineteenth- and early twentieth-century interpretations by which our more recent ones are inevitably informed. Thus the first part of this book includes translations of the two primary ancient literary versions of the myth, the Homeric hymn and Ovid's account in the *Metamorphoses.* My introductory essays in this part of the book also take note of alternative versions of the myth suggested by other literary sources and artistic representations and by the relevant rituals, particularly the Thesmophoria and the Eleusinian mysteries, for attending to a myth entails attending to all its variants; it presumes a love of the variety, a love of the details, a sense of the connections to ritual and to art. Attending to myth also means remembering that a myth is first of all a story, and that stories are told in order to be retold.

Each retelling in some sense presumes the many retellings that precede it. Thus the second part of the book includes an overview of the influential interpretations put forward in the nineteenth century and provides a somewhat more detailed consideration of early depth-psychological interpretations of the myth.

The emphasis of this anthology, however, falls on interpretations put forward in recent decades, particularly, although not exclusively, interpretations proposed by women. We begin with two important precursors of contemporary feminist re-visionings, the imagist poet H.D. and the poet and novelist Meridel Le Sueur. These are followed by a wide range of contemporary voices—psychologists and theologians, feminist theorists, classicists, poets and storytellers. I have included some of my own work and that of friends as well as strangers. I have tried to provide a helpful order and useful contexts, but ultimately I hope to have allowed each piece to *speak* and to contribute to a polyphonic appreciation of the myth.

NOTE

1. James Hillman, *ReVisioning Psychology* (New York: Harper and Row, 1975), 158.

PART ONE

THE
ANCIENT SOURCES

THE
GREEK LITERARY TRADITION

Dɪʀᴇᴄᴛ ᴇɴɢᴀɢᴇᴍᴇɴᴛ with the ancient sources is a pre-requisite for any informed understanding of more recent interpretations of the Demeter/Persephone myth—although ideally one moves back and forth between the earliest retellings and the most recent, and it does not really matter where one begins. There is no original version, no recoverable first telling. Our apprehension of the Greek and Roman versions of the myth is expanded and deepened as we discover what others have seen in them, as our response to contemporary interpretations is clarified as we compare them with our own sense of the sources they adduce.

Thus it is important to look at the role Demeter and Persephone and the myths and rituals associated with them played in the classical and Hellenistic periods. I aim in this first part of the book to provide factual information about the ancient literary and ritual traditions rather than interpretations of them, though of course any account of the classical world involves a judgment about which scholars to rely on and what of their contributions to emphasize. There is still much disagreement among scholars about how to understand and put in proper context not only architecture, reliefs, and vase paintings but even literary sources.

And, or course, it is important to remember not only that most of the recognized scholars in this field have been male and thus have inevitably looked at these materials from their own male perspective but, even more significant, that the evidences we have from the ancient world reflect the perspectives and values of a patriarchal culture, and that this is especially true of the most easily available sources, the literary ones. Nonetheless, the Homeric "Hymn to Demeter" and the extant traditions about the all-women's ritual, the Thesmophoria, may give us more access than most classical material does to women's perspectives, since the hymn looks at the story of Persephone's abduction from a female perspective, from Demeter's viewpoint, and the Thesmophoria is generally regarded as one of the oldest and least changed of Attic rites. Contemporary feminist scholars may seek to penetrate beyond this evidences to an earlier stratum of the tradition, but it is these materials that they must look through ar.d reinterpret. They represent the inevitable beginning points for any interpretation.

Although all the literary and ritual allusions show the two goddesses, Demeter and Persephone, already connected, their names suggest that this was not always so. *Persephonia* is a non–Indo-European name whose precise meaning is not agreed upon but which connects Persephone to Perseis and Perses, the Titan grandmother and father of Hekate, and to Perseus, the slayer of Medusa. As Lewis Richard Farnell says, the name must always have had "an ominous ring," would always have suggested an association with death.[1] Persephone must always, even in pre-Greek cult, have been an underworld deity.

Demeter (Da meter), on the other hand, is Greek; this goddess must have come to what we know as Greece with the Aryan invaders. Although earlier scholars often understood the name to signify "earth mother," it is now generally taken to mean "grain mother." Demeter's name distinguishes her from Ge (or Gaia), the primordial mother goddess whose name directly communicates her association with the earth, with all that grows and not only with cultivated crops, for *ge* is also the common noun meaning "earth." Yet there are hints in the traditions associated with Demeter that she, too, might have originated as a less differentiated great goddess, hints that are picked up in the late classical Orphic literature, which often conflates Demeter and Rhea, a goddess who by Homer's time is represented as an intermediary between Gaia and Demeter, daughter to one and mother of the other, but who was clearly once upon a time a great goddess in her own right.

Even in the archaic period we find Demeter associated with a maiden goddess, Kore. This Greek appellation simply means "maiden"; it is the female form of *kouros,* "youth." Some believe *Kore* may have originally signified simply "the young Demeter." Farnell regards Demeter and Kore as originally identical pre-Homeric offshoots of Ge—each has both agrarian and chthonic (underworld) aspects. Eventually the two distinct names led to there being two distinct goddesses: Demeter, a mature mother goddess who is regularly accompanied by Kore, the maiden.[2] Thus the bond between Demeter and Kore is not due to a joining of two originally separate cults but rather to a sense that mother/maiden (or mother/daughter) are inextricably linked. (As we'll see, interpreters disagree as to whether Persephone is to be viewed primarily as Demeter's maidenly aspect or as her daughter.)

Sometime later, but well before Homer, the Demeter/Kore cult was combined with the pre-Greek cult dedicated to Persephone, probably because of a felt connection between Kore and Persephone perhaps based on the idea that a death goddess will also be a source of fruitfulness. Gunther Zuntz suggests that the maidenly goddess of the first fruit of spring may have already been associated with a tale in which she spent the barren portion of the year in the underworld. Perhaps the myth about Kore's abduction originated in order to create an identity between this seasonal visitor to the underworld and its dread queen.[3] Once accomplished, the identification of Persephone and Kore is complete. Scholars have made all kinds of attempts to impose a logical distinction between Kore and Persephone, to suggest, for example, that the name *Kore* is used only for the yet unabducted goddess of spring,

Persephone only for Hades' bride; unfortunately, the ancient texts seem never to be so consistent in their usage.

The amalgamation of the Persephone and Demeter cults may also have been facilitated by the chthonic aspect of Demeter that seems to have been part of her aboriginal character rather than a derivation of her later association with Persephone. From early on she was known as Demeter Chthonia, as Demeter Erinyes, and as Black Demeter. There is a very ancient temple to Demeter at Phigaleia set within a cave, a locale with definite chthonic implications. Thus Demeter, even apart from Persephone, was seen as having a vindictive, gloomy, death-related aspect. Farnell even suggests that the reunion between Demeter and Persephone celebrated in the Thesmophoria ritual must have been imagined as taking place in the underworld. This representation, "older than and alien to classical legend," assumes a descent of Demeter rather than an ascent of Persephone,[4] imagines a Demeter, unlike the Demeter of the Homeric hymn, not confined to the upper world.

Gunther Zuntz, on the other hand, notes that in ancient Sicily Persephone was so emphatically a goddess of death that there was really no room in the tale for Demeter. The entire focus in the Sicilian version of the myth is on Persephone's abduction and her becoming queen of the underworld. There is no return, no reunion.[5]

The essays included in this book tend to emphasize the agrarian and chthonic significance of the worship of "the two goddesses" (as they were called at Eleusis), but we should at least take cognizance of its political dimension. As the goddess who introduced humankind to agriculture, Demeter is associated with the establishment of polis-centered society. "Cities are the gift of Demeter." Her ancient cult name, Demeter Thesmophoros, may mean "one who gives pleasing ordinances to cities"; many scholars have seen it as implying a recognition of how a stable, social world derives from the settled life of cultivators. Farnell suggests that Demeter may have been the deity around whom the earliest

Greek religious confederacy arose (though contrary to the view of some of the feminist scholars whose work appears later in this volume, he is at pains to assert that this transtribal cult is not a remnant of an archaic matriarchal society but very much part of the development toward the patriarchal world depicted in Homer).[6] What is not in doubt is that Athens used the Eleusinian mysteries to make itself the center of the pan-Hellenic world.[7]

Even in the ancient world, each telling of the myth served a different meaning. Probably the oldest meaning was about Demeter as a grain goddess, about the seasonal cycle and the introduction of agriculture. There are hints of this meaning in parts of the Thesmophoria ritual and in the hymn, though it is not central to either. By the time of Homer, the Greek gods and goddesses were not viewed as aspects of the natural world but as humans writ large; in the Homeric hymn the myth about Demeter, Persephone, and Hades is already understood as primarily about interpersonal relationships.

The earliest literary references to the myth are found in the epic literature. In Homer (whose works most classicists regard as products of the eighth century BCE) neither goddess is important. Persephone appears as goddess of the underworld (Circe, for example, sends Odysseus to consult Teiresias in the "house of Hades and Persephone") and Demeter only as goddess of the grain. Neither really enters into the action of the poems. There is no reference to Persephone's abduction or even to a connection between the two goddesses. From the Homeric perspective the only real life takes place in the upper, daylight world; the only meaningful afterlife is "glory," a heroic reputation among the still living.

In Hesiod's *Theogony* (usually dated as having been composed around 700 BCE), Demeter's birth, her being swallowed by her father, Kronos, who feared that someday one of his children might usurp his power, and her eventual rescue by her youngest sibling, Zeus, are described. Later in the epic Hesiod names Demeter Zeus's fourth consort:

Next Zeus entered the bed of Demeter, the lady who nourished
all life, and she gave birth to Persephone, with her white arms,
whom Hades, with the permission of Zeus, the lord of wisdom,
took forcibly from her mother.
(lines 912–14)

This is the first extant literary reference to the abduction.

Toward the end of the *Theogony* (in a section devoted to liai-
sons between goddesses and mortal men, which many scholars
consider the work of a later poet) there is a reference to another
liaison of Demeter's:

> Demeter, the great goddess, united in sweet love with the hero
> Iasion, in a fallow field ploughed three times, in the fertile land
> of Crete; she bore Plutos (Wealth), a good spirit who goes every-
> where on land and on the sea's broad back, enriching and giving
> great prosperity to whomever he meets and joins hands with.[8]
> (lines 969–74)

Homer, in another version of this same incident, pictures Calypso
taunting Zeus with always being resentful of goddesses who sleep
with mortal men and would happily stay true to them.

> So it was when Demeter of the lovely hair, yielding
> to her desire, lay down with Iasion and loved him
> in a thrice-turned field, it was not long before this was made
>   known
> to Zeus, who struck him down with a cast of the shining
>   thunderbolt.[9]
> (lines 125–28)

Both Hesiod and Homer emphasize not just Demeter's willing-
ness but her active desire for her lover—an image of real love
between women and men utterly absent from the more familiar
Homeric "Hymn to Demeter."

The Homeric "Hymn to Demeter" played a central role in expressing and forming the ancient world's understanding of the

goddesses. Many twentieth-century reinterpretations of the myth are based almost entirely on this hymn, or else on it and on what we know of the Eleusinian mysteries whose initiation it describes and with which it seems to be closely associated. The ascription of the Homeric hymns to Homer signifies that they belong to the epic rather than devotional tradition, to a literary rather than a cultic context. Composed by professional bards, over a long interval beginning in the eighth century, the hymns are clearly stylistically influenced by both Homer and Hesiod. The "Hymn to Demeter" was probably written in the seventh century BCE; its omission of any reference to Athens suggests that at the time of its composition Eleusis was still an independent cult center.

Yet despite its prominence, the hymn's version of the Demeter/ Persephone myth never received canonical status. The Orphic tradition included a very different version, one with which fifth- and fourth-century Athenians such as Sophocles, Euripides, Aristophanes, and Plato were clearly familiar. Unfortunately, most ancient Orphic texts have been preserved only in fragmentary form, and most of the literary references to the Orphic versions of the Demeter/Persephone mythologem during the classical period are indirect, perhaps because the role this myth played in the Orphic mysteries made it a sacred secret.[10] Certainly there are important parallels between the myth of Persephone's abduction and the myth about Orpheus, the eponymous founder of the cult, which focuses on his descent into Hades to retrieve his dead bride, Eurydice.

It is also likely that there may never have been a single coherent "official" Orphic version of the Persephone myth. In the Orphic versions the gods and goddesses seem to keep taking one another's places.[11] Rhea and Demeter are identified, as are Demeter and Persephone; Zeus, Hades, Poseidon, and perhaps even Dionysos all appear in the role of abductor and rapist.

An Orphic tradition represents Zeus in the shape of a serpent violently attacking and raping his mother, Rhea, who had become Demeter after Zeus's birth.[12] Persephone is thus the child of Zeus and Rhea/Demeter. Demeter then hides her daughter in a Sicilian cave guarded by two serpents. But one day while Persephone (now a full-grown maiden) is weaving, Zeus enters the cave in the shape of a serpent, rapes his daughter, and impregnates Persephone with Zagreus/Dionysos, who, according to Orphic belief, is to be his successor, the fifth ruler of the world. (Just to complicate the picture further, Kerenyi cites an Orphic hymn according to which this was not a rape at all but, rather, was all done as Demeter had set it up to happen![13]) Trying somehow to work in the more-familiar tale about Persephone, the Orphic version goes on to say that Hades abducts her (or that Zeus cedes her to Hades) only after she has given birth to Zagreus/Dionysos.[14]

To get a full sense of the dense complexity of the Orphic vision, we need also to note a variant according to which it is Dionysos who rapes Persephone (as the Heracleitos fragment that asserts the identity of Hades and Dionysos and even the Homeric hymn that sets the abduction at the "Nysian plain" may both be hinting). There is an Orphic hymn in which Demeter herself goes to the underworld as part of her search for Persephone.[15] We should also note the tradition that tells of Poseidon raping Demeter, who then gives birth to the always-unnamed underworld goddess (clearly a Persephone figure) whose cult title was Despoina, Mistress.[16] The Baubo incident, the story of grieving Demeter being made to laugh by an obscenely dancing old woman, seems also to be an Orphic contribution to the tale. (In the more sedate Homeric hymn, Baubo's place is taken by Iambe, who indulges only in verbal indecency.)

Thus Persephone plays an important role in Orphism, and Orphism in turn seems to have influenced the Eleusinian cult, since it is only after the rise of Orphism that the Eleusinian rite came to climax around a cry welcoming the birth of a child called Bromios, who is often confused with Zagreus/Dionysos despite the radical difference in basic presuppositions between the Eleusinian and the Orphic mysteries. In Orphism, salvation was won through asceticism and a world-denying morality; at Eleusis, initiation itself was experienced as transformative.[17]

Plato and the Greek tragedians were clearly aware of at least some of these Orphic variant versions of the myth; to them Demeter and Persephone and Hades are not simply the figures portrayed in the Homeric hymn.[18] A fragment attributed to Sophocles makes evident how highly he valued the Eleusinian ritual: "Thrice happy are those of mortals, who having seen these rites depart for Hades; for to them alone is it granted to have true life there; to the rest all there is evil."[19] Nonetheless, his plays suggest the possibility of an initiation into a willing readiness for death won through a soul-searching engagement with the ineluctable tragedy of life rather than through cultic participation. In *Oedipus at Colonos*, the description of Oedipus's death is resonant with allusions to the myth and rituals associated with Demeter and Persephone. The play takes place by Demeter's grove in Colonos. As Oedipus prepares to die, he tells Theseus, who is to be his only witness, that he must never disclose what happens or where:

> These things are mysteries, not to be explained;
> · · · · · · · · · · · · · · · · ·
> Keep it secret always, and when you come
> To the end of life, then you must hand it on
> To your most cherished son, and he in turn
> Must teach it to his heir, and so forever.[20]
>
> (lines 1526, 1530–33)

In his *Helen*, Euripides includes a version of Persephone's abduction that clearly follows the Orphic pattern of conflating Rhea and Demeter. Demeter becomes the "Mountain Mother," surrounded by the "mutter of drums and rattles," and in Euripides' version it is Aphrodite (not Iambe or Baubo) whose song persuades grieving Demeter to smile.[21]

The most important late classical version of the Demeter and Persephone myth is the one included in Ovid's *Metamorphoses*.[22]

Ovid's writings, composed during the first decade of our era in Augustan Rome, twenty years after Virgil's *Aeneid,* are valuable both as an incomparable repository of inherited mythology and as a marvelously sophisticated ironic reworking of that inheritance. To appreciate his work fully requires that we be acquainted with the familiar versions of the stories Ovid retells and thus alert to the subtle ironies of his retellings, for Ovid is a highly conscious artist for whom myths are clearly first and foremost good stories. In his writing, the gods (and the goddesses, too) are reduced to human psychological terms and seen as often arbitrary and cruel. Ovid seeks to make manifest myth's power to illumine human psychology and thus to demonstrate mythology's enduring power even for those who no longer believe in its gods.

Although the more famous of Ovid's retellings of the Demeter/ Persephone myth appears in his *Metamorphoses,* he includes another version in his *Fasti*[23] (which he is believed to have been working on both before and simultaneously with the *Metamorphoses,* but which he never completed). "In my narration," he begins this less-familiar retelling, "you will read much that you knew before; a few particulars will be new to you." Whereas in traditional cultures the emphasis falls on faithfully accurate retelling, here Ovid communicates his belief that the introduction of new details, a new perspective, is a necessary part of good storytelling. Thus we are invited to pay particular attention to the newly invented variations on a familiar tale.

First: the setting of the abduction is different. The nymph Arethusa has invited the mothers of the gods to a picnic. Demeter[24] comes, and so also does her daughter Persephone in the company of her usual companions. The maidens go off into the meadow and begin picking flowers (Ovid goes on and on here describing the bouquets each maiden gathered). Persephone strays off; by chance none of the others follow. Hades, described as her "father's brother," sees her and immediately carries her off. Persephone calls out for her mother, but no one hears her.

Soon her companions miss her; when they shout that she has

disappeared, Demeter hears them and immediately sets out in search of her daughter, hurrying like "Thracian maenads rush with streaming hair." Demeter follows her daughter's footprints and might have succeeded in finding the girl right then had not some pigs come along to foil the trail. She cries out (as desperately, Ovid says, as Philomela cried out for Itys), alternately calling "Persephone" and "daughter," but doesn't get a response with either name. She asks everyone, "Did you see a girl pass this way?"

Eventually she makes her way to Attica and there for the first time pauses in her search. For days she sits motionless on the Sorrowful Rock disguised as an old woman, until Celeus (depicted here as an old shepherd) and his daughter wander by. She greets him: "Be happy! May a parent's joy be yours forever! My daughter has been taken from me. Alas! How much better is your lot than mine!" His sympathetic response leads her to agree to go home with him to see if she can help his dangerously ill son. Upon arrival at their simple cabin she greets the mother, Metanira, and kisses her sick boy, who immediately begins to get better. After the household goes to sleep Demeter puts the child in the fire, as in the more familiar versions, and as usual the mother awakens and interrupts the magic spell designed to make the child immortal. Here Ovid lays less stress than usual on the goddess's anger, more on her disappointment at the failure of her plan, and relates that she promises that despite what has happened Triptolemus (in this version it is he, not Demophoon, who was put in the fire) will be the first to plow and reap and sow.

Demeter then takes off in her dragon-pulled cart, and Ovid provides very detailed descriptions of her flying over all the known world and also through the heavens, asking of all about her daughter's fate, until finally the sun tells her what happened. Demeter promptly accosts Zeus the Thunderer: "You ought to be concerned too, after all you're her father. Persephone didn't deserve a robber husband, nor is it right that we should get a son-in-law in this fashion. What good is it that you're king of heaven if something like this can happen. But I don't care about vengeance, I just want my daughter back." Zeus replies that there's nothing shameful about Hades as a son-in-law, after all, he's just as royal as Zeus himself, but agrees that if she's determined to break the contracted bonds of wedlock he'll try to arrange that Persephone be returned to her mother, provided that she has kept her fast while in the underworld. If not, the marriage is irrevocable. Alas! Hermes returns to tell the parents that the ravished maiden has broken her fast with three pomegranate seeds. Demeter, as bereft as if her daugher had just that moment been taken from her, announces that she too is going to Hades, but at that point Zeus promises that Persephone will spend half of each year in heaven. "Then at last Ceres recovered her looks and her spirits, and set wreaths of corn ears on her hair; and the laggard fields yielded a plenteous harvest."

Ovid's other version of the tale, the one included in the *Metamorphoses,* is more complex and interesting. As always in reading Ovid, it is important to take note of the frame within which a particular tale is told. Here, the story of Persephone becomes a tale of a virgin's rape told by the virgin Muses to the virgin goddess Athene. The Muses have just confided to the goddess how easily frightened their virgin minds are. They have told her how once a fierce warrior called Pyreneus had tried to rape them but had killed himself falling from a high tower as he sought to follow them. They had managed to escape his pursuit by flying away.

Then they tell Athene about the time when they were challenged to a contest by the nine daughters of Pierus and describe both their rivals' song and that of Calliope, the Muse they chose to represent them. The song of the Pieriae praised Typhoeus and the other giants who challenged the Olympian gods and belittled the gods for in fright having concealed themselves from their rivals by adopting animal forms. Because her song was intended to be a response to that of her rivals, Calliope began with a reminder of Typhoeus's defeat by the gods, who in punishment imprisoned him under Sicily.

As the giant strives to free himself, the earth trembles, and even Hades is afraid it might split open and let daylight enter his realm and frighten its trembling ghosts. So he comes up on an inspection tour to make sure there are no weak spots. Aphrodite sees him and hatches a plot so that the underworld, as well as sea, earth, and sky, might come under her dominion and also so that the maiden Persephone won't escape her, as Athene and Artemis have, by staying a virgin forever. She sends Eros to inflame Hades with love for the maiden.

Thus Ovid frames the story so that the focus falls on Aphrodite as the instigator of all that occurs; Hades becomes her tool; the tale becomes a tale of power politics among the gods, not just of lust. (Ovid, I suspect, intends us to note allusions here to the *Aeneid*'s description of Aphrodite's role in bringing Aeneas and Dido together.)

Just as Aphrodite had planned, Hades sees Persephone and loves her and carries her away. Ovid's (or we might better say, Calliope's) version emphasizes Persephone's youth and innocence; Persephone is as upset by losing the flowers tucked in her apron as by the abduction. As one commentator puts it, "Persephone is no more than a frightened girl who wants her mother."[25] The previous exchange has made it evident that to the "virgin minds" of the Muses the abduction of Persephone will be viewed with horror as an unforgivable rape and that Calliope won't realize what her song is inadvertently suggesting about Demeter's own violence and cruelty. Ovid leaves it to us to decide whether Calliope's view of the events she recounts is the only way to understand them.

No doubt because this is the Muses' version, and the nymphs have been asked to judge between Calliope and the Pieriae, there are many nymphs in this telling of the tale. One, Cyane, sees the abduction and is so upset by it that she melts away in grief. The account of Demeter's panic and maenadlike frantic, vain searching puts much more emphasis on the goddess's anger than on her grief. A somewhat cheeky boy dares to tease her; she promptly turns him into a lizard. She doesn't just neglect the fields but actively disrupts agriculture. Another nymph, Arethusa, tells her, "Demeter, this is too much. I saw your daughter. She was sad but she was a queen."

Demeter goes to protest to Zeus, who tells her, "It was love; he's not a bad son-in-law. But if you insist, I'll arrange for her return—on one condition, that she has not eaten in the underworld." But, of course, it turns out that while in the underworld Persephone had innocently picked and eaten a pomegranate. (Here we cannot help but note the allusion to her earlier innocent picking of the narcissus; again there is a subtle criticism of Persephone's exaggerated—or feigned?—innocence.) In Ovid's version it isn't the eating that issues in Persephone's having henceforward to spend half of each year in the underworld but rather that the eating was seen. Ascalaphus happens to be nearby and he tells on her (and pays for being a tattler by becoming a screech owl).

After a description of the happy reunion between mother and daughter, Calliope's song returns to Arethusa and her successful flight from an attempted abduction. Calliope finishes by telling of Demeter instructing Triptolemus to teach humans how to sow grain.

Not too surprisingly, the nymphs who were to judge the contest voted for Calliope, who had presented them so favorably in her song (and the Pieriae become magpies because they had dared to protest the verdict); Athene, too, expresses her approval of the Muses' song. This episode is one of several in the *Metamorphoses* where Ovid reflects on the art of poetry (and thus indirectly on his own art). There are some obvious parallels between this contest and the weaving contest between Athene and Arachne, parallels that Athene is imagined as recognizing, for she is prompted to tell her story as soon as the Muses finish theirs. In both cases what is involved is a contest between human and divine artists. William Anderson thinks Ovid deliberately tells the story of Persephone's abduction awkwardly so readers will be led to doubt whether the Muses really deserved to win their contest.[26] Because we are given only the Muses' version of the Pieriae's song, it is presented in a highly condensed form, yet enough is said to suggest to any attentive reader some parallels between the song and Ovid's own poetry in earlier parts of his book. As Anderson says, Arachne and the Pieriae are no greater detractors of gods than Ovid himself. Ovid's identification with the human challengers turns the received stories upside down. In the case of the myth about Demeter and Persephone, we cannot help but see the goddesses differently from the vision of them suggested to us by the Homeric hymn. We cannot help but wonder about the extravagance of Demeter's rage and of Persephone's maidenly innocence.

NOTES

1. Lewis Richard Farnell, *The Cults of the Greek States,* vol. 3 (Chicago: Aegean Press [1906] 1971, 121.

2. Ibid., 117, 119, 121.

3. Gunther Zuntz, *Persephone* (Oxford: Oxford University Press, 1971), 75–77.

4. Farnell, *Cults,* 48–53, 62, 64, 96.

5. Zuntz, *Persephone,* 150, 401. This Sicilian tradition may lie behind Virgil's (in the *Georgics* 1.39) speaking of Proserpina as "loath to follow Ceres calling her back to earth."

6. Farnell, *Cults,* 72–73, 85.

7. George E. Mylonas, *Eleusis and the Eleusinian Mysteries* (Princeton: Princeton University Press, 1961), 100.

8. The quotations from the *Theogony* are from Norman O. Brown's translation (Indianapolis and New York: The Bobbs-Merrill Company, 1953).

9. The quotation is from Richmond Lattimore's translation of the *Odyssey* (New York: Harper and Row, 1977).

10. Mylonas, *Eleusis*, 290.

11. Carl Kerenyi, *The Gods of the Greeks* (London: Thames and Hudson, 1979), 231.

12. Mylonas, *Eleusis*, 291.

13. Kerenyi, *Gods*, 253.

14. Some of the peculiarly Orphic understandings of the myth are apparent in the Orphic "Hymn to Persephone" included in Apostolos N. Athanassakis, *The Orphic Hymns* (Missoula, Mont.: Scholars Press, 1977), 41, 43.

15. C. Kerenyi, *Eleusis: Archetypal Image of Mother and Daughter* (New York: Pantheon, 1967), 43.

16. Ibid., 31.

17. W. K. C. Guthrie, *The Greeks and Their Gods* (Boston: Beacon Press, 1981), 154.

18. Indeed, it has been suggested that the association between Dionysos and Eleusis may have first been voiced in Sophocles' *Antigone*, lines 1118–21.

19. Mylonas, *Eleusis*, 284.

20. The quotations from Sophocles' *Oedipus at Colonus* are translated by Robert Fitzgerald in *The Complete Greek Tragedies*, edited by David Grene and Richmond Lattimore, vol. 2 (Chicago: University of Chicago Press, 1959).

21. The quotations from Euripides' *Helen* (lines 1301–52) are translated by Richmond Lattimore in *The Complete Greek Tragedies*, edited by David Grene and Richmond Lattimore, vol. 3 Chicago: University of Chicago Press, 1959).

22. For a good indication of what the average Greek toward the end of the classical period knew about Demeter and Persephone, we have no better source than the *Library* of Apollodorus, an uncritical summary of Greek mythology written in the second century BCE. See Michael Simpson's translation, *Gods and Heroes of the Greeks: The "Library" of Apollodorus* (Amherst: University of Massachusetts Press, 1976), 18.

23. Ovid, *Fasti* 4.417–615, translated by James George Frazer (Cambridge, Mass.: Harvard University Press, 1976), 219–35.

24. Ovid, of course, consistently uses the Roman names of the deities that appear in the myth: Persephone becomes Proserpina; Hades, Pluto; Zeus, Jupiter; Aphrodite, Venus; Athene, Minerva; Eros, Cupid.

25. Stephen Hinds, *The Metamorphosis of Persephone: Ovid and the Self-conscious Muse* (New York: Cambridge University Press, 1987), 61.

26. William S. Anderson, *Ovid's "Metamorphoses" Books 6–10* (Norman, Okla.: University of Oklahoma Press, 1982), 19.

The Homeric "Hymn to Demeter"

TRANSLATED BY DAVID G. RICE
AND JOHN E. STAMBAUGH

I BEGIN MY SONG of the holy goddess, fair-haired Demeter, and of her slim-ankled daughter whom Aidoneus snatched away; and Zeus the loud-crashing, the wide-voiced one, granted it. She was playing with the deep-bosomed daughters of Ocean, away from Demeter of the golden weapon and glorious fruit, and she was gathering flowers throughout the luxuriant meadow—roses, saffron, violets, iris, hyacinth, and a narcissus which was a trap planted for the blossoming maiden by Earth in accord with Zeus's plans, a favor to Hades the receiver of many guests; it was radiantly wonderful, inspiring awe in all who saw it, whether immortal god or mortal man; a hundred stems grew from its root; and the whole wide heaven above, the whole earth, and the salt surge of the sea smiled for joy at its fragrance. The girl was charmed by it and reached out both hands to pluck the pretty plaything—suddenly, the earth split open wide along the plain and from it the lord host of many, Kronos's son of many names, darted out on his immortal horses. He grabbed her, resisting and screaming, and took her away in his golden chariot. She lifted her voice in a cry, calling upon Father Zeus, the almighty and good. But no one, god or mortal, heard her voice, not even the glorious-fruited olive trees, except the childish daughter of Perses, Hecate of the glistening veil, who—from her cave—heard, and so did Lord Helios, the glorious son of Hyperion, as the maiden calling upon Father Zeus, though he was sitting, removed from the other gods, in his much-besought temple, receiving fine sacrifices from mortal men.

Her, all unwilling, with the approval of Zeus, he took away on his immortal horses, Kronos's son of many names, brother of her father, designator of many, host of many. As long as the goddess could see the earth and the starry sky, the flowing, fish-filled sea and the rays of the sun, she still had hope that her holy mother and the race of the immortal gods would see her, and there was still much hope in her heart in spite of her distress. . . . The peaks of the mountains and the depths of the sea echoed back the immortal voice, and her blessed mother heard her. Then sharp grief seized the mother's heart; she tore the headdress upon her ambrosial hair and threw her dark veil down from both her shoulders, and like a bird she darted over land and sea, searching. None of the gods or of mortal men would give her a true report, nor would any of the birds come to her as a true messenger.

For nine days then Lady Deo wandered the earth, holding blazing torches in her hands; in her grief she touched neither ambrosia nor the sweetness of nectar, nor did she bathe her body with water. But when the tenth day dawned, Hecate, bearing light in her hands, encountered her and spoke to her this message: "Lady Demeter, bringer of seasons and glorious gifts, who of the gods of heaven or of mortal men has taken Persephone and pained your own heart? I heard her voice but did not see who it was. I am telling you everything promptly and accurately."

So spoke Hecate. The daughter of fair-haired Rheia did not answer a word, but she immediately darted off with her, holding blazing torches in her hands, and they came to Helios, the viewer of gods and men. They stood before his horses, and the divine goddess said, "Helios, as a god, respect me, as a goddess, if ever in word or deed I have warmed your heart. The maiden whom I bore—sweetest blossom—beautiful—I heard her voice, sobbing, as if she were being raped, but I did not see her. But you survey from the bright heaven all the earth and the sea with your rays;

tell me accurately whether you have seen who of gods or mortal men has forced her and taken her away, all unwillingly, in my absence."

So she spoke, and the son of Hyperion answered her, "Lady Demeter, daughter of fair-haired Rheia, you will know all: I have great respect for you and pity you in your grief for your slim-ankled child: none of the immortals is responsible except Zeus, the cloud-gatherer, who has granted to Hades his own brother that she be called his tender wife, and he has taken her, screaming a loud cry, away on his horses down into the misty darkness. So, goddess, stop your loud lament; you should not rashly hold on to this boundless anger; Aidoneus, the designator of many, is after all not an unsuitable son-in-law for you, since you have the same mother and father, and his honor he gained when at the beginning a division into three parts was made, and he dwells with those over whom the lot made him king." When he had said this he called to his horses, and at his command they bore the swift chariot like broad-winged birds.

Then grief still more horrible and oppressive came upon her heart, and in her anger at Zeus, shrouded in clouds she deserted the gatherings of the gods and went far from Olympus to the cities and farms of men and for a long time disguised her appearance. No man, no woman who saw her recognized her, until she arrived at the home of clever Keleos, who was the king of fragrant Eleusis at the time. At the spring Parthenion where the citizens draw water in the shade of a towering olive tree she sat by the side of the road in the guise of an old woman, one who is beyond the age of childbearing and the gifts of Aphrodite who bears the garland of love, one who might be a nurse of royal children or governess of important households. The daughters of Keleos of Eleusis saw her as they came to draw water and carry it in bronze vessels to their father's house. There were four of them, like goddesses in youthful bloom—Kallidike, Klesidike, lovely Demo, and Kallithoe, the eldest of them all. They did not recognize her, for gods are hard for mortals to see. They approached her and said, "Old woman, who are you? Why have you kept away from the city and not approached the settlement? There in the dusky houses there are women as old as you and younger who would treat you kindly in word and deed."

So they spoke, and the goddess mistress said in answer, "Dear children, daughters of womanly mothers, be of good cheer, and I will tell you, for it is right to tell you the truth. The name my lady mother gave to me is Doso. I have just come across the sea from Crete, forced by pirate men who abducted me against my will. They brought their swift ship to shore at Thorikos, and a crowd of women came on board from the land, and they all prepared their dinner by the ship's stern cables. But my heart had no desire for a pleasant supper; instead I got up secretly and escaped those arrogant overlords across the dark countryside, so that they might not enjoy any profit from selling me. I wandered about until I arrived here; but I do not know what land it is nor which people dwell here. May all the gods who dwell on Olympus grant you vigorous husbands and all the progeny they want; but pity me, maidens; dear children, help me come propitiously to some home of a man and woman where I may provide the services of an aged woman for them: I could hold their infant child in my arms and nurse it well, I could keep house, make the master's bed in the inmost chamber, and instruct the women in their tasks."

So said the goddess, and the maiden Kallidike, most beautiful of Keleos's daughters, answered her, "Mother, we humans endure the gifts of the gods, even under grievous compulsion, for they are much mightier. I will explain it all to you clearly and tell you the men who hold the power of authority here and who stand out in the government and direct the defense of the city with their counsels and decisions. There are Triptolemos the clever, Dioklos, Polyxeinos, Eumolpos the blameless, Dolichos, and our father the manly one. Their wives manage everything in their households, and not one of them would dishonor you at first sight by making you depart from their houses. They will receive you, for you are godlike. If you wish, wait here while we go to our father's house

and tell Metaneira, our deep-belted mother, all these things and
see whether she bids you come to our house and not search for
another's. A favorite son, born to her late, is being nursed in the
strongly built palace; she prayed much for him, and rejoiced in
him. If you would nurse him and he would reach adolescence, any
woman would envy the sight of you, for she [Metaneira] would
give you so great a reward for nursing him."

So she spoke, and she nodded her head, and then they filled
their shining jugs with water and carried them proudly. Soon they
reached their father's great house and quickly told their mother
what they had seen and heard. She told them to go quickly and
bid her come, at a vast wage. As deer or heifers frolic across the
meadow eating to their hearts' content, so they darted along the
road down the gully, holding up the folds of their lovely gowns,
and their hair streamed along their shoulders like saffron blossoms. They reached the spot near the road where they had left
the glorious goddess, and they led her to their father's house. She,
grieved at heart, walked behind them with her head veiled, and
the dark robe trailed along around the slender feet of the goddess.

Soon they reached the house of Zeus-descended Keleos and
went through the portico to the place where their lady mother
was sitting beside a column of the carefully made chamber, holding her new baby in her lap. The girls ran to her, but Demeter
trod upon the threshold, and her head reached the roof beam,
and she filled the doorway with a divine radiance. At this, awe,
reverence, and pale fear seized the woman. She rose from her
chair and urged her to be seated, but Demeter the bringer of
seasons and glorious gifts did not wish to be seated on the gleam-
ing chair but silently cast down her beautiful eyes and waited until
Iambe understood and set a jointed stool out for her, and threw a
shining white fleece upon it. She sat down, holding her veil in
front with her hands. For a long time she sat there on the stool
sorrowfully, without speaking, and made no contact with anyone
in word or gesture. Without smiling, without touching food or
drink she sat, consumed with yearning for her daughter, until

Iambe understood and made plenty of jokes and jests and made the holy lady smile with kindly heart, and ever afterward she continues to delight her spirit. Then Metaneira filled a cup of sweet wine and offered it to her, but she refused it, for she said it was not right for her to drink red wine. Instead, she asked her to give her barley groats and water mixed with crusted pennyroyal to drink. She made the compound, the *kykeon,* as she commanded, and offered it to the goddess. Deo, the greatly revered, accepted it for the sake of the ceremony. . . . Fair-belted Metaneira began with these words, "Be of good cheer, woman; I do not expect that you are sprung from base stock, but from good; dignity and grace are manifest in your eyes, like those of kings, stewards of the right. But we humans endure the gifts of the gods, even under grievous compulsion, for a yoke lies upon our neck. But now that you have come here, all that is mine shall be yours. Nurse this child for me, whom the immortals have given me, late-born and unexpected, but much prayed for. If you would nurse him and he would reach adolescence, any woman would envy the sight of you, for I would give you so great a reward for nursing him."

Then Demeter of the fair crown said to her, "May you also be of good cheer, woman, and may the gods grant you all good things; I willingly accept the child, as you bid me. I will nurse him, and I do not expect that he will be injured by nurse's incompetence, supernatural attacks, or magical cuttings, for I know an antidote more mighty than the woodcutter, and I know a fine preventative against malignant attacks.

When she had said this she received him with her immortal hands in her fragrant lap, and the mother's heart rejoiced. So she nursed the glorious son of clever Keleos, Demophon, whom fair-belted Metaneira bore, and he grew like a god, eating no food, being suckled on no milk, for Demeter would [feed and] anoint him with ambrosia, like the progeny of a god, and she breathed sweetly on him and held him in her lap. At night she would hide him like a firebrand within the might of the flame, without his parents' knowledge. It made them wonder greatly how he was so precocious and why his appearance was like the gods'. She would have made him ageless and deathless, if it had not been that fair-belted Metaneira foolishly kept watch one night and watched her from her fragrant bedchamber. She screamed and struck both her thighs in fear for her child and in a frenzy of mindlessness. Wailing, she said, "My child, Demophon, the stranger woman is hiding you in the blazing fire and is making grief and bitter sorrow for me."

So she spoke, lamenting, and the divine goddess heard her. Demeter of the beautiful crown was amazed at her; with her immortal hands she put from her the dear child whom [Metaneira] had borne, all unexpected, in the palace, and threw him at her feet, drawing him out of the fire, terribly angry at heart, and at the same time she said to fair-belted Metaneira, "Humans are short-sighted, stupid, ignorant of the share of good or evil which is coming to them. You by your foolishness have hurt him beyond curing. Let my witness be the oath of the gods sworn by the intractable water of Styx, that I would have made your son deathless and ageless all his days and given him imperishable honor. But now it is not possible to ward off death and destruction. Still he will have imperishable honor forever, since he stood on my knees and slept in my arms; in due season, as the years pass around, the children of the Eleusinians will conduct in his honor war [games] and the terrible battle cry with each other for ever and ever. I am Demeter the Venerable, ready as the greatest boon and joy for immortals and mortals. So now, let the whole people build me a great temple and an altar beneath it, below the city and the towering wall, above Kallirhoe on the ridge which juts forth. I myself will establish rites so that henceforth you may celebrate them purely and propitiate my mind."

With these words the goddess altered size and form and sloughed off old age; beauty wafted about her. A lovely fresh smell radiated from her lovely gown, and the radiance from the skin of the immortal goddess shone afar. Her blond hair flowed down over her shoulders, and the sturdy house was filled with the light like a flash of lightning. She went out through the palace. As for the other, her knees gave way, and for a long time she was speechless. She did not even remember the child, her favorite, to pick him up from the floor. His sisters heard his piteous crying, and they leapt down from their well-covered beds. Then one of them took the child in her hands and put him in her lap, one kindled a fire, and another hurried on gentle feet to rouse her mother out of the fragrant chamber. Crowding around they washed him, covering him with love as he squirmed; his heart was not comforted, however, for less skillful nurses and nursemaids were holding him now.

All night long the women, quaking with fear, propitiated the glorious goddess. As soon as dawn appeared they gave a full report to wide-ruling Keleos, as Demeter of the beautiful garlands commanded. He summoned the people from their many boundaries and ordered them to build an elaborate temple to fair-haired Demeter and an altar on the ridge which juts forth. They obeyed him straightway and hearkened to him as he spoke and started to build as he commanded. And it grew at the dispensation of the divinity. When they finished and ceased from their toil, each person went back to his home. Blond Demeter stayed there, seated far from all the blessed gods, wasting with grief for her deep-belted daughter.

She made the most terrible, most oppressive year for men upon the nourishing land, and the earth sent up no seed, as fair-garlanded Demeter hid it. Cattle drew the many curved plows in vain over the fields, and much white barley seed fell useless on the earth. By now she would have destroyed the entire race of men by grievous famine, and deprived those who dwell on Olympus of the glorious honor of offerings and sacrifices, if Zeus had not taken notice and taken counsel with his mind. First he roused gold-winged Iris to summon fair-haired Demeter, of the very desirable beauty. So he spoke, and she obeyed Zeus wrapped in clouds, the son of Kronos. She rushed down the middle and arrived at the citadel of fragrant Eleusis. In the temple she found Demeter dark-clad and addressed her with winged words. "Demeter, Father Zeus who understands imperishable things summons you to come among the race of the immortal gods. So come, and let my message from Zeus not be fruitless."

So she spoke in supplication, but Her heart was not persuaded. Therefore the Father sent out the blessed, ever-living gods one after another, and they went in turn and implored her, and offered her many fine gifts and whatever honors she might choose among the immortal gods. None, however, was able to persuade the heart and mind of the angry goddess. She rejected their speeches firmly and claimed that she would never set foot upon fragrant Olympus, nor allow any fruit to grow on the earth, until she saw with her eyes the beautiful face of her daughter.

When Zeus the loud-crashing, the wide-voiced one, heard this, he sent Hermes the slayer of Argos with his golden wand to Erebos, to use smooth words on Hades and lead pure Persephone out of the misty darkness into the light to join the deities, in order that her mother might see her with her eyes and turn from her anger. Hermes obeyed and eagerly rushed down under the recesses of the earth, leaving the seat of Olympus. He found the lord inside his house, seated on couches with his modest and very unwilling wife, yearning for her mother. . . .

The mighty slayer of Argos came near and said, "Dark-haired Hades, ruler of the departed, Father Zeus has ordered me to lead glorious Persephone out of Erebos to join them, in order that her mother might see her with her eyes and cease from her anger and terrible wrath, since she is contriving a tremendous deed, to destroy the fragile race of earth-born men, hiding the seed under the earth and obliterating the honors of the immortals. Her anger is terrible; she has no contact with the gods but sits apart inside her fragrant temple, holding the rocky citadel of Eleusis."

So he spoke, and Aidoneus, the lord of the underworld, smiled with his brows and did not disobey the injunctions of Zeus, the king. Promptly he gave the command to diligent Persephone: "Go, Persephone, to your dark-clad mother, and keep gentle the strength and heart in your breast. Do not be despondent to excess beyond all others. I shall not be an inappropriate husband for you among the immortals; I am a brother of Father Zeus. Being there, you will rule over all that lives and moves, enjoying the greatest honors among the immortals. And there shall be punishment forever on those who act unjustly and who do not propitiate your might with sacrifices, performing the pious acts and offering appropriate gifts."

So he spoke, and Persephone, the discreet, was glad and swiftly leapt up for joy. But he gave her a honey-sweet pomegranate seed to eat, having secretly passed it around [himself?], so that she might not stay forever there by modest, dark-clad Demeter. Aidoneus, designator of many, harnessed the immortal horses in front of the golden chariot, and she stepped on the chariot; beside her the mighty slayer of Argos took the reins and a whip in his hands and drove out of the palace. The pair of horses flew willingly. They finished the long journey quickly. Neither sea nor rivers nor grassy glens nor mountain peaks held back the rush of the immortal horses; they went above them and cut through the high air. He drove them where Demeter of the fair crown waited in front of her fragrant temple, and he stopped them there. Seeing them, she darted up like a maenad in the woods on a thick-shaded mountain.

[Demeter asked Persephone if she had eaten anything in the underworld. If not,] "you will come up and dwell with me and Zeus of the dark clouds and be honored by all the immortals. But if you have tasted anything, then you shall go back down and dwell there for the third part of the season, and for the other two, here with me and the other immortals. Whenever the earth blossoms with all the sweet-smelling flowers of spring, then you will come back up from the misty darkness, a great wonder to gods and to mortal men. But what trick did the powerful host of many use to deceive you?"

Persephone, the exceedingly beautiful, gave her this response: "I will tell you, Mother, everything accurately. When the swift slayer of Argos came to me from Father Zeus and the others in heaven with the message to come out of Erebos, so that seeing me with your eyes you might cease from your anger and terrible wrath, I leapt up for joy. But he secretly insinuated a pomegranate seed, honey-sweet food, and though I was unwilling, he compelled me by force to taste it. How he snatched me away through the clever plan of Zeus and carried me off, down into the recesses of the earth, I will tell you, and I will go through it all as you ask. We were all there in the lovely meadow—Leukippe, Phaino, Elektre, Ianthe, Melite, Iache, Rhodeia, Kallirhoe, Melobosis, Tyche, Okyrhoe of the flowering face, Chryseis, Ianeira, Akaste, Admete, Rhodope, Plouto, charming Kalypso, Styx, Ouranie, lovely Galax-aure, Pallas the inciter of battles, Artemis the shooter of arrows— playing and picking the lovely flowers, a profusion of gentle saffron blossoms, iris, hyacinth, rosebuds and lilies, a marvel to see, and narcissus, which the broad land grew like saffron. Full of joy, I was picking them, but the earth under me moved, and the powerful lord, the host of many, leapt out. And he took me under the earth on his golden chariot, against my will, and I screamed loudly with my voice. Grieved though I am, I am telling you the whole truth."

Then with minds in concord they spent the whole day warming their hearts and minds, showering much love on each other, and her mind found respite from its griefs, as they gave and received joys from each other. And there came near them Hecate of the glistening veil, and she also showered much love on the daughter of holy Demeter, and ever since she has been her attendant and lady-in-waiting.

Zeus the loud-crashing, the wide-voiced one, sent fair-haired Rheia as a messenger to them, to bring dark-gowned Demeter among the race of the gods; he promised to give her whatever honors she might choose among the immortal gods. He granted that her daughter should spend the third portion of the year in its cycle down in the misty darkness but the other two with her mother and the other immortals.

So he spoke, and the goddess obeyed the biddings of Zeus. Promptly she darted along the peaks of Olympus and came to the

Rarian plain, the life-bringing udder of plow land formerly, but at that time not life-bringing at all, as it stood all barren and leafless. The white barley was concealed according to the plans of fair-ankled Demeter, but at this time it was about to grow shaggy with waves of grain as it became spring. In the field the rich furrows were to be loaded with the grain, and they were to be bound in sheaves. Here she first alighted from the boundless ether, and they saw each other gladly and rejoiced in their hearts.

Rheia of the glistening veil said to her, "Come here, child. Zeus the loud-crashing, the wide-voiced one, summons you to come among the race of the immortal gods, and he has promised to give whatever honors you might choose among the immortal gods. He has granted that your daughter will spend the third portion of the year in its cycle down in the misty darkness, but the other two with you and the other immortals. So has he promised, and nodded his head in affirmation. Go, now, my child, and obey; do not be obdurately angry at Zeus of the dark clouds but give prompt increase to the fruit, bringer of life to men."

So she spoke, and Demeter of the fair crown obeyed. Promptly she sent up fruit on the rich-soiled fields, and the whole broad land was loaded with leaves and flowers. She went to the royal stewards of the right and to Triptolemos; Diokles, the driver of horses; mighty Eumolpos; and Keleos, the leader of the people. She showed the tendance of the holy things and explicated the rites to them all, to Triptolemos, to Polyxeinos, and to Diokles— sacred rites which it is forbidden to transgress, to inquire into, or to speak about, for great reverence of the gods constrains the voice. Blessed of earthbound men is he who has seen the things, but he who dies without fulfilling the holy things, and he who is without a share of them, has no claim ever on such blessings, even when departed down to the moldy darkness.

When the divine goddess had ordained all this, she went to Olympus among the assembly of the other gods. And there they dwell, sacred and reverent, with Zeus who revels in thunder. Greatly blessed of earthbound men is he whom they propitiously love: to him they promptly send to the hearth of his great house Ploutos [wealth], who gives abundance to mortal men.

Now, ye that hold the people of fragrant Eleusis and sea-girt Paros and rocky Antron, Lady mistress Deo, bringer of seasons and glorious gifts, thou thyself and Persephone, the exceedingly beautiful, do ye bestow a heartwarming livelihood in exchange for my song. Now I shall recall thee, and also another song.

The Rape of Proserpine

From the *Metamorphoses* of Ovid

TRANSLATED BY MARY INNES

THE VAST ISLAND OF SICILY had been piled on top of Typhoeus' limbs, and the giant who had dared to hope for a home in heaven was crushed and held under by its mighty mass. He struggled, it is true, and often tried to rise again: but his right hand was pinned under Ausonian Pelorus, his left under Pachynus, while his legs were fastened down by Lilybaeum. Etna weighed heavily upon his head; as he lay stretched on his back beneath it, he spat forth ashes and flame from his cruel jaws. Often he strove to throw aside the weight of earth and roll off the towns and massive hills that secured him. At such times the earth trembled, and even the king of the silent shades was afraid lest the ground should split and gape wide open and the daylight thus admitted to his kingdom frighten the trembling ghosts.

Dreading such a disaster, the tyrant had come up from his dark dwelling and, in his chariot drawn by black horses, was cautiously driving around the foundations of the Sicilian land. He had made sufficiently sure that there were no weak places, and his fears had been set at rest: but meanwhile the lady of Eryx, who was seated on her mountainside, saw him on his travels. Embracing her winged son, she said; "My son, you who are arms and hands to me, and all my power, take those all-conquering darts, my Cupid, and shoot your swift arrows into the heart of the god to whose lot fell the last of the three kingdoms. You have conquered the divinities of the upper air, including Jupiter himself, and hold them in subjection; yes, and the gods of the sea, also, not excepting their overlord. Why is Tartarus left alone? Why not extend your mother's domain, and your own? A third part of the world is at stake, while we display such tolerance that we are being scorned in heaven. The powers of the god of love are dwindling, no less than my own. Don't you see how Pallas and the huntress Diana have been lost to me? Ceres' daughter, too, will remain a virgin, if we allow it, for she has that same ambition. But do you, if you have any feeling for the kingdom which we share, bring about a union between the goddess and her uncle." Such were Venus' words. Cupid opened his quiver and, at his mother's wish, selected one of his thousand arrows, the sharpest and surest, and most obedient to the bow. Then, bending his pliant bow against his knee, he struck Pluto to the heart with the barbed shaft.

Not far from Henna's walls, there is a deep lake, called Pergus. The music of its swans rivals the songs that Cayster hears on its gliding waters. A ring of trees encircles the pool, clothing the lakeside all around, and the leaves of the trees shelter the spot from Phoebus' rays, like a screen. Their boughs afford cool shade, and the lush meadow is bright with flowers. There it is always spring. In this glade Proserpine was playing, picking violets or shining lilies. With childlike eagerness she gathered the flowers into baskets and into the folds of her gown, trying to pick more than any of her companions. Almost at one and the same time, Pluto saw her, and loved her, and bore her off—so swift is love. With wailing cries the terrified goddess called to her mother, and to her comrades, but more often to her mother. She rent and tore the upper edge of her garment, till the flowers she had gathered fell from its loosened folds; and she was so young and innocent that even this loss caused her fresh distress. Her captor urged on his chariot, called each of his horses by name, encouraging them to greater efforts, and shook his reins, dyed a dark and somber hue, above their necks and manes. On they raced, across deep lakes and over the sulfurous pools of the Palici, that boil up, bubbling, through the earth; past the place where the Bacchiadae, a people who came originally from Corinth on its isthmus, had built their city walls between two harbors, a larger and a smaller one.

Halfway between Cyane and Pisaean Arethusa there is a narrowing stretch of sea, shut in by jutting headlands. Cyane herself lived there; she was the most famous of the Sicilian nymphs, and from her the pool itself took its name. She rose from the midst of her waters as far as her waist, and recognized the goddess. "You will go no further, Pluto!" she cried. "You cannot be the son-in-law of Ceres, if she does not wish it. You should have asked for the girl, instead of snatching her away. If I may make a humble comparison, I too have been loved, by Anapis. But it was after he had won me by his prayers that I became his bride, I was not frightened into marriage like this child." As she spoke, she stretched out her arms on either side, to block their path. Pluto, Saturn's son, contained his wrath no longer, but urged on his grim steeds, and with his strong arm hurled his royal scepter into the depths of the pool. Where it struck the bottom, the ground opened up to afford a road into Tartarus, and the yawning crater received his chariot as it hurtled down. As for Cyane, she lamented the rape of the goddess, and the contempt shown for her fountain's rights, nursing silently in her heart a wound that none could heal; until, entirely wasted away with weeping, she dissolved into those waters of which she had lately been the powerful spirit. Her limbs could be seen melting away, her bones growing flexible, her nails losing their firmness. The slenderest parts of her body dissolved first of all, her dark hair, her fingers, her legs and feet. It needed but a little change to transform her slight limbs into chill water; after that her shoulders, her back, her sides, her breasts disappeared, fading away into insubstantial streams, till at last, instead of living blood, water flowed through her softened veins, and nothing remained for anyone to grasp.

Meanwhile Proserpine's mother, Ceres, with panic in her heart, vainly sought her daughter over all lands and over all the sea.

When Aurora came forth, with dewy tresses, she never found the goddess resting, nor did Hesperus, the evening star. Holding in either hand a blazing pine torch kindled at Etna's fires, she bore them through the darkness of the frosty nights, never relaxing her search. When kindly day had dimmed the stars, still she sought her daughter from the rising to the setting sun. She grew weary with her efforts, and thirsty too, but before she found a spring of water to moisten her lips, she chanced to see a thatched cottage. She knocked at the humble door, and an old woman came out. When she saw the goddess and heard that she wanted some water, she gave her a sweet drink, into which she had sprinkled roasted barley. While Ceres was drinking this, a cheeky bold-faced boy stopped in front of her, taunting her, and calling her greedy. While he was still speaking, the offended goddess threw in his face the mixture of liquid and barley grains, which she had not yet finished. As it soaked into his skin his complexion became spotted; he developed legs where previously he had had arms, and in his changed shape he acquired a tail as well. To prevent him from doing much mischief, he shriveled up until he was like a tiny lizard, but even smaller. The old woman wondered and wept; she put out her hand to touch the strange creature, but it fled away, seeking a hiding place; and now it bears a name appropriate to its disgrace, derived from the multicolored spots which star its body.

It would take a long time to name the lands and seas over which the goddess wandered. She searched the whole world—in vain; and when there was no place left for her to search, she came back to Sicily. As she journeyed over the length and breadth of the island, she visited Cyane, among other places. Had the nymph not been changed to water, she could have told Ceres everything; but though she wished to speak, she had no mouth, no tongue, nothing with which to talk. However, she did give the mother an obvious clue, by displaying on the surface of the water Proserpine's girdle, which happened to have fallen in her sacred pool. Ceres knew it well, and as soon as she recognized it, tore her disheveled hair, as if she had only then learned of her loss: again and again she beat her breast. She still did not know where her daughter was, but she reproached all the lands of the earth, calling them ungrateful, undeserving of the gift of corn. More than all the rest, she blamed Sicily, where she had found traces of her lost one. So, in that island, she broke with cruel hands the ploughs which turned up the earth, and in her anger condemned the farmers and the oxen which worked their fields to perish alike by plague. She ordered the fields to betray their trust, and caused seeds to be diseased. The land whose fertility had been vaunted throughout the whole world lay barren, treacherously disappointing men's hopes. Crops perished as soon as their first shoots appeared. They were destroyed, now by too much sun, now by torrential rain; winds and stormy seasons harmed them, and greedy birds pecked up the seeds as they were sown. Tares and thistles and grass, which could not be kept down, ruined the corn harvest.

Then the nymph whom Alpheus loved, Arethusa of Elis, raised her head from her pool and, shaking back the dripping locks from her brow, said to Ceres: "Great mother of the corn crops, you who have sought your daughter throughout the whole world, enough of unending toil, enough of violent rage against the faithful earth! No blame attaches to the earth: if it gaped open to receive that robber, it did so reluctantly. It is not for my own land that I plead; I was born in Elis, Pisa was my birthplace. I came here as a stranger, but though I am not a native of Sicily, I love this land beyond all others. This is now Arethusa's home, and this her dwelling. Do you, most gentle goddess, keep it safe. As to why I left my country and traveled across such a stretch of sea to Ortygian Sicily, it will be time enough to tell of that later, when you are relieved of your anxieties, and can look more cheerful; suffice it now, that the earth opened up a way for me, and, after passing deep down through its lowest caverns, I lifted up my head again in these regions, and saw the stars, which had grown strange to me. So it happened that, while I was gliding through the Stygian pool beneath the earth, there I saw your Proserpine, with my own eyes. She was sad, certainly, and her face still showed signs of fear;

nonetheless, she was a queen, the greatest in that world of shadows, the powerful consort of the tyrant of the underworld."

When she heard these words, the mother stood, as if turned to stone, and for a long time seemed to be dazed, till her crushing distress was replaced by bitter indignation and she went soaring up in her chariot, into the realms of aether. There she stood before Jupiter, with clouded brow, her hair all disarrayed, and said accusingly, "I have come, Jupiter, to intercede for one who is your child as well as mine. If her mother has no influence with you, at least let your daughter move her father's heart to pity. Do not regard her with any less affection because she is my child. For behold, the daughter I have sought so long has now at last been found—if you call it 'finding' to be more certain that I have lost her, or if knowing where she is is finding her. But I shall overlook the theft, provided she be returned. A pirate is no fit husband for your daughter, even if she is no longer mine." Jupiter answered her: "Our child is as dear to me as she is to you, and I feel my responsibility no less. But if you will only call things by their proper names, this deed was no crime, but an act of love. Only give your consent, and this son-in-law will not disgrace us. Though he had no other qualities to recommend him, it is a great thing to be the brother of Jove. What then, when he does possess other qualities, and yields place to me only because of the luck of the draw? However, if you are so eager to separate them, Proserpine may return to heaven, but on one definite condition, that no food has passed her lips in that other world. Such is the provision made by the decree of the fates." Jupiter had finished. Ceres was still resolved to rescue her daughter, but the fates would not allow it to be so, for the girl had broken her fast. While wandering in the well-tended gardens, she had innocently picked a pomegranate from a drooping branch, and had placed in her mouth seven seeds taken from its pale husk. The only person who saw her was Ascalaphus, the son whom Orphne bore, so men say, to her own Acheron long ago in the dusky woods of Avernus, where she herself was not the least famous of the nymphs of the grove. He saw

Proserpine and, by telling what he had seen, cruelly prevented her return. Then the queen of Erebus moaned in distress, and changed the informer into a bird of evil omen. Sprinkling his head with water from Phlegethon, she gave him a beak and feathers and huge eyes. He lost his human shape, and found himself clad in tawny wings; his head increased in size in proportion to his body, he developed long hooked talons, and he could scarcely raise the feathers which had sprouted along his languid arms. He became a sluggish screech owl, a loathsome bird, which heralds impending disaster, a harbinger of woe for mortals.

Now, Ascalaphus may be thought to have earned his punishment, by revealing what he knew about Proserpine. But how did the daughters of Achelous come to have feathers and claws like birds, while retaining their human faces? Was it because these skillful singers were among Proserpine's companions, when she was gathering the spring flowers? And after seeking her in vain the world over, they prayed that they might fly across the waves on beating wings, so that the seas, too, might know of their anxiety. The gods consented, and suddenly they saw their limbs covered with golden plumage. But in case those melodies that fell so sweetly on the ear should be silenced, if the maidens lost their tongues, and their rich gift of song be denied expression, they retained the features of young girls, and kept their human voices.

Jupiter, however, intervening between his brother and his sorrowing sister, divided the circling year in equal parts, and now the goddess whose divinity is shared by two kingdoms spends the same number of months with her husband and with her mother. Her expression and her temperament change instantly: at one moment she is so melancholy as to seem sad to Dis himself; the next, she appears with radiant face, as when the sun breaks through and disperses the watery clouds that have previously concealed him. Then kindly Ceres, restored to cheerfulness by the return of her daughter, inquired the reason for Arethusa's flight, and why she was now a holy spring. The waters were stilled as their goddess raised her head from the pool and, wringing the moisture from her green tresses, told the story, now an old one, of the love of the Elean river.

"I was one of the nymphs who dwelt in Achaea," she said, "and none took more delight than I in roaming the forests and spreading my hunting nets. Though I was a maid of action and never sought a reputation for beauty, still, I was famous for my loveliness. But my appearance, all too highly praised, gave me no pleasure; in my simplicity, I blushed for those attractive looks on which other girls pride themselves, and thought it wicked to please men's eyes.

"I was returning from the Stymphalian wood, I remember, quite tired out. It was very hot, and my exertions had made the heat seem twice as fierce. I came to a stream that flowed silently and smoothly, so clear that I could see right to the bottom and count every pebble in its depths. You would scarcely have thought that it was moving at all. Silvery willows and poplars, drawing nourishment from the water, spread natural shade over its sloping banks. I went up and dipped my feet in the stream, and then my legs, up to the knees. Not content with that, I unfastened my girdle, hung my soft garments on a drooping willow, and plunged naked into the waters. As I swam with a thousand twists and turns, striking the water and drawing it toward me, threshing my arms about, I felt a kind of murmuring in the midst of the pool and, growing frightened, leapt onto the nearer bank. 'Whither away so fast, Arethusa?' cried Alpheus from his waters, and then again, in harsh tones, 'Whither away so fast?' I fled, just as I was, naked, for my garments were on the other bank: all the more passionately did he pursue me, and because I was undressed I seemed more ready for his assault. I ran on, and he pressed fiercely after, just as doves flee from the hawk on fluttering wings and the hawk closely pursues the trembling doves. Right on past Orchomenus and Psophis, past Cyllene and the ridges of Maenalus, past chill Erymanthus and Elis, I kept on running, and he was no swifter than I. But my strength was no match for his, and I could not keep up my pace for long, whereas he could make a sustained effort. Still, over the open plains and the tree-clad mountain slopes, over rocks and crags, and where there was no path, on I sped. The sun was behind me. I saw a long shadow stretching before my feet—unless fear made me imagine it—but certainly the sound of his footsteps terrified me, and as he panted heavily behind me his breath stirred my hair. Weary with my efforts to escape, I cried out to Dictynna: 'Help me, or I am lost! Help your armour-bearer, to whom you have so often given the task of carrying your bow, and your quiver full of arrows!' The goddess was moved by my cry, and sent a thick cloud which she cast over and around me. The river god circled about me as I stood shrouded in darkness, and, not knowing what had happened, searched all round the hollow cloud. Twice, unwittingly, he walked round the place where the goddess had hidden me, and twice he called: 'Ho there, Arethusa! Hallo, Arethusa!' Alas, what feelings did I have then! Assuredly I was like a lamb when it hears the wolves howling round the high sheepfold, or like a hare, hiding in the brambles, watching the jaws of hostile hounds, and not daring to move. Still Achelous did not depart, for he did not see any footprints leading further on. He kept watch on the spot where the mist was. A cold sweat broke out on my limbs, when I was thus trapped, and dark drops fell from my whole body. Wherever I moved my foot, a pool flowed out; moisture dripped from my hair. More quickly than I can tell of it, I was changed into a stream. Then, indeed, the river recognized the waters that he loved, divested himself of the human shape he had adopted, and resumed his proper form, to join his waves with mine. But the Delian maiden split open the earth, and I plunged into its gloomy caverns. By that route I reached Ortygia: this land, dear to me because it bears the name of my own goddess, first restored me to the upper air."

That was the end of Arethusa's tale. The goddess of fertile fields then yoked her two dragons to her car, fastening the bits in their mouths, and rode off through the air, midway between heaven and earth. She guided her light chariot to the city of Pallas, where she handed it over to Triptolemus, bidding him scatter the seeds she gave him, partly in virgin soil, partly in fields that had long lain fallow.

The boy drove high above Europe and the land of Asia, and then turned his course towards the realm of Scythia where Lyncus was king. He entered the royal palace and, when asked to tell his name and country, how he had come, and why, he answered thus: "My name is Triptolemus, and famous Athens is my native city. I did not come by sea, nor yet by land, neither on board ship, nor on foot: the skies were my highway. I bring the gifts of Ceres, which, if they are scattered widely over the fields, will produce fruitful harvests and cultivated crops." The barbarian king was jealous. Hoping that he himself might have the honor of bestowing so great a blessing on mankind, he welcomed Triptolemus into his house and then, when his guest lay fast asleep, attacked him with a sword. But, as he tried to pierce the boy's breast, Ceres turned the villain into a lynx. Then she told the young Athenian to continue his journey through the air, borne by her sacred team.

ART AND RITUAL

Although we have begun our exploration of the ancient Greek understanding of Demeter and Persephone by looking at literary evidences, it is generally agreed that the rituals celebrated in honor of the two goddesses, including both the Attic Thesmophoria and the Eleusinian mysteries, are far older than the hymn and thus provide us with important clues to the beliefs and practices of a more archaic period.

Archaeologists have found indications that a mystery cult was already established at Eleusis by the middle of the second millennium BCE. The place name, Eleusis, probably refers to the underworld in a favorable sense; it may mean something like "place of happy arrival"; the name suggests an allusion to Elysian, the realm of the blessed.[1] Unlike most Greek temple sites, at Eleusis the temple complex is built around a megaron, a subterranean chamber, making evident the connections to archaic chthonic tradition.

Vincent Scully says that Demeter's temples (like Minoan sanctuaries) evoke "the interior, life-giving, death-bringing forces of the earth." He sees Demeter as "an Olympian only by courtesy" and believes the increasing importance of her mysteries in the Hellenistic period represents a renewal and reinterpretation of older rites that had been suppressed by the Dorian invaders. He sees in the temple architecture itself an attempt "to integrate the ancient chthonic deities into the intellectual and emotional life of the polis." The temple at Eleusis differs from other Greek temples in its emphasis on interior, enclosed space; the design of the temple leads to a "fixed conclusion," not the continued free movement about the site characteristic of most Greek religious architecture. Like temples dedicated to Dionysus, the temple at Eleusis seems specifically designed to encourage a visionary experience.[2]

It seems clear that the Homeric "Hymn to Demeter" gives us the official Eleusinian version of the Demeter/Persephone mythologem and that the hymn serves to validate the Eleusinian cult at a particular stage in its evolution, for the ritual surely changed during the perhaps two thousand years of its existence. We know at least something of the changes that took place during the thousand years between the writing of the hymn and the destruction of the temple complex at Eleusis by the Goths around 400 CE and can deduce some of the changes introduced earlier. Even more important than changes in what was done during the ceremonies are the changes in the meaning attributed to the ritual acts. Originally the Eleusinian ritual seems to have had important agrarian significance, although there was probably always also a chthonic element. In the Hellenistic period the emphasis seems to have fallen almost entirely on the mysteries' power to assuage the fear of death. And in a sense the meaning may *still* be changing!—as we will discover when we look at the many meanings contemporary women find in the myth and the rituals associated with it, some clearly different from any meaning consciously acknowledged in the ancient world.

The relatively minor emphasis given to Triptolemus (the youth whom Demeter sends forth to teach humankind about the cultivation of corn) in the hymn, in contrast to the importance attributed to him in many reliefs and vase paintings, suggests that at the time of the hymn's composition the main purpose of the ritual was no longer associated with agricultural fertility. Indeed, the hymn's description of vain plowing and fruitless sowing during the period when Demeter is consumed with rage and grief implies that agriculture already exists at the time of Persephone's abduction.

On the other hand, the omission of Iacchus from the hymn suggests that the cry welcoming his birth was not part of the ritual when the hymn was written and thus not originally central to the mysteries. Iacchus was probably introduced into the rite during the fifth century in response to Orphic influence—though it is important to insist again on the enormous difference between the cults devoted to Demeter/Persephone and those devoted to Dionysus. There is no evidence that at any point in its development the Eleusinian cult included the emphasis on ecstatic, orgiastic communion with the god characteristic of the Dionysian cult.

Originally Eleusis was undoubtedly the center of a local cult devoted to the two goddesses and closed to strangers, but in 760 BCE the oracle at Delphi, in response to a great famine sweeping over all of Greece, ordered Athens to offer a sacrifice to Eleusinian Demeter in the name of all Greeks. The famine ended, and thereafter it became a custom that each year as an expression of gratitude, all the Greek states would send first-fruit offerings to Eleusis. By the time of Pericles (fifth century), Eleusis was clearly under the hegemony of Athens, and the pan-Greek importance of the cult served Athenian political ambitions. The "lesser mysteries," celebrated in the outskirts of Athens in the spring and, according to tradition, first celebrated so that Heracles might be purified of bloodguilt and so made eligible for participation in the "greater mysteries," which were celebrated at Eleusis in the fall, were probably introduced when Athens took over the Eleusinian cult.

Differing in this respect from most Greek religious cults, participation in the Eleusinian rite was not open to the general public but only to those who underwent a ritual initiation and who took a vow to keep this ritual secret. It may be that at one time the Eleusinian rites were open only to women (as the Thesmophoria always continued to be); it is certain that priestesses always played a central role in the administration of the cult. But in historical times the Eleusinian cult was the most inclusive of all Greek cults, open to all who spoke Greek and were free of bloodguilt.

Unlike many other rituals in which one participates on a regular basis, it was felt that to have seen the mystery once was sufficient, although a different status in the celebration was reserved for repeaters. Participation in the ritual created no ongoing bonds among the initiates and implied no further ritual or ethical obligations. The initiates returned to their ordinary life outwardly unchanged. But inwardly, as testimony after testimony confirms, they were transformed. As Pindar exclaimed, "Happy is he who, having seen these rites, goes below the hollow earth; for he knows the end of life and he knows its god-sent beginning."[3]

What the initiates saw at the climax of the rites is still a mystery, still a secret. The hymn was, of course, public; the myth was known to everyone. The myth was part of the open preparation; elements of it are clearly paralleled by various parts of the preparatory phases of the celebration, about which no one felt the need to be silent: the procession carrying the sacred objects from Athens to Eleusis, the purification in the sea, the pig sacrifice, the obscene cursing at the bridge. Aristophanes felt perfectly free to include a detailed, somewhat mocking description of these parts of the ritual in his comedy *The Frogs*.

But what was enacted, what sacred things were shown at the climax of the rite, which took place within the temple and at night, we do not know. As Mylonas says, the maintenance of the secret is amazing when one considers that these rites were celebrated for almost two thousand years and that multitudes from everywhere were initiated.[4] We know of the anger directed at Aeschylus for allegedly having revealed some forbidden aspect of the mysteries in one of his plays. We know that Alcibiades was banished from Athens for violating the oath of secrecy. We have the testimony attributed to Aristotle that the focus in the secret part of the rite was on something seen and done that had a transformative psychological effect, not on something taught: the initiates, he says, don't learn anything but suffer, feel certain emotions, are put in a certain frame of mind.[5] We have the Homeric hymn, of course, teasing allusions scattered here and there, and the testimony of Christian authors who claimed to know what the sacred objects were and who speculated about what was done with them.

We also have the evidence of vase paintings and reliefs, though I agree with Mylonas and others that the secret will no more be revealed in art than it is in literature. What the artistic representations do reveal are how important corn and poppies, pig and serpent are as symbolic emblems of the goddesses. They also show how little there is to help us distinguish Demeter from Persephone; in the most ancient vases and terracottas the two goddesses often appear almost like twin sisters, and there is often disagreement among scholars as to which is which![6] Many vases and reliefs also suggest a different understanding of Hades from that of the hymn. Hades is often depicted not as a ravisher of Persephone but simply as her beloved consort; there are portrayals of a Demeter reconciled to Hades and blessing his union with her daughter.[7] The reunion of Persephone and Demeter, the sending forth of Triptolemus, the initiation of Heracles—these are among the most popular themes. But none of these touch upon the heart of the mystery.

On these inadequate sources we must base our knowledge, our assumptions, and our flights of imagination. The essays in Parts Two and Three of this book will make abundantly clear how varied these guesses and imaginings can be—though most of the writers seem to agree with Mylonas that "whatever the substance and meaning of the Mysteries was, the fact remains that the cult of Eleusis satisfied the most sincere yearnings and the deepest longings of the human heart."[8]

If we want to understand how Demeter and Persephone were experienced in the ancient world, we must also take into account another ritual, the Thesmophoria. This all-women's ritual was celebrated in the fall in honor of Demeter. The precise meaning of the ritual's name is in dispute; it is usually interpreted as referring to Demeter's association with the gifts of agriculture, settled life, and marriage.[9] Pamela Berger suggests it may refer to Demeter as the goddess who brought women the gift of the rites celebrating women's mysteries.[10] Though there are elements in the ritual that make evident its continuing agrarian significance, the emphasis, at least in the classical period, does seem to be on the social, inter-human aspect, on this as a women's festival that provided married women (children and virgins were excluded) an occasion to share with one another the sorrows of motherhood and the anger women felt at men and, some believe, an opportunity to reclaim their own sexuality.

Walter Burkert notes that the Thesmophoria, the most widely celebrated of all Greek festivals, was a very ancient rite that remained remarkably unchanged over a long period. It gave the cloistered wives of the classical period their only opportunity to leave home for a three-day period. Husbands were obligated to support their going, and men were ruthlessly excluded from participation.[11] Great stress was laid on the secretive nature of the rites—which means that again there is much dispute about just what happened and what it meant. We do know that the ritual was associated with the mysteries of death and decay, sexuality and fertility, that it included a pig sacrifice in commemoration of Persephone's rape and an indulgence of obscenity and aggression in honor of Demeter's grief and rage. "At the core of the festival," Burkett concludes, is "the dissolution of family, the separation of the sexes, the constitution of a society of women."

NOTES

1. Carl Kerenyi, *Eleusis: Archetypal Image of Mother and Daughter* (New York: Pantheon, 1967), 23.
2. Vincent Scully, *The Earth, the Temple, and the Gods* (New Haven: Yale University Press, 1979), 70–79.
3. George E. Mylonas, *Eleusis and the Eleusinian Mysteries* (Princeton: Princeton University Press, 1961), 285.

4. Ibid., 226.
5. Ibid., 228, 262.
6. Lewis Richard Farnell, *The Cults of the Greek States,* vol. 3 (Chicago: Aegean Press, [1906] 1971, 259, 263.
7. See Mylonas, *Eleusis,* 99; Farnell, *Cults,* 136, 225.
8. Mylonas, *Eleusis,* 284.
9. Farnell, *Cults,* 107.
10. Pamela Berger, *The Goddess Obscured* (Boston: Beacon Press, 1985), 17.
11. Walter Burkert, *Greek Religion* (Cambridge, Mass.: Harvard University Press, 1985), 245.

PART TWO

PRECURSORS

OF

CONTEMPORARY

PERSPECTIVES

MYTHOGRAPHY AND
DEPTH PSYCHOLOGY

A REVIVED INTEREST in Greek mythology during the eighteenth century accelerated in the nineteenth when radically new approaches to mythography (the scholarly study of mythology) and new interpretations of mythology were put forward, approaches and interpretations that inevitably form a kind of backdrop for the more recent re-visionings that we will be focusing on in the last part of this book.

Perhaps the most revolutionary interpretation was J. J. Bachofen's, whose *Mutterrecht (Mother Right)* appeared in 1861, the same year as Darwin's *Origins of the Species*. Bachofen's aim in looking at myth was not simply to retell the ancient stories as Bullfinch, for example, had, but to learn how to look through symbol and myth as sources of historical information. Myths, if we learn to read them rightly, are in his view an indispensable source for clues as to how earlier peoples imagined themselves and their world.

Bachofen believed that the only way we can properly understand the creative expressions of cultures other than our own is through the exercise of the empathic imagination, through our activating in ourselves psychological capacities analogous to those involved in the creation of those cultural artifacts. Thus Bachofen emphasized the important role imagination and intuition play in

scholarly investigation. "Aroused by direct contact with the ancient remains, the imagination [*Phantasie*] grasps the truth at one
stroke."[1] Bachofen also understood that this kind of imaginative
entrance into the mental processes of those who lived in earlier
times demands an inner transformation, a sloughing off of acquired sophistications: "The divine can only be understood by a
divine mind and not by the rationalistic self-conceit that sets itself
above history."[2] Bachofen's validation of imagination as a historical method makes him a precursor (though not necessarily a recognized precursor) of feminist scholars like Charlene Spretnak
who have sought to look through the patriarchal traditions about
Demeter and Persephone to discover a prepatriarchal perspective.

Bachofen's attempts to explore the religious life of pre-Homeric Greece were undertaken well before any of the archaeological excavations at Mycenae, Troy, or Knossos. He is best known
for his conviction that behind the patriarchal social and religious
organization of classical Greece lay a period of "mother right" or
matriarchy. His basis for this belief was not archaeology or anthropology but myth—and perhaps also something that we might call
a kind of rudimentary "depth psychology." For Bachofen says that
he saw, in what he regarded as man's unquenchable (though
mostly unacknowledged) "nostalgia" for the rule of women, a clue
that such rule once obtained.

Bachofen (perhaps influenced consciously or unconsciously by
Hegel) divided Greek history into three phases characterized, re-
spectively, by promiscuity, mother right, and father right.

In the first stage, the period before the discovery of agriculture
and before the institution of marriage, relations between the sexes
were solely governed by lust; there was as yet no recognition of
the relation between intercourse and conception. Bachofen views
Aphrodite as the most appropriate symbol of this period when
promiscuity reigned. The next stage, that of mother right, arises
because women come to protest the abuses they suffer under the
conditions of promiscuity; for although there are as yet no stable

bonds between women and men, mothers were already strongly attached to their children. "The relationship which stands at the origin of all culture, of every virtue, of every nobler aspect of existence is that between mother and child. . . . Woman at this stage is the repository of all culture, of all benevolence, of all devotion, of all concern for the living and grief for the dead."[3] By *mother right* Bachofen does not mean female political rule but, rather, the change to settled life and monogamy that comes with the introduction of agriculture. In these new circumstances the basis for the relation between the sexes becomes not just lust but the desire for progeny. He regards his descriptions of this stage in human history (which he identifies with Demeter and which he sees as appearing universally, not only in Greece) as his most important contribution. Bachofen honors Demeter's association with the development of a more spiritual religion than the earth-focused one of the first stage, for the move to agriculture brings an engagement with seed grain that discloses "death as the indispensable forerunner of a higher rebirth." But Bachofen has nothing to say about the relationship between Demeter and Persephone nor about the latter's connection to a religious cult that frees humans from their fear of death.

Indeed, Bachofen includes few specific references to the Greek myths involving Aphrodite or Demeter. In his writing, these goddesses have become what Jung would call archetypes, emblems of universally occurring ways of ordering experience. And though Bachofen is deeply invested in his insistence on the historicity of a "matriarchal" period and on the virtues of the Demetrian order, he nonetheless upholds the third (or "solar") phase, the phase of father right, of the patriarchal family, private property, and the division of labor, as a "higher" phase because it represents a turn to a more abstract, more spiritual consciousness. Yet Bachofen also realizes that it is not quite that simple, that the emphasis on the masculine, heroic virtues may lead to a painful separation from the natural world and a radical suppression of emotion. Thus the nostalgia for mother right, for the order symbolized by Demeter, an order that Bachofen comes to recognize represents not just a long-vanished period in history but a never fully erased layer in our souls.

Even more emphatically than Bachofen, James George Frazer (under the acknowledged influence of Darwin) adopts an evolutionary approach to human culture—though he is far less appreciative of the value of the earlier, now outgrown stages. His understanding of the Demeter/Persephone mythologem as presented in his monumental *Golden Bough* (first published in 1890), though enormously influential in his own time, now seems largely outmoded. It is important to give it attention primarily in order to take note of some approaches to myth that are likely to lead one astray.

Although Frazer was quite dogmatic in his insistence that myths are based on rituals, that they are the spoken correlative of sacred rites, he remained wedded to a rather intellectualistic view of mythology as having only an etiological function. A product of the "primitive mind" not yet able to devise more rational explanations, myths in his view were created to explain the origin and structure of the natural world. Rituals are designed to effect change through the exercise of magic; they purport to offer protection against the terrors of the hostile universe, which inspires them; they rely on analogical rather than cause/effect thinking. Thus both myth and ritual are regarded by Frazer as protoscientific ways of responding to the natural world, ways long since fully superseded by science itself. Frazer pays little heed to the story aspect of myth nor to the emotional needs that myth or ritual assuage. Despite his interest in a comparative approach to mythology and his fascination with the great variety of myths and rituals, Frazier is ultimately committed to the notion of a monomyth: all rituals arise as fertility rituals; all myths are concerned with the theme of death and rebirth.

Frazer's discussion of Demeter and Persephone concludes a section of his book devoted to "dying and reviving Gods," divinities whom he regards as "mythic embodiments of fertility." He begins by emphasizing the commonalties between the Demeter/Persephone myth and other myths about a goddess mourning the loss of a loved one who personifies the corn that dies in winter and revives in spring. If we ask, "What was, after all, stripped of later accretions, the original kernel of the myth?" it is easy to recognize that the two goddesses "resolve themselves into personifications of the corn." He identifies Demeter with cultivated corn and with the teaching of agriculture. Demeter is the ripe ear, Persephone the seed corn. Frazer finds what he calls a "substantial unity" between mother and daughter borne out by art in which the two are often almost indistinguishable. Frazer is determined somehow to fit the myth's account of Demeter's mourning and the earth's barrenness with what he knows about the time of year when the rites were performed and about Greek agricultural practices, though he acknowledges that it doesn't all quite fit. (The most charming part of the whole essay comes when, perhaps as a way of diverting attention from the inescapability of the contradictions, he recalls his own delight in the beauties of the Greek landscape in both autumn and spring.)

Yet it is not really fair to say that Frazer sees the Eleusinian mysteries only in terms of agrarian rite. Though he sees this as their original meaning, he says this is

> not to deny that in the long course of religious evolution high moral and spiritual conceptions were grafted on this simple original stock and blossomed out into fairer flower than the bloom of the barley and the wheat. Above all, the thought of the seed buried in the earth in order to spring up to new and higher life readily suggested a comparison with human destiny, and strengthened the hope that for man too the grave may be but the beginning of a better and happier existence in some brighter world unknown.

But then he goes on to add in what I cannot help but experience as his smug nineteenth-century voice:

No doubt it is easy for us to discern the flimsiness of the logical foundations on which such high hopes were built. But drowning men clutch at straws, and we need not wonder that the Greeks like ourselves, with death before them and a great love of life in their hearts, should not have stopped to weigh with too nice a hand the arguments that told for and against the prospect of human immortality.[4]

It is easy to criticize Frazer, and the emphasis on the fertility elements in his interpretation of the myths and rituals associated with Demeter and Persephone has long been out of favor—and yet we may now be beginning to see that this, too, is a prejudice: renewal of the earth's fertility *was* one aspect of the myth's original meaning, and in a time when we have real reason to be deeply concerned about the continuity of life on this planet, some feminists are rediscovering the present-day relevance of this dimension of the myth.

Unlike Frazer, who so clearly regarded his own time as superior to all earlier periods of human history, Walter Otto (a figure who comes from a time much closer to our own, since his major writings were published in 1929 and 1933) presents himself as a self-conscious pagan who has chosen Greece over Christianity.[5]

In his *Homeric Gods*, Otto hoped to be able to communicate the uniqueness of each particular deity as in some real sense "out there," existing independently of our experience of them. The gods of Greece are, Otto believes, *Urformen*, archetypes; they represent eternally valid aspects of the world.

The figures in which this world was divinely revealed to the Greeks—do they not demonstrate their truth by the fact that they are still alive today, that we still encounter them when we raise ourselves out of petty constraints to an enlarged vision? Zeus, Apollo, Athena, Artemis, Dionysus, Aphrodite . . . they will endure as long as the European spirit, which in them has attained its most significant objectivation, is not wholly subju-

gated to the spirit of the Orient or to that of utilitarian ratio-
nality.[6]

I remember very clearly the impact this passage made on me
when I first read it thirty years ago. I felt a deep kinship with this
man who knew, as I had felt I was alone in knowing, that the gods
of Greece are still alive—and who knew each one as a unique and
living presence.

> The images of individual divine personages are firmly deline-
> ated. Each of them possesses its special character, clearly de-
> fined in all its traits. . . . Always divinity is a totality, a whole
> world in its perfection. . . . None of the [gods] represents a
> single virtue, none is to be encountered in only one direction of
> teeming life; each desires to fill, shape, and illumine the whole
> compass of human existence with his peculiar spirit.[7]

What Otto calls a sense of the living actuality of the "peculiar
spirit" of Persephone and Demeter lies behind all the years of my
own engagement with the two goddesses.

In his book on the Homeric gods Otto has little to say about
Demeter or Persephone, for he recognizes how small a role Demeter plays in Homer, where the sphere of the dead has lost its
sanctity; the gods belong wholly to life and are by their essence
separated from all that is death's. A later essay on the Eleusinian
mysteries presented at one of the Eranos gatherings organized by
Jung represents Demeter's love of Persephone as unique, different from Aphrodite's for Adonis or Ishtar's for Tammuz, because
it is "love for a daughter who resembles her and gives the impression of a double." Otto refuses to reduce the mysteries to the
agrarian element. Don't "belittle these mysteries . . . by reducing
them to the level of agricultural ritual, offering only a metaphoric
consolation," he cries.[8] Rather, he says, we must see that the
meaning of these rites is much more profound. They help us to
understand that death is a prerequisite to the growth of the grain,
that "generation and fertility . . . are indissolubly bound up with

death." Without death there would be no procreation. "The inevitability of death is not a destiny decreed by some hostile power. In birth itself, in the very act of procreation, death is at work."[9]

The secret of the mysteries is not some teaching about rebirth, he insists. It is something *seen,* a real event. Otto reminds us of Aristotle's testimony that the initiates were not meant to learn anything, but to suffer an experience and be moved. The secret cannot possibly just be that we survive in our progeny—for every noninitiate knows that.

Otto concludes that what happens in the rite is that Persephone is called and she comes. "What was involved in the Mysteries was an epiphany: 'the real presence of the supernatural.' "

> The queen of the underworld is present. And Demeter, of course, as well. Demeter with her grief, her lament, her search and rediscovery. . . . The gods are at hand as they were at the beginning of time, not only as majestic figures demanding reverence, but as what they are: supreme realities of the here and now, primal phenomena of the movement of being, creating and suffering powers of the living moment which also encompasses death. Without death there can be no life; without dying, no fertility. . . . The mystai are witnesses of this event, which in essence is not a play, but divine presence, realized myth. . . .
> The Eleusinian mystes lived the miracle of intimacy with the goddesses, he experienced their presence. He was received into the sphere of their acts and sufferings, into the immediate reality of their sublime beings. His famous vision was no mere looking on. It was sublimation to a higher existence, a transformation of his being. . . . And is that not a rebirth?[10]

As I read this and recall that it was written in 1939, I sense that Otto's engagement with the goddesses of Eleusis was a source of consolation and hope to him in a time of deep need—as it may continue to be for some of us.

Otto turned to Dionysus and to Eleusis only after an intense engagement with the Homeric gods; Carl Kerenyi says that as a young man in 1920 he was already deeply absorbed in trying to understand the mysteries, though clarification came only twenty years later when he discovered extensive parallels between the Eleusinian rituals and the initiation rites of an Indonesian tribe. These parallels seemed to him to be meaningful only on the basis of an assumption of a "common human foundation," because even if the commonalities are due to historical transmission rather than spontaneous acquisition, the assimilation presupposes what Kerenyi, borrowing from Jung, calls an "archetypal foundation."[11]

The recognition that the significance of the Eleusinian mysteries can only be apprehended if we see them not simply in terms of the role they played in Greek life but rather in relation to perennial human concerns led Kerenyi to write his seminal essay, "Kore."[12] But the writing of this essay did not mean he was finished with Eleusis. Intead, he continued to write essay after essay devoted to the shrine and the goddesses it served, culminating in the 1966 volume *Eleusis: Archetypal Image of Mother and Daughter.*

To Kerenyi the ultimate identity of mother and daughter is central to the "mystery" of Eleusis. Through the mysteries a "feminine" perspective was made available to all initiates, irrespective of gender. He communicates a profound appreciation of Demeter's human dimension, her embodiment of a universal principle of life: the inescapability of experiences of loss and suffering. Men, too, he believes, entered into the figure of Demeter through whom they were able to experience what it is like "to be pursued, robbed, raped, to fail to understand, to rage and to grieve, but then to get everything back and be born again." Part of the point of the ritual as he understands it was for both men and women to identify with the goddess, with the feminine, and like Demeter to experience the possibility of getting beyond grief, beyond not understanding. The secret of the mysteries was a wordless knowledge, an experience, not an idea, that freed the initiates from an identification with their individual ego and thus from their need for an assurance of individual immortality.

Almost as important as the classicists in helping to shape present-day response to the Demeter/Persephone myth have been the early depth psychologists. Carl Jung's essay "The Psychological Aspects of the Kore" was inspired by Kerenyi's essay on the Kore. Kerenyi came to believe that part of the value of his study was that it led Jung to his psychological appraisal; he acknowledged how deeply moved he was by the possibility that his work as a classical scholar through its influence on Jung "might be of help to suffering humans."[13]

In his essay Jung recognizes the difference between the anima, the unconscious feminine aspect of men, and the psyche of women themselves and consciously struggles to honor the difference more than in perhaps any other of his writings. He acknowledges that the Demeter/Persephone mythologem is in origin really about female experience, not about men's experience of their feminine side nor about their relation to women—and admits that, precisely because of its basis in women's experience, the mythologem is difficult for a man to understand fully: "The mother/daughter experience is alien to man and shuts him out." Jung's essay, as its title suggests, is really about the Kore, not about Persephone, about the maiden/daughter as a universal archetype rather than about the details of any particular myth. Like many other interpreters of the myth, he sees the relationship between Demeter and Kore as more that of adult woman and maiden than of mother and daughter. Kore appears in a woman's dreams as an "unknown young woman," as her unconscious, helpless aspect. "Demeter and Kore extend feminine consciousness both upward and downward. They add an 'older and younger,' 'stronger and weaker dimension,'" to a woman's personality, a sense of extending "backwards into one's mother and forwards into her daughter," "a conviction of being outside time, a feeling of immortality."[14]

In *The Great Mother,* Jung's student Erich Neumann gives us a more extended interpretation of the Demeter/Persephone myth. Earlier in his book Neumann focuses on the role that the archetype of the great mother plays in the individuation process of men, in their journey toward psychological transformation; now, as Neumann turns to the Eleusinian mysteries, he proposes to consider instead their relevance to women's self-understanding. Neumann recognizes that in the historical period the Eleusinian mysteries had been usurped by males but believes that it is possible to remove the patriarchal overlay and discover the original matriarchal version of the mysteries that focused on the relationship between mother and daughter and on a commitment to the preservation of their primordial bond. From the matriarchal perspective, males are always perceived as alien, as violent intruders. Thus abduction, rape, separation, and reunion are the primary themes of the Eleusinian mysteries. This leads to Neumann's astounding assertion that the reunion of Demeter and Persephone "signifies the *annulment* of the male rape and incursion"! (emphasis added) Once mother and daughter are reconnected, the painful experience of separation has been erased.

Yet even Neumann recognizes that Persephone does not return to her mother unchanged; it is not as though nothing has happened. What has happened in his view is that while in the underworld Persephone was impregnated and after her return she gives birth; she becomes a mother. The daughter becomes a mother, thus making manifest "the twofold unity of the goddess."

This he regards as the central content of the mysteries, the maiden becoming a mother, giving herself not to Hades but to the Great Mother, to womanhood, to the spiritual aspect of the feminine. The turn to "spirituality" is represented by Persephone becoming an Olympian, a goddess of the heavens as well as of the underworld. As in his reading of the Psyche myth,[15] Neumann imagines here that the goal of woman's journey toward self is transcendence, moving beyond earth, beyond the physical, a goal that many feminists would reject.

He also proposes that the fruit of this transformative process is not simply that the maiden becomes a mother but that she mothers a son, gives birth to something entirely different from herself, something wholly new. Male lovers may be intruders from a matriarchal perspective, but male sons bring fulfillment to women.

It is not surprising then that at the end of his essay Neumann should ask about the meaning of the Eleusinian mysteries for the male initiates who participated in them. Like Kerenyi he sees that the men must have sought to identify themselves with Demeter. For Neumann this means simply that the men identify with their "own feminine aspect," not that they have to participate imaginally in the sufferings characteristic of female experience. Demeter becomes simply an anima figure, an aspect of male psychology.

Notes

1. J. J. Bachofen, *Myth, Religion, and Mother Right* (Princeton: Princeton University Press, 1973), 12.

2. Ibid., 16

3. Ibid., 79.

4. Excerpted and paraphrase from Theodor Gaster, ed., *The New Golden Bough: A New Abridgment of the Classic Work by Sir James George Frazer* (Garden City, N.J.: Doubleday, 1961), 202–9.

5. Walter Burkert, *Greek Religion* (Cambridge, Mass.: Harvard University Press, 1985), 1.

6. Walter F. Otto, *The Homeric Gods* (Boston: Beacon Press, 1964), 11.

7. Ibid., 15, 160–61.

8. Walter F. Otto, "The Meaning of the Eleusinian Mysteries," in Joseph Campbell, ed., *The Mysteries: Papers from the Eranos Yearbooks* (New York: Pantheon, 1955), 21.

9. Ibid., 20.

10. Ibid., 29, 30.

11. Carl Kerenyi, *Eleusis: Archetypal Image of Mother and Daughter* (New York: Pantheon, 1967), xxvi.

12. Carl Kerenyi, "Kore," in C. G. Jung and C. Kerenyi, *Essays on a Science of Mythology* (Princeton: Princeton University Press, 1969), 103–55.

13. Kerenyi, *Eleusis,* xxiv, xxviii, xxix.

14. Carl Jung, "The Psychological Aspects of the Kore," in Jung and Kerenyi, *Essays,* 156–62.

15. See Erich Neumann, *Amor and Psyche* (New York: Harper and Row), 1962.

The Woman's Experience of Herself and the Eleusinian Mysteries

ERICH NEUMANN

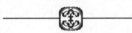

IN OUR EXPOSITION of the transformative character, we have thus far stressed the reaction of the male object of transformation. But this must not blind us to the importance of the woman's experience of her own transformative character for her understanding of herself.

The woman experiences herself first and foremost as the source of life. Fashioned in the likeness of the Great Goddess, she is bound up with the all-generating life principle, which is creative nature and a culture-creating principle in one. The close connection between mother and daughter, who form the nucleus of the female group, is reflected in the preservation of the "primordial relationship" between them. In the eyes of this female group, the male is an alien who comes from without and by violence takes the daughter from the mother. This is true even if he remains in the place of the female group, but much more so if he carries the woman off to his own group.

Abduction, rape, marriage of death, and separation are the great motifs underlying the Eleusinian mysteries. Although these are late mysteries that in a certain sense were usurped by the males, it is to them that we owe much of our knowledge of the matriarchal mysteries. Unquestionably the patriarchal development, which began very early, effaced or at least overlaid many elements of the old matriarchal culture, so that, as in studying a palimpsest, we must first remove the upper layer before we can see the matriarchal culture beneath.

The unity of Demeter and Kore is the central content of the Eleusinian mysteries. The one essential motif in the Eleusinian mysteries and hence in all matriarchal mysteries is the *heuresis* of the daughter by the mother, the "finding again" of Kore by Demeter, the reunion of mother and daughter.

Psychologically, this "finding again" signifies the annulment of the male rape and incursion, the restoration after marriage of the matriarchal unity of mother and daughter. In other words, the nuclear situation of the matriarchal group, the primordial relation of daughter to mother, which has been endangered by the incursion of the male into the female world, is renewed and secured in the mystery. And here Kore's sojourn in Hades signifies not only rape by the male—for originally Kore-Persephone was herself the Queen of the Underworld—but fascination by the male earth aspect, that is to say, by sexuality.

In the myth this is reflected by two symbols, the pomegranate and the narcissus. The redness of the pomegranate symbolizes the woman's womb, the abundance of seeds its fertility. Outwitted by Hades, persuaded to taste of the "sweet morsel," the pomegranate seeds, she consummates her marriage with him and belongs to him for at least part of the year. With regard to the other symbol, the seductive narcissus, "which beguiled the maiden," we read in the Homeric "Hymn to Demeter":

> It was a thing of awe whether for deathless gods or mortal men to see; from its root grew a hundred blooms and it smelled most sweetly, so that all wide heaven above and the whole earth and the sea's salt swell laughed for joy. And the girl was amazed and reached out with both hands to take the lovely toy; but the wide-pathed earth yawned . . .

Through this embodiment of the seduction that fills the whole world, through desire to seize the phallus, she "succumbs" to

Hades and is carried off by the male from "Mycone," the moon country of virginal dreams.

Kore's resurrection from the earth—the archetypal spring motif—signifies her finding by Demeter, for whom Kore had "died," and her reunion with her. But the true mystery, through which the primordial situation is restored on a new plane, is this: the daughter becomes identical with the mother; she becomes a mother and is so transformed into Demeter. Precisely because Demeter and Kore are archetypal poles of the Eternal Womanly, the mature woman and the virgin, the mystery of the Feminine is susceptible of endless renewal. Within the female group, the old are always Demeter, the mother; the young are always Kore, the maiden.

The second element of the mystery is the birth of the son. Here the woman experiences an authentic miracle that is essential to the orientation of the matriarchate: not only is the female, her image, born of woman but the male as well. The miracle of the male's containment in the female is expressed at the primitive level by the self-evident subordination of the male to the female: even as lover and husband, he remains her son. But he is also the fecundating phallus, which on the most spiritual plane is experienced as the instrument of a transpersonal and suprapersonal male principle. Thus, at the lowest level of the matriarchate, the male offspring remains merely that which is necessary for fertility.

But at the mystery level, where the Kore who reappears is not only she who was raped and vanished but also a Kore transformed in every respect; her childbearing too is transfigured, and the son is a very special son, namely, the luminous son, the "divine child."

In connection with the *heuresis,* the finding again of Kore by Demeter, or rather their reunion, the mystery of the marriage of death expresses the transformative character of the Feminine as manifested in the experience of growing from girlhood to womanhood. Rape, victimization, downfall as a girl, death, and sacrifice stand at the center of these events, whether they are experienced through the impersonal god, the paternal uroboros, or, as later, personalized and placed in relation to a male who is in every sense "alien."

But Kore is not merely overcome by the male; her adventure is in the profoundest sense a self-sacrifice, a being-given-to-womanhood, to the Great Goddess as the female self. Only when this has been perceived, or emotionally suffered and experienced in the mystery, has the *heuresis*, the reunion of the young Kore turned woman, with Demeter, the Great Mother, been fulfilled. Only then has the Feminine undergone a central transformation, not so much by becoming a woman and a mother, and thus guaranteeing earthly fertility and the survival of life, as by achieving union on a higher plane with the spiritual aspect of the Feminine, the Sophia aspect of the Great Mother, and thus becoming a moon goddess.

For the renascent Kore no longer dwells as before on the earth, or only in the underworld as Persephone, but in conjunction with Demeter becomes the Olympian Kore, the immortal and divine principle, the beatific light. Like Demeter herself she becomes the goddess of the three worlds: the earth, the underworld, and the heavens.

With the birth of her son, the woman accomplishes the miracle of nature, which gives birth to something different from itself and antithetical to itself. Moreover, the divine son is totally new, not only as to sex but also in quality. Not only does he engender, while she conceives and bears; he is also light in contrast to her natural darkness, motion in contrast to her static character. Thus the woman experiences her power to bring forth light and spirit, to generate a luminous spirit that despite all changes and catastrophes is enduring and immortal.

Her delight at being able to bear a living creature, a son who complements her by his otherness, is increased by the greater delight of creating spirit, light, and immortality, the divine son, through the transformation of her own nature. For in the mystery, she who gives birth renews herself. No doubt the Eleusinian cry, "The noble goddess has borne a sacred child. Brimo has borne Brimos," preserves the name of an ancient and presumably "primitive" goddess. But the mystery action teaches that the resurrected Kore is no longer a Kore who can be abducted by Hades. In the mystery the late psychological insight that matriarchal consciousness was the true native soil of the processes of spiritual growth becomes the "knowledge" of woman, and it is no accident that she experiences Brimos, the male, as a mere variant of her own self as Brimo.

The woman gives birth to this divine son, this unconscious spiritual aspect of herself; she thrusts it out of herself not in order that she herself may become spirit or go the way of this spirit, but in order that she herself may be fructified by it, may receive it and let it grow within her and then send it forth once more in a new birth, never totally transforming herself into it.

This brings us to the question of why *men* were initiated into the Eleusinian mysteries and what these mysteries, which deal exclusively with the central events in the mysterious life of woman, could mean to men. For in the Homeric "Hymn to Demeter" we read:

> Happy is he among men upon earth who has seen these mysteries; but he who is uninitiate and who has no part in them, never has lot of like good things once he is dead, down in the darkness and gloom.

And if we consider the awe in which all antiquity stood of these mysteries, it is clear that they must have constituted a genuine mystery experience for men as well as women.

The nature of the experience was this: the male initiate, as we can see from many particulars in the accounts, sought to identify himself with Demeter, i.e., with his own feminine aspect. Here it should be stressed that in Eleusis, as in all mysteries, the experience was predominantly emotional and unconscious, so that even in a late epoch, when the male consciousness had long become patriarchal, such a prepatriarchal experience was possible in a mystery.

WOMEN'S RE-VISIONINGS

THUS FAR every retelling or interpretation of the Demeter and Persephone myth that we have looked at has been composed by a man. We are now ready to look at responses to the myth put forward by women during the first half of this century.

Jane Ellen Harrison was an important figure among a remarkable group of classicists known as the Cambridge Ritualists, all of whom felt they took Frazer's notion of the primacy of ritual over myth and the central role that anthropological perspectives must play in the study of the ancient world more seriously than in practice Frazer himself had. Most members of the group evinced a clear preference for Greece's classical age and the Olympian gods it honored, whereas Harrison was fascinated with the archaic period and with chthonic cult.

Although space considerations have prevented including excerpts from her work in this anthology, we cannot proceed without some discussion of its primary themes.

Harrison's biographer, Sandra J. Peacock, is wholly persuasive in her claim that Harrison's scholarly work represented a kind of "personal quest," that in some ways it was as much a repudiation of the Victorian society in which she lived, whose emotional and sexual repressiveness she deeply resented (in part because of her painful awareness of the degree to which she had internalized it), as it was a study of Greek religion.[1] Harrison focused on pre-Olympian Greece because there religion still clearly had an emotional content. Religion arises out of desire to express and represent emotion; the aim of ritual is to summon the divine, to create an experience of its presence, to wit, epiphany. Harrison seems to have recognized that her focus on the emotional aspect of religion, which set her apart even from her good men friends among the Ritualist group, represented a clearly female perspective, though she wanted it understood that her approach derived not from some unconscious "welling up of feminine intuition and imagination"[2] but was, rather, consciously and deliberately chosen.

Particularly in her later writings she clearly accepts Bachofen's hypothesis about the historicity of matriarchy. Indeed, the vision of earlier matriarchal societies she presents is even more idealistic than his—perhaps because she longs for a world where women and their nurturing capacity are valued and where women's lives are defined primarily by their intense emotional bonds with one another. Unlike Bachofen, who saw human intellectual and spiritual evolution as dependent on the rise of patriarchy, she emphatically asserted the superiority of matriarchy. For Bachofen matriarchy is inferior because of its closer association to nature; just this Harrison saw as evidence of its superiority.

Harrison seems to have adopted Nietzsche's sense of the conflict between Dionysus and Apollo, emotion and intellect, chthonic and Olympian religion with an even more definite valorization than his of the Dionysian side. Her high regard for Dionysian religion derives at least in part because this god alone among the major male deities of the classical period never broke his connection to the matriarchal world.[3] Her discussion of the Eleusinian mysteries in her *Prolegomena to the Study of Greek Religion* attributes the spiritual depth that these mysteries received during the Hellenistic period almost entirely to the influence of the mysteries of Dionysus.[4]

The chapter from her *Prolegomena* titled "The Making of Goddess" reflects her regret at how radically the Olympian goddesses (not only the male gods) have departed from the matriarchal realm that gave them birth. The gods and goddesses seem to her much less truly divine when they "only mirror human individuality," when they have lost their connections with the natural world.[5] The rigid distinction between gods and humans, immortals and mortals characteristic of Olympian religion made impossible that sense of communion with the divine that Harrison feels essential to an authentic religiosity. She values the mystery religions "because they are still alive with the life-blood of all living things from which they sprang."[6] Her discussion of Demeter and Persephone traces the gradual differentiation, dictated by the storytelling, not the religious instinct, of the two goddesses that at first were merely the older and younger forms of the same person. "Mythology might work its will, but primitive art never clearly distinguished between the Mother and the Maid, never lost hold of the truth that they were one goddess."[7] But in mythology and at Eleusis Demeter comes to have as her sphere the things of this life, and Persephone becomes identified with things below and beyond. Harrison laments the separation of the earthly and underworld sphere thus symbolized, a separation that she sees as representing a betrayal of the truly religious recognition of their unity. Harrison's writing is infused with nostalgia for the religion of the more archaic period.

H.D. (Hilda Doolittle) says that her poetry grew out of "nostalgia for a lost land. I call it Hellas." It was not Greece in any literal way but an imagined *mother*land that inspired her writing. Indeed, as her analysis with Freud helped her to understand, H.D.'s whole way of being in the world was profoundly shaped by her sense of emotional separation from her mother.

Greece was a natural image for this lost land because, as Alicia Ostriker recognizes, H.D. was a "visionary poet," a poet for whom there exist permanent sacred realities that are both supremely beautiful and supremely forceful, realities that the poet experiences as presences, as epiphanies.[8] Like some of the other writers we have discussed, H.D. experienced these archetypal realities to be embodied in the myths of ancient Greece, though much of her poetry expresses her sense that the dominant patriarchal interpretations of these myths must be displaced. These myths will look different when re-visioned from a perspective that acknowledges the primacy of femal experience.

H.D. is particularly drawn to those embodiments of primal sacred energy that have the power to overwhelm us, to force us to surrender to them, to passion, to sexuality—figures like Bacchus, Circe, Aphrodite, and Demeter. Her poem "At Eleusis," written in the persona of an Eleusinian priestess, begins:

> *What they did,*
> *they did for Dionysos,*
> *for ecstasy's sake.*

The priestess sees how unbearably difficult the god's demand is. Union with Dionysus requires a full acceptance of self, an entering into the foulest part of one's own interior underworld, a supplication and conjuration of the moment in our life it would be most painful for us to acknowledge.

"Demeter," written from the goddess's perspective, voices Demeter's resentment of the elaborate rituals men have instituted in her honor, the heavy sculptures in which they have sought to enclose her, and expresses her awareness that this treatment derives from their fear of her who is both "greatest and least" of all the gods. Men may find it easy to deal lightly with the maiden goddess, but the mother frightens them. In the final section of the poem, the goddess turns to her relation to her daughter, the beloved daughter whom Hades stole and who is now the awesome "Mistress of Death."

> Ah, strong were the arms that took
> (Ah, evil the heart and graceless),
> but the kiss was less passionate.

The goddess voices her anger at Hades' violence and at the same time affirms that her love, her kiss, the love between mother and daughter is far more passionate than his male lust.

H.D. begins another poem, "The Master," written in response to her work with Freud, with an avowal of her anger at patriarchy, at male mysteries:

> I was angry with the old man
> with his talk of the man-strength,
> I was angry with his mystery, his mysteries,
> I argued until daybreak.

But then the poem becomes a paean in praise of the female mysteries, which she imagines taking their place:

> No man will be present in those mysteries
> yet all men will kneel,
> no man will be potent,
> important,
> yet all men will feel
> what it is to be a woman.[9]

Meridel Le Sueur dedicated *Ripening,* the collection of her work that she published in 1982, to "the continuous matriarchal root" that begins with her great-grandmother and goes on to include her daughters' granddaughters, "the root cycle turning into view."

All Le Sueur's writing seems to circle around the theme of the connection between mothers and daughters and the pain each feels when that connection is broken. Le Sueur began writing "Persephone," the story included in this volume, at a time when she felt violently cut off from her mother, adrift in a male-dominated world, spiritually dead, and suicidal. She finished it while pregnant with her daughter, a child she had consciously chosen to have in a very Demeter-like way, as *her* child, as her way of participating in that matriarchal chain of life that her dedication honors. Looking back at that period in her life fifty years later, she said that writing the story, which enabled her to look at her own experience refracted through the Demeter/Persephone myth, "saved her life."[10]

In the story an innocent young girl, whose peaceful life with her mother had been violently disrupted when she was abducted by a dark and fearful man, is now on her way to a hospital evidently fatally ill. This Persephone is lost in an underworld experience of which she can make no sense and from which there seems to be no rescue. There are many other Persephone figures in Le Sueur's later stories. Some are stories of sexual awakening rather than death. Some communicate Le Sueur's growing recognition that the underworld, although always frightening, may represent a fructifying chaos out of which something new might be born. Engagement with the dark side of life and creativity come to be seen as inextricably intertwined, and Le Sueur comes to emphasize Persephone's reunion with her mother, a theme completely absent from that first story. Even when Le Sueur was in her eighties, this myth continued to inspire her writing, though by then she had come to speak as Demeter rather than as Persephone, as a Demeter who is "grieving but protective, strong and fierce," and identified with the natural cycle of birth, death, and renewal.[11]

NOTES

1. Sandra J. Peacock, *Jane Ellen Harrison: The Mask and the Self* (New Haven: Yale University Press, 1988), 165.

2. Ibid., 131.

3. Jane Ellen Harrison, *Themis: A Study of the Social Origins of Greek Religion* (Gloucester, Mass.: Peter Smith, 1974), 562.

4. Jane Ellen Harrison, *Prolegomena to the Study of Greek Religion* (Cambridge: Cambridge University Press, 1903), 271.

5. Harrison, *Themis*, 447.

6. Ibid., 450.

7. Harrison, *Prolegomena*, 288.

8. Alicia Ostriker, *Writing Like a Woman* (Ann Arbor: University of Michigan Press, 1983), 8.

9. H.D., "The Master," quoted in Dianne Chisholm, *H.D.'s Freudian Poetics* (Ithaca: Cornell University Press, 1992), 26. This uncollected poem is used here by permission of H.D.'s daughter Perdita Schaffner. Permission for the use of other poems cited in this chapter has been given by New Directions Publishing Corporation.

10. Meridel Le Sueur, "On the Far Edge of the Circle," *Lady Unique* 2 (Autumn 1977): 14.

11. See Elaine Hedges's introduction to Meridel Le Sueur, *Ripening* (Old Westbury, N.Y.: The Feminist Press, 1982), 19.

Demeter

H.D.

I

Men, fires, feasts,
steps of temple, fore-stone, lintel,
step of white altar, fire and after-fire,
slaughter before,
fragrant of burnt meat,
deep mystery, grapple of mind to reach
the tense thought,
power and wealth, purpose and prayer alike,
(men, fires, feasts, temple steps)—useless.

Useless to me who plant
wide feet on a mighty plinth,
useless to me who sit,
wide of shoulder, great of thigh,
heavy in gold, to press
gold back against solid back
of the marble seat:
useless the dragons wrought on the arms,
useless the poppy-buds and the gold inset
of the spray of wheat.

Ah they have wrought me heavy
and great of limb—
she is slender of waist,
slight of breast, made of many fashions;
they have set *her* small feet
on many a plinth;
she they have known,
she they have spoken with,
she they have smiled upon,
she they have caught
and flattered with praise and gifts.

But useless the flattery
of the mighty power
they have granted me;
for I will not stay in her breast,
the great of limb,
though perfect the shell they have
fashioned me, these men!

Do I sit in the market-place—
do I smile, does a noble brow
bend like the brow of Zeus—
am I a spouse, his or any,
am I a woman, or goddess or queen,
to be met by a god with a smile—and left?

II

Do you ask for a scroll,
parchment, oracle, prophecy, precedent;
do you ask for tablets marked with thought
or words cut deep on the marble surface,
do you seek measured utterance or the mystic trance?

Sleep on the stones of Delphi—
dare the ledges of Pallas

but keep me foremost,
keep me before you, after you, with you,
never forget when you start
for the Delphic precipice,
never forget when you seek Pallas
and meet in thought
yourself drawn out from yourself
like the holy serpent,
never forget
in thought or mysterious trance—
I am greatest and least.

IV

What of her—
mistress of Death?

Form of a golden wreath
were my hands that girt her head,
fingers that strove to meet,
and met where the whisps escaped
from the fillet, of tenderest gold,
small circlet and slim
were my fingers then.

Now they are wrought of iron
to wrest from earth
secrets; strong to protect,
strong to keep back the winter
when winter tracks too soon
blanch the forest:
strong to break dead things,
the young tree, drained of sap,
the old tree, ready to drop,
to lift from the rotting bed
of leaves, the old

crumbling pine tree stock,
to heap bole and knot of fir
and pine and resinous oak,
till fire shatter the dark
and hope of spring
rise in the hearts of men.

What of her—
mistress of Death—
what of his kiss?

Ah, strong were his arms to wrest
slight limbs from the beautiful earth,
young hands that plucked the first
buds of the chill narcissus,
soft fingers that broke
and fastened the thorny stalk
with the flower of wild acanthus.

Ah, strong were the arms that took
(ah, evil the heart and graceless),
but the kiss was less passionate!

Persephone

Meridel Le Sueur

WE BOARDED THE TRAIN at a Kansas town. Its black houses sat low amidst the fields, were hardening and darkening now the summer was over. The corn had been shocked, the seed lay in the granaries, the earth had closed, and now the sun hung naked in the sky. All was over—the festival, the flowering, the harvesting. Dark days had come, and I was taking the daughter of Freda away to discover, if I could, the malady which made her suffer.

As the train moved from the station, I watched Freda standing on the platform, her rounded face shadowed by the train as it passed between her and the low sun. The daughter leaned against the window for the last sight of her mother; as we left the town she sat with her small head bent as if half broken from her body.

We sped through the dying country, fleeing through the low land. Upon the fields as they lay upturned and dark, clear to the round swinging sky-line, there fell the eerie wan light of the dying season. The train as it traveled through this dim sea of light became uncanny and frail, touched, too, with the bright delicacy of decay. But upon the daughter of Freda the last light dwelt intimately as she lay half sleeping, like the fields, fatally within the cycle of the dying earth.

Fatigued after the preparations for the journey, she rested in utter weariness. Her black garments hung, about to exhaust her, while out from them, like sudden flowers, sprang her hands and face. Over her great eyes the lids were lowered and gave to her whole being a magical abstraction, as if she looked eternally within, or down through the earth. Only her mouth had tasted of violent fruit; it drooped in her face and turned red when she coughed, which she did frequently, dipping her head like a blind bird.

As I watched her an old pain brewed within me; a faint nostalgia which had come upon me all my life when looking upon her, or when in the presence of her mother, as if upon seeing these two women a kind of budding came about on all the secret unflowered tendrils of my being, to blossom and break in the spaces of a strange world, far from my eyes and hands.

Just when the round and naked sun hung on the horizon, three bulls, standing in the dim, nether light, turned and loped toward our train.

"The black bull," I said, "looked like your husband's."

She lifted the white lids from her eyes, but did not speak. When I repeated what I said, she turned away without answering and sat with her hands in her lap, her eyes lowered, in an attitude so fatal and hopeless that I knew it was of no use to take her on this train, through these fields, past these rivers and houses to our destination. Nothing lay in these things that could mitigate her illness. The malady was too deep.

As we sped through the fields, the fantastic conquering of distance threw a magic over us so that terrible and vast things became possible. With the dying of the sun the train traveled through a colossal cave, between the closed earth and the closed sky, and I half forgot our departure and our destination.

I have always expected some metamorphosis to take place in Freda and her daughter—a moment when the distant look would, by miracle, go from their eyes and they would reveal their nativity in some awful gesture. Nothing had ever happened beyond the natural ritual of our common farm life. But there came upon me now the old mystic credulity as I watched Freda's daughter sitting motionless, her white lids rounding over her eyes, her face glowing in the gloom.

Lying there she contained, like a white seed, the mystery of her origin. The marks of living were slight upon her, for from the first she seemed to carry most strongly the mark of a perpetual death. Paradoxically, I thought that because death was her intimate I could never come nearer her mystery than to her birth on the prairies, in the spring as the first white violets bloomed.

For the women of the Kansas town, shading their eyes, had seen Freda coming from the prairies, walking and carrying the child.

"Whose baby is that?" the women asked her when she had come to them.

And she answered, "Mine." And uncovered for them to see, bending down to them.

"When was it born?" these women, to whom birth was a great dread, asked.

She answered, smiling. "In the night." And she went into a store and bought some goods with little flowers marked on it in which she wrapped the baby.

That year the days were bright and the earth bountiful. For each ear of corn heretofore, there were now two. The sun ripened all that had been sown. The soil was so hot we could not suffer our bare feet upon it. Freda's lands were the most fertile of all.

Her husband, Frantz, the strongest man in the country, was a ploughman. We saw him in the fields, dark and stocky, driving his big flanked horses, astride the black furrows that turned behind him. When he came to our fields we were frightened by his narrow eyes buried in the flesh, and by his hands matted with hair.

Together, Frantz and Freda ploughed the fields; there was a feeling abroad that never had Freda sown a seed that had not come to fruition. It was true that for her everything blossomed.

In the spring we met her in the fields or in the thickets, where the first flowers were springing alone. In the full, golden light she came towards us, full-bosomed, with baskets of wild berries hanging on her bright arms. When we ran to her, she gave us gifts, berries, nuts, and wild fruits unknown to us.

At harvest time she worked in the fields with the men. When we brought her water she straightened from the earth to loom above us, curving against the sky; a strong odor would come from her, like the odor of the earth when it is just turned; her yellow hair would glisten around her face and we thought it grew from her head exactly as the wheat grew from the earth. Once when she leaned over me, I grew faint with the fertile odor and at the same time drops of perspiration fell from her temples on my face.

When her mare was seen hitched outside the houses of the town, we knew that a great, natural, and dreadful thing was taking place within. The house became, after that, marked, possessing a strange significance of birth. We children, while the mare waited, sat on the curb watching for Freda, who, when she came, passed in a kind of confusion of her great body, the golden hair, and the strong, sweet odor. We would watch the hips of the horse, with Freda upon her, diasppearing down the road, past the houses of the town, out into the open plains.

The child of Freda, delicate and pale from the first, was not much known or seen about. She came to town on the first spring days, with her mother, riding in the wagon atop the early vegetables. She carried with her always, falling from her hands, the first white violets. It did not astonish us that she was thus privy to the first stirrings of the season, since we glimpsed her through all the year in the prairies, by the streams, or hidden in the nooks of the fragrant hills. In the fall, returning from berry hunting, she brushed past us in the chill dusk. In the winter, as we went to the frozen creek, we glimpsed her peering from the naked bush. In the spring we saw her come by her mother, with the first violets. She never spoke to us, but covered her enormous eyes with her lids, standing quite still, before us but irrevocably hidden.

On Saturdays as Freda went about the town she hid behind her skirts, her eyes lowered in her slim, pale face. Some women would stop in the streets and say she was idiotic because of her little head. To me, however, she had a strange grace, with her swelling body, her little head and pale face, her eyes like minerals, and her hair light like her mother's, but fine and thin as if it had grown outside the light of the sun.

When Freda and her husband were ploughing the fields, the girl, who grew very tall, would run in the wake of the plough, singing. Frantz hated her, as everyone knew, and he hated her singing. When Freda with her horses went plunging through the black waves to the horizon, he would leave his plough and strike at the girl. She would veer away as if only the wind had struck her, still singing.

When I could run away from the town I used to lie in the damp thicket which bordered their field and watch them; the dark man straddling the furrows, following the rumps of his horses, holding the plough to the heavy soil; Freda with her skirts on the earth, the horses turning their great eyes to look back at her, the fields lying about her with their living secrets—I watched with satisfaction these two heavy figures, turning the vast earth, moving upon her stillnesses, and the slim girl, like an antelope, running in the fields beside them, singing high and shrill.

She coughed beside me, dipping her little head like a bird. Now no song was in her.

Outside rapidly past us moved the thickets, the fields, the villages. A woman stood in a doorway, half invisible in the dusk, hoisting a baby on her hip—a man came down the road with his team, the white breath of the horses flying from them in the dusk.

The visible world was sinking into another sea, into a faint dusk. The daughter of Freda lay like a fallen and despoiled angel, traveling through darkness, lost to the realm of her nativity, with neither memory nor anticipation. Still I watched her trying to spin around her the stuff of reality. Did there exist for her the seed of our common life, or had she eaten only the fruit of perpetual strangeness and death? All that had happened to her, all the incidents of her life, I brought to bear upon her, but I had easier made a mark upon the wind. These things had made no mark upon her. The only mark was her mark upon life, upon all of us who saw her as a frail lost child in the fields of her mother, as a woman ravished by strangeness.

The young farm boys, still delicate with the wind and the fire, which is the mark of light and air before the fields harden them, were the only ones who came close to Freda's daughter. They often told us in the evenings that they had met her in the thickets or coming across the fields and had talked with her. But then they would say no more.

The older youths found it impossible to snare the footsteps of the delicate girl. Strange to say, on the other hand, the firm and serious farm youth were convinced of her wantonness, while old ladies rocking on their porches hinted dark things of her.

But one night a man came to town, from the west, driving his cattle, packed and bellowing, through the deserted streets.

The next morning people said to each other, "Did you hear the cattle going by in the night?" We children thought it had been only a dream until, early in the morning, we saw on the lawn the deep prints of cloven hoofs. When I went for the morning milk, just outside the town, I saw the cattle where they stood sleeping, knee deep in the grass and mist. As I was passing a man sat up, from where he too had been sleeping, and looked at me from the grasses. His beard stood out like bracken. From his low forehead the black hair sprang. When I saw him about to rise, I ran into the town, shouting to my brothers that the cattle they had heard and thought were only the sound in a dream had really gone down our streets and had stopped on the outskirts of the town.

It came to be known that the man I had seen in the grasses went by the name of March. Saturday he came into the town riding a splendid horse. He went about the streets talking in a loud voice to the country people. He was to be seen, too, at the horse barns, or at public auctions. Saturday nights he herded what cattle he had purchased, sometimes only a fine bull, to the pasture he had bought next to Freda's land. He became famous through the countryside for his pedigreed bulls. The farmers came in season to lead them to their own pastures for breeding.

It happened in a very subtle way that the countryside came to think of Freda and her daughter and the man March, all three together, as somehow of the same blood. All the vital acts of farm life came to move around one or the other of them. Freda and her husband seemed intimate with the fields and the half-mystical rites of planting and reaping. It was said in wonder that Freda even brought in the lambs as they were dropped in the fields in the spring as if she knew their time. She appeared to the women at the oven, and her appearance augured good bread. It was out their road the farmers went for the breeding of their cows. The very lay of the land with its rich dark color was strange; so was the magic they had with the earth and with natural things. Freda's daughter held a more strange mystery. She seemed half evil at times. But after she saved the life of a boy, when his body had turned black, they sought her out for palliatives.

So that it came about that the country people, as they dreamed over their work in the spring and autumn, were half unconsciously touched by the mystery of their tasks—a mystery between their own action and the secret of what they acted upon, by virtue of which alliance everything they did prospered and yielded in the field, the vine, the flesh. Probably because they were, in a manner of speaking, without a god, when in their dream, in a kind of blind ecstasy over the earth, within the heat, they attributed dimly to the figure of Freda, and with her the other two, an alliance and an intimacy with the virtue and the mystery, along with something sinister, of the natural things of which their lives were made.

After the corn had been husked and the dreary Kansas cold had set in, I was wandering in the thicket which ran along the stream in a little curve of the fields below Freda's. The pale sun, casting no shadow, shone on the naked sod, and the land, low and flat, swelled a little to the sky. This side of Freda's, the bulls stood in the wind, quite still.

I had just left the path and gone further into the thickets for berries, when out of the dying woods, with only slight sound like a bird's, ran the daughter of Freda. March came after her. I could hear his feet strike the bare ground, and saw as he ran past me, his black beard and hair struck by the wind as he ran into the open. She had climbed the barbed fence and was running in the bull pasture, through the crisp grasses toward her mother's. But three bulls turned at the farthest fence and eyed her. When she turned back, frightened, March was running to her. Then she stood binding her skirts around her, her small head, like a dying bird's thrown back. As she seemed about to cry out, he came upon her and bore her with him into the grasses. A young bull struck the ground with his forefeet and loped toward the sun. I ran back into the thicket.

The next days I was filled with terror because of what I had seen. I dared not go upon the road to the fields, or even out under the sky. The third day I came home and there in the dusk was Freda, leaning in our door.

"She is gone," I heard her say.

My mother spoke from the dark kitchen. "And is he gone, too, with all the cattle?"

"Yes," said Freda and stood suffering in the dusk. After a while she walked away down the dim road.

Frantz came in the night, knocking and pounding at our door to know where she had gone.

That winter she grew very old. The farmers, through the frosty moonlight, saw her wandering the barren plains. Children screamed when she approached the town. She seemed like an old woman whose time of fertility had gone. In the nights she came knocking at the doors of the village to ask for her daughter.

That year the spring never came. The flowers died beneath the ground and the fields burned in the sun.

Through the hot days of summer we saw her far off, unreal in the simmering heat. We found her by the old well in our orchard, sitting, sorrowing on the stones, her hair wild and white. We were young girls from school with bright ribbons in our hair. We had come to cool our faces over the black opening of the well and to cry down its sides to hear the sweet, far echo answer us. But when we saw her there we drew together, whispering and peering at her. She rose and came toward us, no longer bright and bold, but still terrible, looming above us. She went among us as we hid our faces in our aprons, stroking our hair and arms, calling each of us by the same name. It was a name I had never heard before and I could never, after that, remember it. She peered at each of us so close that we trembled when her breath came upon us. When she turned her sad eyes to the well again we ran from her in every direction, through the orchard, and for the rest of the afternoon watched her from behind the trees as she sat on the stones of the well, sorrowing.

One evening late in summer, as the land still lay beneath the drought, my brother came from the fields, and standing before us with the heat of the day on his face he said, "I saw Freda's daughter walking toward her mother's."

That night the country people thought it strange that the first rains fell, plunging ceaselessly into the earth.

The train stopped at a siding amidst the prairies in a sudden silence. The woman, aroused, sat up with her eyes wide open.

"How far are we?" she asked in a light voice.

I answered her very low, "From where?"

Before she could answer, a fit of coughing shook her and the train started again.

The lights were lit. She was timid about going into the diner, but at last, with vague gestures, lifting her pale hands she put over her head an old velvet hat and rose and went down the aisle, forlorn and pale, with a kind of assaulted and pathetic dignity.

I came behind her, looking at the tall body as it moved with its peculiar grace. It was like this she had come back to Freda's, with this delicate, hopeless grace, as if she had touched strange fruits and eaten pale and deathless seeds.

After the summer, March had come back, driving his bulls

through the street to the old pasture. He had knocked at Freda's door, and Freda had given her daughter back to him. She had gone to live in his low hut. When we passed we saw her come out of the door to throw the dishwater over the bare ground. Her thick black skirts, given her now by the women of the town, would be pulling and dragging about her, her little head would swirl up from them, free as a serpent's. After she had thrown the water she would stand still, tall and hopeless, in that terrible abstraction, looking toward us with her blind, deep eyes.

In the diner she seated herself with timid, quick movements, then sat with her eyes lowered. Some arrangement of the heavy skirt annoyed her; she fingered it delicately beneath the table. She coughed, turning her head and frowning. In an effort to suppress it the tears started, and did not fall, but hung there magnifying her great eyes. Suddenly, unable to bear the light, she closed them. Again as the lids covered her eyes, by some bewitchment her face became beautiful and eternal. I felt imminent metamorphosis as if she were about to change before my eyes, and as always in haste as if to prevent a phenomenon which I both hoped for and dreaded, I spoke.

"Did you see the fine bulls that ran toward our train?"

She lifted her eyes and looked at me, but did not answer.

"I believe the black one was the one your husband sold the upstate farmer." She was looking at me. "Did you see the bulls just before dark?"

"No," she said, and the answer startled me.

Whether it was the natural desolateness of traveling between places, likely to give to the form of what reality we know a vast and fabulous temper, or the sorrow of the dying year, I do not know, but back in the car, I became desolate and afraid.

For the remaining hours I sat opposite, watching her sleeping. I brooded over her, half expectant, as if about to startle from the mist that covered her, the winged bird which was the secret of her being. I watched her with pain as she moved me with her ancient mystery, as of something half remembered.

What strange realms had thrust her forth to be born of her mother in the night, to put upon her the burdens of endless movement through fields, upon the earth, through many days under the burden of shadowless nights, marked with the mark of strangeness to be usurped by an unfamiliar man, to walk through unfamiliar places, and to carry unfamiliar burdens.

Watching her glow before me with her terrible veiled identity, a strangeness of everything came upon me and a terror. I felt suddenly that after this journey, in which after all nothing had happened, I should never be the same; that by looking upon her I was partaking of some poisonous drug, like the poison of early spring flowers and the poison of late berries.

I dared not move in my terror, afraid she might stir, but she sat still, preoccupied, with her eyes hidden, dreaming of what she had never forgotten. Cautiously I came near to her mystery. She among us all had known that living was a kind of dying. When in these realms, she had refused to partake of our fruits and so become enamored, but had closed herself in the dream which is real and from which we die when we are born.

Soon, now, we would come upon the city glittering on the plain, above the bluffs of the river. A terror of all that lived came upon me; a terror of Freda's daughter who lay as if dead, glowing already in the mineral worlds of her strange lord. Because of the terror I said to myself, this woman is only the wife of a Kansas stockman—but who is the stockman? We saw him driving his bulls through the night, but who is he? Who is her mother? We saw her in the ripe fields, and turning the soil to fertility—but who is she?

All in that town came to me, all I had known passed before me, and I said, who are they? And I did not know.

PART THREE

CONTEMPORARY WOMEN'S RETELLINGS

A RICHLY FILLED CORNUCOPIA

THIS SECTION of the book explores the many different ways in which contemporary women have interpreted the myth of Demeter and Persephone and related aspects of it to their own lives or the lives of others close to them. I have sought to order this book in a way that makes evident the diverse themes that have been taken as central to the myth's meaning: its hints of the worldview of matristic cultures, its representation of the patriarchal conquest of a woman-centered world, its valorization of the love that connects mothers and daughters and in a more extended way all women, its recognition of women's vulnerability to male violence, its providing the basis for several female rites of passage, its relevance to our hopes for creating a postpatriarchal world in which concern for the earth might again become a central value.

There is a sense in which each of the interpretations imagines the myth forward, perhaps by imagining a Demeter who has come to terms with loss or a Persephone who has wholeheartedly taken on her role as goddess of the underworld. The themes of reunion and renewal so prominent in the end of the Homeric hymn seem to encourage such hopeful, though often cautiously hopeful, retellings.

In attempting to fit the essays I had chosen to include in this book into one or another of these subsections, I have often had to decide which of several themes an essay considers is central to it. However, I am well aware that many of these pieces really belong in more than one place. I am also aware that inevitably almost all the essays touch on the difficulties of overcoming or coming to terms with violence and separation, loss and death. To have ordered the book around these themes would, I believe, have obscured the diversity I hoped to highlight.

The myth gives rise to many interpretations, many appropriations. Many of us have experienced that our own understanding of its meaning keeps changing, keeps growing. At a particular time, at a particular life stage, or in relation to a particular life crisis, a new meaning may suddenly emerge. We learn to appreciate a wide range of such meanings by continuing to return to the myth itself, by continuing to seek to understand our own lives in terms of their mythic dimensions—and by listening to what others have found in the myth that speaks to them.

IN SEARCH OF A
PREPATRIARCHAL VERSION

A LMOST SIXTY YEARS AGO the Jungian analyst Esther Harding wrote a book, *Woman's Mysteries,* in which she suggested that the myths and rituals associated with the goddesses of the ancient world might provide contemporary women with images of "the feminine" that would help us toward a more complex and satisfying understanding of ourselves. She was most interested in the virgin goddesses who display an "in-oneselfness," a sense of having their center in themselves, and thus are not defined by their relation to father, husband, or son. The self-sufficiency of these divine females, Harding suggested, might serve as an empowering image for modern women. She also spoke of the important role in ancient religion played by mother goddesses, though she claims that they, too, were in a sense "virgins," powerfully autonomous figures. Viewing these mother goddesses primarily as the mothers of sons, she emphasized that the myths suggest that it is as important for the mother to let go of her sons as it is for them to become independent of her. But Harding had almost nothing to say about the mythological representation of the mother-daughter bond and included no references to either Persephone or Demeter.[1]

This book was rediscovered about twenty years ago as I and other women all across the country, apparently independently of one another, rediscovered the goddess and the goddesses and their power to stir our imagination, our pride, and our hope. We were deeply moved by these representations of female deities as powerful and beneficent sources of life and nurturance, wisdom and art, as caretakers of the earth and givers of the laws that sustain culture, as figures who embodied energies and capabilities that we had been taught to think of as masculine, as well as those familiarly identified as feminine. As Carol Christ says, we felt ourselves filled with a "fierce, new love" for the divine in its female manifestations.[2] Discovery of the ancient symbols and rituals encouraged us to reclaim our bodies and our sexuality, to celebrate our solidarity with other women, and to act on behalf of our concern for the planet. Telling the stories, sharing images, was itself a way of creating community.

Many of us were drawn to the archaic great mother goddesses of whom Marija Gimbutas has written with such scholarly eloquence,[3] but some, like myself, were pulled instead to the goddesses of Greece, sharing Bachofen's and Harrison's determination to learn as much as we could about who these goddesses had been before they were absorbed into the Zeus-dominated pantheon and what they had meant to the women who worshiped them.

More consciously perhaps than Harrison, certainly more avowedly, we felt that the rediscovery of these ancient images of female power as sacred and transformative could be transformative in our own lives, both individually and socially. We hoped that the discovery of a prepatriarchal world might help us imagine forward to a postpatriarchal one. We sought to learn as much as we could about that pre-Olympian world and, like Bachofen, recognized that looking through evidence from a patriarchal culture to discern the lineaments of an earlier matristic one called for the disciplined use of imagination and intuition.

Among the first books in this wave of goddess research was Merlin Stone's *When God Was a Woman.* The first pages of that book, with their bold appeal, "In the beginning God was a woman.

Do you remember?" communicate what was happening. We were all busy re-membering, trying to gather all available evidences and clues and then putting them together in order to glimpse a long-lost past. We also took up Monique Wittig's encouraging challenge: "Remember. Make an effort to remember. Or failing that, invent."[4]

Thus some of our re-creations of the ancient matristic world were admittedly in part inventions, imaginative projections. Among such creations, the most important was Charlene Spretnak's *The Lost Goddesses of Early Greece.* The subtitle, *A Collection of Pre-Hellenic Myths,* is somewhat misleading, for Spretnak is careful in her introduction to acknowledge that these myths about the goddesses of pre-Homeric Greece couldn't be "collected," they are not "inert found objects."[5] Her book represents a "reimagining" of a lost tradition that was oral, not written, and her work is undertaken in the spirit of oral tradition: there is no text to follow; each retelling is inevitably a new telling. Spretnak names the resources she consulted as a starting point for her reimaginings; most of them are the same ancient or scholarly sources included or discussed in this book. She tells us that in preparing to write each myth she would begin by assembling the "surviving clues," including art and artifacts that had the power to bring the ancient deities to life as living presences, not just as ideas. Then through meditation she would access a consciousness of the mythic presence of the particular deity being invoked.

If we ask, Are her versions of the myths true? we have to answer yes—yes, as myths that have had powerful resonance for us. As she herself declares, "The goal of such work is not the reinstatement of prehistoric cultural structures, but rather the transmission of *possibilities.*"[6] Her book has not only inspired an untold number of readers but has often been used as a basis for the construction of contemporary rituals, rites of passage, particularly for adolescent girls, and rites marking the passage of the seasons. Many feminists who have written about the Demeter/Persephone myth cite Spretnak's retelling in a way that grants it the full authority of myth.

In her book Spretnak saves the Demeter and Persephone myth for last, perhaps because of her conviction that of all the pre-Homeric goddesses Demeter is the least changed by the male-dominated tradition. She remains a goddess of the earth rather than making her home on Olympus; she claims her daughter as fully her own child. Spretnak's version of the myth proceeds from her assumption that the story of Persephone's rape was added to the Persephone traditions after the rise of patriarchy, indeed, that it is a disguised representation of the patriarchal invasion. In her introduction she reminds us of the many artistic representations of Persephone's descent that omit the rape, and she sees them as reminders of this earlier account.

"There was once a land with no winter"—thus Spretnak begins her tale. Demeter is goddess of both grain and underworld, but she admits to her beautiful and beloved daughter Persephone that she is so concerned with providing food for the living that she has had to neglect her underworld domain. Persephone chooses to go to the underworld and welcome the confused newly dead. Finding them in despair, she initiates them into their new world and restores them to tranquillity and wisdom. Demeter accepts her daughter's choice but nevertheless grieves at her absence. The fields become barren; winter comes for the first time. But in the spring Persephone returns and the grain and flowers reappear, as they will every year.

The myth paints a picture of an idealized world, a world free of violence, deceit, jealousy; a world filled with peace and harmony; a world in many ways similar to the one Gimbutas paints. Others, even Harrison, despite her nostalgic rendering of the prepatriarchal world, would say there was never such a time. There was blood sacrifice, orgiastic worship, even when the goddesses ruled. The ancient religion was inspired by terror as well as by joy. The ancient goddesses were less insipid, less unambivalently benevolent than the ones pictured here. But myths need not describe a world that *was;* they may also picture a world that might have been or that might be.

Among those deeply indebted to Spretnak's re-visioning of the myth is Mara Lynn Keller. Her essay "The Eleusinian Mysteries of Demeter and Persephone: Fertility, Sexuality and Rebirth," regrettably not included in this volume, is a careful, scholarly attempt to recover the matristic origins of the Demeter/Persephone mythologem and to underscore how much these origins are still discernible in the myths and rituals of a later period. She believes that the ancient mother/daughter mysteries were "mysteries of love" designed to show love as present in the most important moments of human life—birth, sexual passion, and death/rebirth. Keller incorporates Spretnak's version of the myth but also imagines another alternative to the story of Hades' rape of Persephone—a scene (loosely based on Homer's and Hesiod's accounts of Demeter's choosing to have intercourse with Iasion) of Persephone in passionate affirmation of her own active sexual desire choosing to lie with Hades in the field. Spretnak's vision is essentially asexual; Keller sees sexuality as one path of initiation into life's mysteries.[7]

NOTES

1. M. Esther Harding, *Woman's Mysteries* (New York: Bantam, 1973); see especially chapter 9.

2. Carol Christ, "Why We Need the Goddess" in *The Laughter of Aphrodite* (San Francisco: Harper and Row, 1987), 117.

3. See Marija Gimbutas, *The Language of the Goddess* (San Francisco: Harper and Row, 1990).

4. Monique Wittig, *Les guerilleres* (New York: Avon, 1971), 89.

5. Charlene Spretnak, *The Lost Goddesses of Early Greece* (Boston: Beacon Press, 1992), 24.

6. Ibid., 38.

7. Mara Lynn Keller, "The Eleusinian Mysteries of Demeter and Persephone," *Journal of Feminist Studies in Religion* 4, no. 1 (Spring 1988): 27–54.

The Myth of Demeter and Persephone

CHARLENE SPRETNAK

THERE ONCE WAS NO WINTER. Leaves and vines, flowers and grass grew into fullness and faded into decay, then began again in unceasing rhythms.

Men joined with other men of their mother's clan and foraged in the evergreen woods for game. Women with their children or grandchildren toddling behind explored the thick growth of plants encircling their homes. They learned eventually which bore fruits that sated hunger, which bore leaves and roots that chased illness and pain, and which worked magic on the eye, mouth, and head.

The Goddess Demeter watched fondly as the mortals learned more and more about Her plants. Seeing that their lives were difficult and their food supply sporadic, She was moved to give them the gift of wheat. She showed them how to plant the seed, cultivate, and finally harvest the wheat and grind it. Always the mortals entrusted the essential process of planting food to the women, in the hope that their fecundity of womb might be transferred to the fields they touched.

Demeter had a fair-born Daughter, Persephone, who watched over the crops with Her Mother. Persephone was drawn especially to the new sprouts of wheat that pushed their way through the soil in Her favorite shade of tender green. She loved to walk among the young plants, beckoning them upward and stroking the weaker shoots.

Later, when the plants approached maturity, Persephone would leave their care to Her Mother and wander over the hills, gathering narcissus, hyacinth, and garlands of myrtle for Demeter's hair. Persephone Herself favored the bold red poppies that sprang up among the wheat. It was not unusual to see Demeter and Persephone, decked with flowers, dancing together through open fields and gently sloping valleys. When Demeter felt especially fine, tiny shoots of barley or oats would spring up in the footprints She left.

One day They were sitting on the slope of a high hill looking out in many directions over Demeter's fields of grain. Persephone lay on Her back while Her Mother stroked Her long hair idly.

"Mother, sometimes in My wanderings I have met the spirits of the dead hovering around their earthly homes, and sometimes the mortals, too, can see them in the dark of the moon by the light of their fires and torches."

"There are those spirits who drift about restlessly, but they mean no harm."

"I spoke to them, Mother. They seem confused, and many do not even understand their own state. Is there no one in the netherworld who receives the newly dead?"

Demeter sighed and answered softly, "It is I who have domain over the underworld. From beneath the surface of the earth I draw forth the crops and the wild plants. And in pits beneath the surface of the earth I have instructed the mortals to store My seed from harvest until sowing, in order that contact with the spirits of My underworld will fertilize the seed. Yes, I know very well the realm of the dead, but My most important work is here. I must feed the living."

Persephone rolled over and thought about the ghostly spirits She had seen, about their faces drawn with pain and bewilderment.

"The dead need us, Mother. I will go to them."

Demeter abruptly sat upright as a chill passed through Her and rustled the grass around Them. She was speechless for a moment, but then hurriedly began recounting all the pleasures They enjoyed in Their world of sunshine, warmth, and fragrant flowers. She told Her Daughter of the dark gloom of the underworld and begged Her to reconsider.

Persephone sat up and hugged Her Mother and rocked Her with silent tears. For a long while They held each other, radiating rainbow auras of love and protection. Yet Persephone's response was unchanged.

They stood and walked in silence down the slope toward the fields. Finally They stopped, surrounded by Demeter's grain, and shared weary smiles.

"Very well. You are loving and giving and We cannot give only to Ourselves. I understand why You must go. Still, You are My Daughter and for every day that You remain in the underworld, I will mourn Your absence."

Persephone gathered three poppies and three sheaves of wheat. Then Demeter led Her to a long, deep chasm and produced a torch for Her to carry. She stood and watched Her Daughter go down farther and farther into the cleft in the earth.

In the crook of Her arm Persephone held Her Mother's grain close to Her breast, while Her other arm held the torch aloft. She was startled by the chill as She descended, but She was not afraid. Deeper and deeper into the darkness She continued, picking Her way slowly along the rocky path. For many hours She was surrounded only by silence. Gradually She became aware of a low moaning sound. It grew in intensity until She rounded a corner and entered an enormous cavern, where thousands of spirits of the dead milled about aimlessly, hugging themselves, shaking their heads, and moaning in despair.

Persephone moved through the forms to a large, flat rock and ascended. She produced a stand for Her torch, a vase for Demeter's grain, and a large shallow bowl piled with pomegranate seeds, the food of the dead. As She stood before them, Her aura increased in brightness and in warmth.

"I am Persephone and I have come to be your Queen. Each of you has left your earthly body and now resides in the realm of the dead. If you come to Me, I will initiate you into your new world."

She beckoned those nearest to step up onto the rock and enter Her aura. As each spirit crossed before Her, Persephone embraced the form and then stepped back and gazed into the eyes. She reached for a few of the pomegranate seeds, squeezing them between Her fingers. She painted the forehead with a broad swatch of the red juice and slowly pronounced:

> You have waxed into the fullness of life
> And waned into darkness;
> May you be renewed in tranquillity and wisdom.

For months Persephone received and renewed the dead without ever resting or even growing weary. All the while Her Mother remained disconsolate. Demeter roamed the earth hoping to find Her Daughter emerging from one of the secret clefts. In Her sorrow She withdrew Her power from the crops, the trees, and plants. She forbade any new growth to blanket the earth. The mortals planted their seed, but the fields remained barren. Demeter was consumed with loneliness and finally settled on a bare hillside to gaze out at nothing from sunken eyes. For days and nights, weeks and months She sat waiting.

One morning a ring of purple crocus quietly pushed their way through the soil and surrounded Demeter. She looked with surprise at the new arrivals from below and thought what a shame it was that She was too weakened to feel rage at Her injunction being broken. Then She leaned forward and heard them whisper in the warm breeze: "Persephone returns! Persephone returns!"

Demeter leapt to Her feet and ran down the hill through the fields into the forests. She waved Her arms and cried: "Persephone returns!" Everywhere Her energy was stirring, pushing, bursting forth into tender greenery and pale young petals. Animals shed old fur and rolled in the fresh, clean grass while birds sang out: "Persephone returns! Persephone returns!"

When Persephone ascended from a dark chasm, there was Demeter with a cape of white crocus for Her Daughter. They ran to each other and hugged and cried and laughed and hugged and danced and danced and danced. The mortals saw everywhere the miracles of Demeter's bliss and rejoiced in the new life of spring. Each winter they join Demeter in waiting through the bleak season of Her Daughter's absence. Each spring they are renewed by the signs of Persephone's return.

THE
MOTHER-DAUGHTER BOND

I FIRST HEARD the story of Demeter and Persephone from my mother. Or so I've always said. But actually what she told me was how profoundly Demeter had longed for a daughter to whom she could give the love that filled her heart and how wholly she had delighted in the daughter whom she bore. My mother's telling focused on the love that flowed back and forth between this mother and daughter of ancient times. There was no abduction, no separation forced or chosen, only a mother and daughter, each full of love for the other.

Or so I remember. And yet when I now read the poems by my mother, Herta Rosenblatt, included in this volume, I wonder, "Is that what she told, or only what I remember? Only what I was ready to hear, willing to hear?" When I read "The Dance of Mother Woman," I discover a Demeter who knew, who foreknew, "how much of motherhood is loss" (to use Kerenyi's beautiful phrase). When I now read "A Last Game of Childhood," I find a Demeter, aware that Persephone stands poised at the precarious and beautiful transition between childhood and womanhood, who watches her daughter prepare to join her lover and blesses her eagerness. When I now read "Were You Weeping?" which I also view as written from Demeter's perspective, I see Demeter's recognition that though her daughter may miss the upper world, she loves the Hades with whom she shares rule of the nether realm. I see Demeter's awareness of how painful it must be for Persephone to yield to Orpheus's plea that she assuage his almost unendurable loss, knowing as he does not that he is yet to suffer an immeasurably deeper one.

I read these poems and I sense that my mother has always known of the separation that tears Demeter and Persephone apart. I see that her Demeter had accepted the inevitability of the separation long before it occurred, that her Demeter blessed her daughter's eager embrace of her lover, that her Demeter took pride in her daughter's graceful exercise of her adult powers. And I realize that perhaps it was always I who was attached to the fantasy of a never-broken bond.

Of course, I realize that my mother's vision is still one that idealizes the mother-daughter bond, still a vision of how it might have been, of how she wishes it had been. I could name all the ways it was never quite thus, but then, so could she. But the image of Demeter as a representation of the all-powerful, all-loving mother for whom we all yearn still has enormous power for her, for me, for many of us. Of course, I also know that there are other versions of Demeter, other interpretations that will find their place within this book, visions of Demeter as a devouring mother, as a narcissistic mother, as a cruel and vengeful goddess, and they, too, have their truth.

Nonetheless, for many the predominant meaning of this myth lies in its powerful evocation of the strength and beauty of the bond that connects mothers and daughters.

Adrienne Rich sees the myth of Demeter and Persephone and the Eleusinian mysteries celebrated in their honor as an "enduring recognition of mother-daughter passion and rapture." What is most important to her about the story of Hades' rape of Persephone is that it means that the separation of Demeter and Persephone is unwilling and unwilled. "It is neither a question of the daughter's rebellion against the mother, nor the mother's rejection of the daughter." Rich honors the sustained, passionate power of Demeter's commitment to her daughter. "It is a mother whose wrath crystallizes the miracle" of Persephone's return.[1]

Carol Christ is also moved by this myth as a tale of a mother who puts her relation to her daughter above all else:

> Unwilling to accept this state of affairs, Demeter rages and withholds fertility from the earth until her daughter is returned to her. What is important for women in this story is that a mother fights for her daughter and for her relation to her daughter. This is completely different from the mother's relation to her daughter in patriarchy. The "mood" created by the story of Demeter and Persephone is one of celebration of the mother-daughter bond, and the "motivation" is for mothers and daughters to affirm the heritage passed on from mother to daughter and to reject the patriarchal pattern where the primary loyalties of mother and daughter must be to men.[2]

And Catherine Keller, too, sees the myth as offering us "a tale of protection by the mother." "How extraordinary," she says, "to find a woman's power, indeed her anger, celebrated as effective and soteriological."[3] Kathie Carlson exclaims that in this myth "the Mother isn't simply overcome." She "fights back" and "Zeus has to give in."[4]

Those of us profoundly aware of how more flawed, more ambivalent, our own experience of the mother-daughter bond has been may nonetheless find that viewing our struggles and suffering in the light of the myth subtly transforms them. Thus Alma Luz Villanueva's poem "The Crux" is at one level a mother's confession that she has loved her daughter badly—and exquisitely, a confession and an offering of love—but it is also clearly a retelling of the Demeter myth in which the mother figure acknowledges that she had to let her daughter go in order that she might become herself. Become Woman. And not only Mother. Separation and continuing love are not incompatible; indeed, they may be necessary correlates. "We will live and die separately, each one virgin in her soul. The crux of loving unsolved, but lived."

In "Learning From My Mother Dying" Carol Christ writes of how, as a young woman, the myth's powerful evocation of Demeter's commitment to her daughter only made her aware of all she had not received from her own mother and how great the distance between them was. She thought she knew what the myth had to say to her. But she has discovered that she keeps discovering new layers of meaning. She came to feel that the separation of daughter from mother that the myth describes is integral to it, not an anomalous interruption. Misunderstandings, estrangement, jealousy, guilt, and shame are painful, but the myth may help us see that they do not so much destroy the deep, complex bond of identification between mother and daughter as give it its particular shape, color, taste. Christ had been helped by the myth to give up her longing for the confluence for which she once yearned. From her participation in her mother's dying she has discovered that dimension of the myth that is centered not on the personal relation of mothers and daughters but on the mystery of death—and now understands as she had not before why the Greeks imagined the mystery of death as a mother-daughter mystery. In the myth Demeter is initiated into an understanding of death by the loss of her daughter; Christ feels she has been initiated into that same understanding through the loss of her mother. "Mother and Daughter. We are Two. We are One. We are and are not the same. And as I now know from experience, we initiate one another into the mysteries not only of life, but also of death."

Notes

1. Adrienne Rich, *Of Woman Born* (New York: Norton, 1976), 240–43.

2. Carol Christ, *The Laughter of Aphrodite* (San Francisco: Harper and Row, 1987), 130–31.

3. Catherine Keller, *From a Broken Web* (Boston: Beacon Press, 1986), 152.

4. Kathie Carlson, *In Her Image* (Boston: Shambhala Publications, 1989), 86.

Three Poems

HERTA ROSENBLATT

THE DANCE OF MOTHER WOMAN

Demeter
    it is spring
have I surprised you, alone
in your garden of roses
where you gaze to mountains
     —of yesterday
       the yesterday you must not mention
       only when it comes around you
       as today—
across the valley
     —of spring—of asphodel
       where fall moves as silence
       to the song and laughter of your daughter
you are so still, Demeter
       hearing
       behind you
       Poseidon's horses
       (the phantom horses of the night)
       raging the sea
       the serpent rising

and the dolphin
hurrying, hurrying
where the singer is in peril
you are silent, Demeter
waiting
are you weeping behind your veil?
must you go to Gaea's place
of darkness
of birthing?
Rise then
and meet the mothers—
meet Leto and Niobe
meet Sara and Mary
Eve and Rebecca
dance the dance of mother-woman
then find your daughter
and send her dancing
to her spring meadow
who will sing the song
of Clytemnestra
of Jocasta
of Medea

A LAST GAME OF CHILDHOOD

Through the leaves, rustling,
who is running?
In stillness, even the nymphs wait—
Persephone, laughing—
in a last game of childhood;
and your mother, breathless, smiling
and you, skipping, making a happy noise
on the path by the lake?
Eager to join your dark lover?
Calling across the water

and Echo answering?
What flowers do you find now
that summer has died
and daffodils are memory?
By the fountain
a last red rose—
Your mother watches you break it,
blessing your eagerness.
Don't look back!
Carry your rose
to the spring meadow
where he will find you—
while behind you it snows,
On the now still path
your mother walks
slowly
to the white fields
sown with wheat.

WERE YOU WEEPING?

Were you weeping, Persephone, pale on your throne,
next to your king-husband,
when Orpheus sang, enchanting
the shades in the darkness of forgetting?
Reaching into the depths, calling
the sleepers to life?
Were you weeping, remembering
the sun, and the flowers,
the running in light—
voices, laughter, singing
and the heaven of solitude and silence
beckoning
when the dark god appeared, in his glory and power,
and, ravished, you died the death of love?

Were you weeping, and your hand
pressing that of your husband?
Were you humming the tune
of that spring day
and he smiled the smile of remembering:
"Go! Euridice!"
Were your arms open and your shoulder ready
to welcome back Euridice,
twice a shadow?

The Crux

Alma Luz Villanueva

1

Girl-child and amazon,
who I raised in the image
of She-who-I-couldn't-name,
but dreamt and knew when

your body slid out of mine;
daughter. Loving you, I loved
myself—badly, exquisitely,
We clung, we fought, we separated;

you to the world of men,
and I in exile. I journeyed
to the Earth and back, seeking
you in the iris, stone, the seemingly

dead bulb; and, finally, I
had to let you go, forget you,
the features of my daughter,
until my own features became

clear, distinct: separate.
Myself. Woman. And I will

die alone, and so will you.
The rose never tires of blooming.

2

She-who-I-couldn't-name
comes to me in dreams
as I walk with dark-skinned
women. She is huge and

I can't take her all in;
a belt of rainbow snakes encircles
her waist, gift of sun and storm.
Between us, daughter, lies a virgin land

where sun and moon rule,
equally; and in our loving
the land appears, vividly—
its mountains, deserts, orchards,

and the waves of natural boundaries.
Now I love myself badly, exquisitely.
Now I name the unnameable.
Now, I am your mother.

We will live and die separately,
each one virgin in her soul. The crux
of loving unsolved, but lived. The dream.
This wild rose belongs to no one.

But I offer it to you, anyway.

Learning from My Mother Dying

CAROL P. CHRIST

CONTEMPORARY WOMEN have been drawn to the myth of Demeter and Persephone because it suggests that in the struggle to understand our relationships with mother and daughter we will gain insight into the great mysteries. Many of us have found different meanings in the myth at different stages in our lives. When I was a young feminist with aspirations and hopes my mother did not understand, pursuing a career in a field in which there were few female role models, I found in the story of Demeter the image of the mother I longed for. It was my experience that my feminist sisters and I were fighting the fathers on our own. While sisterhood was indeed powerful, it was not always powerful enough. I lamented that most of the mothers, including my own, sat on the sidelines or actively supported the fathers. In the story of Demeter's anger at her daughter's abduction and rape, I found the image of the powerful mother who would side with me in my battle against those who had violated me. In the story of the reunion of Demeter and Persephone, I saw reflected the reconciliation I hoped would occur with my mother at some time in the future. The myths and rituals of Demeter and Persephone have also helped me to persevere in the face of great loss, and to understand my responsibility to my spiritual daughters. In the months following my mother's death, the myth speaks to me of the intertwining of the lives of mother and daughter, and of a mystery learned at the hour of death. I am astonished at how the stories of Demeter and her daughter continue to illuminate and shape my understanding of my experience.

Now I begin to understand that the union, separation, and re-union depicted in the myth are not poles in the relation of mother and daughter. Each is a point in the circle whose center is "the flow of energy between two biologically alike bodies, one of which has lain in amniotic bliss inside the other, one of which has labored to give birth to the other."[1] In this highly charged circle, the bond between mother and daughter is woven of love, admiration, and delight, but also, because none of us loves the self or the other perfectly, with fear, jealousy, and shame. Since the sense of identity and identification between mother and daughter provokes such wildly mixed emotions, separation is necessary for both, but it is painful. Separation, too, is charged from the center, as feelings of elation and relief mix with feelings of loss and guilt. From every point in the circle, the bond remains, as mothers and daughters continually measure the self against the other.

The myth of Demeter and Persephone, though based in a story of mother and daughter, was said by the ancients to convey the meaning of life and death. All who learned this "mystery" in the initiation rituals performed in the Greek city of Eleusis were sworn to secrecy. Those who spoke of it did so in veiled terms, indicating only that the knowledge of the mystery provided great happiness in life and in death. As my mother died, an aspect of this mystery was, I believe, revealed to me. Not having been sworn to secrecy, I speak more directly of what I learned than did the ancients, while at the same time recognizing that because the mystery cannot be encompassed in words, I will reveal nothing to those who do not already know.

From one perspective it is true to say that my mother and I were separated by a feminism that affirmed and inspired my desire to live a life very different from hers. Yet our separation began long before I named myself feminist in my second year of graduate school. A therapist sensed that my mother's feelings of separation from me began in the first months of my life. With a sense of wonder, my mother often told me the following story: "You took your first steps when you were about eight months old. Then you stopped walking. On your first birthday, your father told you that because you were tearing your dresses when you crawled, you could not wear dresses again until you learned to walk. You got right up and started to walk, and you never stopped." After I told this story, my therapist responded, "I see you sitting on the floor knowing all along that you could walk, but waiting until you gained your parents' approval of what you knew you could do. I think," she continued, "that your mother realized that you were precocious when you were just a few months old. She was inse-cure. She was afraid of you and afraid for you because she knew that being too smart could bring problems to a girl and a woman in the society into which you were born." My mother's fear was conditioned by our both being born into a social world in which too much intelligence in a girl was considered a liability. Had I been a boy, she would never have worried that being smart might hinder my chances of getting married.

"Your mother was in awe of you," her good friend Fran told me a few days after my mother died. "Your mother did not always understand you. Often she did not know what to say to you. But when she spoke of you, she always spoke with the deepest love in her voice." "But Fran," I protested, "practically the last thing my mother said to me was that I should lose weight. My brothers and my sister-in-law need to lose weight, too, but she never criticized them. Why did she always have to criticize me?" "Your mother struggled with her weight too," Fran replied. "Whatever she said, she said because she identified with you. Maybe she thought you were the only one who was capable of becoming perfect."

While my mother's sense of separation from me probably began very early in my life, my sense of separation from her came later. When I was young, I identified closely with my mother and never imagined that my life would be different from hers. When I was ten and a half years old, my mother gave birth to her second son, my baby brother. I identified closely with my mother's pregnancy. I felt almost as if my brother were my own child, and because my mother was working in the first years of his life, I helped her raise him. To this day, my brother and I share a special bond born of this early closeness. Three years later, when my mother was pregnant again, I looked forward to having another baby to care for. Born with Hylan's membrane, like the Kennedy baby born at about the same time, my brother died a few days after his birth. Because children were not allowed into the hospital, I saw this baby for the first time in his tiny coffin. After the funeral, I begged my mother to have another baby. My mother, who was in her early forties, replied, "I'll never have another baby. It is too sad to lose a baby."

Later, my mother admitted that her grief for her lost baby developed into deep depression that only lifted many years later, when she realized that she was neglecting her living children. My mother's grief is reflected in the image of Demeter, who as Naomi Goldenberg has caused us to recognize, allowed her grief to overpower all else, threatening death to all the children of the earth.[2]

Many years later, as my thirtieth birthday approached and I had neither married nor conceived a child, I was haunted by images of this dead baby. I began to understand that one of the reasons I was drawn to feminism's rejection of the mother role was because I imagined that I could escape my mother's sadness by not becoming a mother. Paradoxically, as it perhaps always is between mothers and daughters, it was my deep identification with my mother that drove me to try to separate from her. In my late thirties (not having escaped at all the sadness of a woman's life), I decided I wanted to have a child. I tried to nurture my husband's daughter, and I tried to conceive. My mother was puzzled when I told her I was thinking of having a baby. "I thought you rejected all of that when you decided to have a career," was her only reply.

The years of my twenties and thirties, years when I was involved with the antiwar, radical, feminist, antinuclear, and peace movements, were years when my mother and I rarely understood one another, often felt estranged, often hurt one another. In recent years something softened in both of us and in my father. We stopped trying to change each other, and we began to enjoy one another's company once again. From my side, at least, I began to appreciate and feel proud of the many ways in which my mother and I are alike.

When my mother was diagnosed last July with the cancer that took her life in early December, she was as happy as she had ever been. My parents' economic struggles during the years of my brothers' and my childhoods had enabled them to be able to afford a beautiful home that she loved and a garden filled with flowers that gave her endless joy. When my younger brother married and left the home, my parents fell back in love. Recent years had brought the birth of three new grandchildren. My father's retirement left my parents free to travel and enjoy life.

After I bought an apartment in Athens, my mother and my father began to plan a trip to visit me and to see my new home. I understood that my parents' desire to visit me in Greece for the first time in the five years that I had lived there was their way of affirming the life I had chosen, a life very different from their own. Though my mother and I had reconciled in her home, I knew that her coming across the ocean to my home would add another and much-longed-for dimension to the healing of our relationship. As I renovated and furnished my new home, I thought constantly, "Mom will like this. Mom will like that." When my parents had to cancel their trip because of my mother's cancer treatments, I took pictures of every nook and cranny of my new apartment to show to my Mom, in the hope that her seeing the pictures would substitute for the visit that probably would never happen.

Shortly after my mother's diagnosis, my older brother arranged for me and his grown children to come home for Mom's seventy-second birthday in August. He told me that though Mom was convinced that she had a good chance for a remission, a doctor friend of the family had told him and my other brother that "this is going to be her last birthday, and she won't be here for Christmas." It was hard to believe these words when I saw my mom. Though she had started both chemotherapy and radiation treatments, she looked beautiful and healthy. The illness caused her to lose the extra pounds that had plagued her later years. She was cheerful and full of life. A sadness in her eyes, evident in photographs taken at the time, is the only indication that she was not well.

When she looked at the pictures of my home, Mom seemed distracted, and she didn't say much. I guessed that her energies were engaged in the struggle with her illness and that she would never share my enthusiasm for my new home, that she would never "be there" with me. With great difficulty, I began to accept that the knowledge that my parents had planned to come to Greece would have to substitute for their actually coming. Then my older brother picked up the photos I had brought with me and commented, "But this looks just like Mom's house." Though I had not realized it until he said it, I was pleased to admit that he was right.

During my visit, Mom told us that she didn't want to die and that she intended to fight for her life. But she added that she felt she had lived a very happy and blessed life and that if her time was up, she had no regrets. I was relieved when she said that she did not intend to go into the hospital and that she had signed a living will so that she would not be put into the hospital even if she got very sick. Mom confided in my older brother that if it became clear she would not recover, she didn't intend to linger. That was as close as she would ever come to talking to any of us about her death. Mom sent me back to Greece after three weeks, insisting that she felt fine and didn't need my help.

My mother's illness affected me more deeply than I had ever imagined it would. It is one thing to hear from a friend or to read that "the loss of a mother is the hardest loss you will ever face." Or that "your mother's death is something you will never get over." Or that "the mother-child bond is the strongest bond." It is quite another to learn that what had sounded like clichés when spoken by others is deeply personal truth. Though I loved my mother and enjoyed being with her, it was also true that I had left her when I went to college and never come back to live near her. For twenty-some years I had made my life living apart from her, separated sometimes by the American continent, sometimes by the Atlantic ocean, and never by less than four hundred miles. I was quite unprepared for the depth of feeling her dying would evoke in me.

The knowledge that my mother was dying and that she might never ask for my help tormented me throughout the fall as I tried to go about my daily life in Athens. Whenever I spoke with my mother on the telephone, she insisted that she was "doing fine" and "didn't need any help." In the late fall, a good friend made me realize that I was not calling or writing my mother as frequently as I wanted to out of fear that I would learn that she was getting worse. I sat down and wrote my Mom the truth I now recognized: that I had never loved anyone as much as I loved her and that nothing was more important in my life than being with her at this time. When I reread this letter before sending it, I discovered, as I would several other times over the next months, that where I had meant to write "nothing is more important than what is happening to you right now." I had instead written "than what is happening to me." Shortly after my mother died, I wrote a friend that "I died," when I meant to write that "my mother died." Though I corrected my "mistakes," I realized that in another sense they were not mistakes: Mom's dying was a passage I was experiencing with her. Though we were not in any literal sense the same person, it was also true that we were, "in fact, merely the older and younger form of the same person: hence [the] easy confusion."[3] My mother (who received cards and letters from her friends every day of her illness) said that my letter "was the nicest letter" she had "ever received." It enabled her to call and tell me that in fact she wasn't "doing fine" any more and that she would like me to come "home." I still had no idea how sick she really was.

I arrived home the Saturday before Thanksgiving. I was

shocked to see that Mom had lost more weight, had very little appetite, and took many seconds to get up from a chair or out of the car. She was also losing her hair because of the chemotherapy. Still, I was relieved to see that she got out of bed every morning, dressed herself, came down the stairs, and went out of the house almost every day. She insisted that a friend with similar cancer had looked worse that she did and was now in remission. Her spirit was so strong, it was difficult not to believe her.

A few days later I heard her mutter to herself, "I hope I don't have to go through too much more of this." I took the opportunity to say, "Mom, if it gets too hard, I want you to know I am here to help you to let go." Her response was abrupt, and her tone was harsh. "I don't want to talk about that," she said. "O.K.," I said meekly and left the room. A few minutes later she came to me and apologized. "I don't want to talk about it," she said, "but I heard what you said, and I appreciate it."

On Friday afternoon, her friend Fran took me out to lunch alone, after Mom said that she wasn't up to coming with us. Even though I scarcely knew Fran, I reminded her that when she had taken my Mom and me out to lunch in August she had said that "if I ever needed anything I could ask." What I really needed was to cry and talk about my mother's dying. I hadn't been able to talk to anyone about it, because my mother hadn't been able to acknowledge that she was dying and neither had my Dad. Fran and I held back nothing as we talked, ate, and drank several glasses of red wine. Fran spoke to me about her husband's dying. "I said goodbye to him after his stroke," she said, "because after that he never was himself again. Still, years later, when he slipped into a coma, he didn't seem to be able to let go. Finally the priest told me I had to go in and tell my husband that it was all right with me for him to die. He passed on soon afterward." On the way back from lunch Fran told me that though we had only gotten to know each other since my mom's illness, she really liked me and felt we had a special openness and ease in communicating. She announced that she was going to "adopt" me. Later I understood my "adoption" to be a symbol and a sign of the mystery I would learn as my mother was dying.

When we got back to the house, Mom sat up in bed and talked with the two of us for some time, even raising her nightgown like Baubo and joking about her skinny legs. The old woman Baubo, according to several traditions, raises her skirt in front of Demeter, causing her to laugh and forget her sorrow. Fran told Mom that it was wrong to think that God would not help her. "God comes to anyone who asks Him," she insisted.

That night we moved Mom's bed downstairs because the stairs made her short of breath. I worried that we might not hear her if she called, and I slept fitfully. Sometime during the night I had the clear sense that her mother, her father, her baby sister who died, and her own baby who died were waiting for her. Shortly before dawn I heard her call. She was struggling for breath and asked me to turn up the oxygen. My Dad came downstairs and turned it up, but it didn't seem to help. As it became clear that she was dying, I told Mom that "Gramma and Grandpa and baby Alice and baby Alan are waiting for you." Though she could not speak, she showed me with gestures that she was still conscious.

As my mother was dying, I had an absolutely clear sense that she was going "to love." Not necessarily to Goddess or God, not necessarily to Mom and Dad, but simply "to love." I told Mom several times not to be afraid because she was going "to love." Remembering Fran's words, I turned to my dad and said, "Dad, Fran says you have to tell Mom it's all right with you for her to die." He spoke quietly to her, and a few minutes later she died, peacefully, in her own bed as she had chosen, with my dad and me holding her hands. . . .

The mysteries of Demeter and Persephone, Mother and Daughter, Mother and Maid, Older and Younger forms of the same person are mysteries rooted in the bond of identification between Mother and Daughter. We are Two, we are One, we are and are not the same. And as I now know from experience, we initiate one another into the mysteries not only of life but also of death.

I learned many things from my mother dying. I learned to respect her courage and strength of will. I learned that, in many cases at least, we can control the circumstances of our dying. I learned that it is possible to die with dignity, at home, in our own bed if that is what we choose. I am certain that my mother hoped until the last week that there was still a chance for a remission from the cancer. I know that she waited to die until I was there to be with her and to be with my father after she was gone. I believe that when she realized that she could fight the inevitable no longer, she quietly gave up and died very quickly. She had told my brother that she did not intend to linger if there was no hope. And she did not. Thirty-two years earlier my mother had seen her mother-in-law die a terrible death in the hospital hooked up to tubes keeping her body alive when her soul was gone, and she told all of us then that this would never happen to her. It did not, because she refused to let it happen.

Looking back on my mother's illness, I am sorry that the doctors did not tell her in July that treatment would not do her any good and that she should go to Greece and fill her life with as much joy as possible in her last months. My mother suffered more from treatment than from the cancer itself. She was burned during radiation therapy and was bedridden at home while the burns healed. Chemotherapy caused her to lose her hair, which can never be anything but humiliating. I doubt that either treatment prolonged her life. The only thing that keeps me from becoming furious with her doctors is that I know that if her doctors had told her there was only a 5 percent chance of remission, she would have chosen the treatment. After seeing what happened to her, I have decided that in a similar situation, I would not choose treatment.

From my mother dying and from an aunt who died before her, I learned that we who will live on do not need to fear the process of dying. The opportunity to be with and care for those who are dying can be one of the most profound experiences of life. In shielding us from intimacy with those who are very ill, modern medical practices and hospitals have also deprived us of the opportunity to learn from the dying.

The mystery that I learned through my mother's dying cannot be reduced to a few simple words. According to George Mylonas, excavator of the archaeological site at Eleusis, there are those who believe that the substance of the Eleusinian mysteries "was so simple that it escapes us just because of its simplicity." In my experience this is so.

I do not know where my mother is now. I know only that as she passed from this life she was surrounded by love—not only mine and my father's but that of the family and friends who called her and wrote her letters during every day of her illness. Love did not abandon her as she died. From my mother dying I learned to trust the power of love in my own life, even when it does not take the shape and form that I think it should. I have learned to accept the situation I find myself in now: living alone without the husband, lover, or companion I used to think I could not live without. I rejoice every day in the love that I do have, from my father, from my adopted mother Fran, from my many friends, and from my cat. For the first time in my life, I know that this very real love is enough. I know that I am surrounded by love and always will be. This knowledge is a great mystery. I do not know why it took me so long to learn it, and I know that I cannot communicate it to others, because the words alone mean nothing.

NOTES

1. Adrienne Rich, *Of Woman Born* (New York: Norton, 1976), 223.

2. See Naomi R. Goldenberg, *Returning Words to Flesh* (Boston: Beacon Press, 1990), 167–69; also see her essay in this volume.

3. Jane Ellen Harrison, *Prolegomena to the Study of Greek Religion* (London, Merlin Press, 1962), 274.

LOVE AMONG WOMEN

T HE LOVE between Demeter and Persephone has been felt by many to symbolize not only the mother-daughter bond but more generally the intense, intimate connections among women whose loyalty to one another takes precedence over their relationships with men. Thus the myth has been taken to provide us with what Karin Carrington calls "an archetype of lesbian love."[1] But it is important to recognize here that by "lesbian" one may mean women sexually involved with other women or simply woman-affirming women. Thus in *Lesbian Nation* Jill Johnston writes:

> All women are lesbians except those who don't know it naturally they are but don't know it yet I am a woman who is lesbian because I am a woman and a woman who loves herself.[2]

Johnston is impressed by the similarities between contemporary lesbian women and the women of early matristic history:

> A similarity between her virility and freedom from the fetters of being an object of the male makes the homosexual woman resemble the image of woman in matriarchal times. This similarity applies particularly to the more masculine type of lesbian. The wide range of activities, the undoubted capacity to manage her life without dependence on men, is the ideal of the homosexual

woman. Female homosexuality is inseparable from the very
qualities which were the perogatives of women in early history.
It is of no consequence to these conclusions whether the matriarchate existed as a definite period of history, which I believe it
did, or in mythology only. Mythology *is* history, transcending
concrete data and revealing their true meaning.[3]

Not too surprisingly, she finds in the Demeter/Persephone myth
a powerful representation of these early women-focused societies.
"An understanding of the Demeter-Persephone myth . . . seems
extremely important to the recovery of the feminine principle."
The barrenness over the land that is the correlate of Demeter's
rage at Persephone's abduction she regards as representing "the
real power that women once held exclusively in the world of
mother-right." Demeter's retention of "the power to yield or
withhold her fruits" signifies that she is a woman "still in control
of the disposition of her own body." Johnston particularly emphasizes the significance of the reunion of mother and daughter,
which she sees as expressing "the psychological archetype of feminine reintegration": "Persephone is the primordial virgin. Her return to her mother is the return to the mother of her primordial
maidenhood, her intactness, her inviolate integrity as woman or
total being."[4]

Judy Grahn, too, sees this myth as having "many Lesbian un-
dertones" and means this in a more explicitly sexual sense than
does Johnston. Grahn claims that the "innermost secret rites" of
the mysteries may have been lesbian, "or to use a more specific
description, tribadic." She reminds us that only Hecate joined Demeter in her search for Persephone, "whose title was Kore, meaning the Maid, the unmarried one, the Dyke," and says that when
Persephone was found, "Hecate embraced her several times" and
then became her "companion for the rest of their lives, that is,
eternally." Grahn recalls that Baubo made Demeter laugh "by
telling her obscene sexual jokes and lifting up her skirts so Demeter could see her genitals."[5] She believes that the pomegranate

means not just women's fertility but "the blood and sex powers special to women":

> The bowl-shaped red "Chinese apple" has tightly grouped seeds in clusters, clear, red, living fruit crystals. More profoundly, they mean female power, menstrual and clitoral, from the intense red of their coloring and the oblong bud shape of each luscious seed. They *feel* like a clitoris, especially to the tongue. To Lesbians the Pom Grannie is the "rubyfruit," the delicate, sexual, acid-sweet crystal-psychic universe of women at the essence of existence, of women who "eat each other out" from one living world of perception into another.[6]

Carrington discovers in the Demeter/Persephone myth hints of some important differences between heterosexual and lesbian patterns of female individuation. Though the separation from the mother, represented in the myth by the intervention of Hades, may, indeed, as Nancy Chodorow and others have suggested, be a centrally important phase in heterosexual development, Carrington argues that "in understanding lesbian individuation the emphasis is placed on the original *union* and the *reunion*," not on separation. Carrington believes that lesbian love typically involves a union with another that echoes the original bond with one's personal mother but believes the lesbian perspective may also lead to a reunion with what Susan Griffin has called "the mother at the center of the earth," the deep source of all life. Thus lesbian experience may lead to the adoption of a new ethos that values fluidity, interconnectedness, and diversity. For Carrington, viewing lesbian love in the context of the myth not only illumines the personal dimension of the love that women may share with one another but also helps women to recognize the earth-focused spiritual perspective that is implicit in their union with one another.[7]

Although my emphases are somewhat different, the essay included here from my *Myths and Mysteries of Same-Sex Love* also reflects on ways that the union and reunion of the two goddesses may deepen our appreciation of a particular aspect of lesbian love.

NOTES

1. Karin Lofthus Carrington, "The Alchemy of Women Loving Women," *Psychological Perspectives*, no. 23, 64–82.

2. Jill Johnston, *Lesbian Nation: The Feminist Solution* (New York: Simon and Schuster, 1973), 266.

3. Ibid., 247.

4. Ibid., 253–54.

5. Judy Grahn, *Another Mother Tongue* (Boston: Beacon Press, 1984), 9, 34–35.

6. Ibid., 35.

7. Carrington, "Alchemy," 69, 72–73, 79–80.

The Return to the Mother

CHRISTINE DOWNING

DEMETER IS IN GREEK MYTHOLOGY clearly a woman-identified goddess. Having been separated from her own mother at birth when her father, Cronus, fearful that one of his children might grow up to overthrow him as he had overthrown his father, swallowed her, she seems to epitomize an idealization of mother love. She longs to have a daughter to whom she might give the love she herself never received. Representing a generation of goddesses who no longer had the parthenogenetic capacity of the original mother/earth goddess, Gaia, Demeter cannot conceive without a male. Therefore she allows Zeus to father her child but refuses him any participation in the child's rearing. Her daughter, Persephone, is to be hers alone and to be the object of all her love. Although it would go beyond the myth to say that Demeter *rapes* Zeus, who raped so many divine and mortal women, one could say that even in the myth *she* uses *him* (almost like a sperm bank). She also deliberately chooses her brother to be her lover, a male as like her as any she could find. She is a mother but emphatically not a wife; she chooses to be a single mother, solely responsible for her daughter's upbringing.

The bond between mother and daughter as Demeter and Persephone exemplify it is a bond of fusion—the intimate connection preceding the recognition of separate existence that we all imagine to have been there "in the beginning." Demeter hopes to maintain this closeness forever, to keep her daughter for herself—and seeks especially to protect their love from any male intruder. Almost inevitably, her daughter ends up being abducted by the male god of the underworld, Hades, and Demeter ends up devastated.

After her daughter's disappearance, Demeter is so overtaken by her grief and rage that she no longer attends to the growth of the grain on which all human life depends but wanders desolate over the earth disguised as an old woman. During this time she spends an evening in the company of an aged dry nurse, Baubo (or, in some versions, Iambe), who succeeds even if only momentarily in getting the goddess to smile and even to laugh aloud. She does so by entertaining her with a lewd dance; she takes off her clothes, she spreads her legs, she displays her vulva. Long past her child-bearing years, withered, wrinkled, and probably flabby, Baubo communicates her joy in her own body, her pride in her female organs, her conviction that her sexuality is *hers*, defined neither by the men who might once have desired her nor the children she may have borne. Conventional beauty, youth, reproductive capacity are all beside the point—she celebrates the pleasure her body can receive and give. The Greeks acknowledged that Baubo was a goddess, that the self-sufficient female sexuality she represents is a sacred reality. They depicted her seated on a pig with legs outspread, holding a ladder by which one might mount to the gods.

Demeter's laugh suggests that she catches on (if only for a moment) to Baubo's message that there is life, female life, even after one is no longer mother. It is that insight that prepares her to be able to accept a new relationship to Persephone after Zeus arranges for the maiden's return. For, henceforward, Persephone will spend some time with her mother each year but some time away, in her own life, in the underworld realm that is now her domain. Demeter has been initiated into a mode of relationship that can tolerate separation and change—and into an understanding of self not dependent on the other. But to Greek women Demeter remains associated primarily with the love that flows between mothers and daughters and with the griefs and losses that seem to be an inevitable correlate of motherhood. (She is also the goddess of the cultivated grain and, through her connection to Persephone, associated with chthonic mysteries; but in those regards she was worshiped by men as well as women. We are interested particularly in her relation to women.)

During the Thesmophoria, the major ritual associated with Demeter alone (in contrast to the Eleusinian rites, where she and her daughter were worshiped together as "the Two Goddesses"), the women celebrated on their own at the expense of men with obscene exposure and mocking songs (called *Iambos*), which expressed their antagonism toward men. The Thesmophoria was an extremely ancient festival; because men played no part in it and because of what Burkert calls "the natural conservatism of women," the ritual was preserved into late classical time in its archaic form and thus provides some of our best evidence of pre-Olympian religiosity. A late autumn festival, it undoubtedly had some agrarian function related to the sowing of crops, but it was much more important as a festival of women. The ritual was "liminal"—it represented a cultic inversion of everyday reality that paradoxically may have served to maintain everyday norms and structures. Thus this temporary dissolution of marital bonds may have strengthened marriage by providing a ritual outlet for expressing frustration, grief, and anger.

"At the core of the festival," says Burkert, "[is] the dissolution of the family, the separation of the sexes and the constitution of a society of women." For most women the Thesmophoria provided the only occasion when they could leave their family and home for three entire days and nights. Men were rigorously excluded from the ritual, as were children and (most scholars believe) virgins. "The absence of men gives a secret and uncanny quality to the festival." Much about this gathering of women reminds us of the maenads. Herodotus's claim that the festival was brought to

Greece by the Danaids, husband-murdering sisters, communicates the dread it inspired in men.

Sexual abstinence—that is, abstinence from intercourse with men—was demanded before and during the festival. On the first day pigs were sacrificed to commemorate the death/rape of Persephone (according to the myth, a herd of swine as well as the maiden were swallowed up in the chasm that appeared when the maiden plucked the narcissus) and then tossed down into a serpent-filled chamber. Later the rotten flesh (perhaps the remnants of the previous year's sacrifice) was brought up from the chasm and mixed with seed corn. In addition to its agrarian meaning, this part of the ritual served as a reminder of the inescapability of loss and grief. During the second day, the women fasted; they sat on the ground in remembrance of grieving Demeter sitting on "the smileless stone" at Eleusis (on the day whose evening she would spend with Baubo) and shared their grief with one another. The women ate pomegranates, whose juice symbolized blood, whose fallen pips belonged to the dead. As Burkert says, they were occupied with blood and death. Their hostility to men is expressed in highly exaggerated form; there are even traditions attesting that the women castrated men who tried to spy on the festival. There was a real indulgence of obscenity and indecent speech (reminiscent of Baubo's self-delighting vulgarity). A late source reveals that the women worshiped a representation of the female pudenda, and at least in Sicily cakes of this shape were baked and eaten.

The ritual put considerable emphasis on sexuality and conception—but not on intercourse, not on the male role. At Eleusis, too (where Demeter and Persephone were worshiped together, and where the focus was on preparation for death rather than on coming to terms with one's life as a woman), the rites were somehow connected to conception and birth (there, as a symbol of ongoing life after death). But there, too, there is no hint of ritual intercourse having been part of the ceremonies.

The Thesmophoria provided women an opportunity to vent

their anger against men, to share the difficulties and sorrows associated with their own experiences of motherhood—confident that Demeter, the grieving mother goddess, would empathize with and dignify their lot. The rite was one that encouraged abandonment—not only to anger and tribulation but to "obscenity," that is, to a self-indulgent sexuality. In the temple of the mother, all is permitted.

That licit transgression of boundaries relates closely to what I see as Demeter's most important signification with respect to same-sex love among women, for Demeter reminds us of a time when there were no boundaries, when lover and beloved were one. I believe that all close bonds among women inevitably conjure up memories and feelings associated with our first connection to a woman, the all-powerful mother of infancy. They remind us of a time in which one neither required the phallus nor rebelled against its power, when it was merely irrelevant. The *pull* to reexperience that bond of fusion, that sense of being totally loved, totally known, totally one with another—*and* the *fear* of reexperiencing that bond of fusion, of being swallowed up by a relationship, of losing one's own hard-won identity—enter powerfully into all woman-woman relationships. This does not mean that in a relationship between two women one partner will play the mother role, the other the daughter role, but rather that it is likely both will experience the profound longing to be *fully* embraced once again as by the mother of infancy—and the imperious need to break away. Much of the intensity, the emotional intimacy, women discover in one another comes from the Demeter-Persephone dimension of their bond. The particular beauty and power—and the particular danger and limitation—of love between women is here made manifest. For it is questionable whether this love really allows for personal relationship between two individuals, for what Buber called an I-Thou relationship. Certainly before Demeter loses Persephone she has allowed her no identity of her own; the daughter exists only as an extension of the mother.

The connection to the mother is always also a connection to

one's own mysterious origins, and in this sense Demeter is also relevant to the particular power that the sexual dimension of women's love for one another may have. Because to enter another woman's vagina is to touch upon the whole mystery of one's own beginnings, it may seem for many women a more sacred experience than heterosexual intercourse (no matter how physically pleasurable) can provide. Even though women's lovemaking with women is not biologically connected to reproduction, experientially it touches on that mystery through a mutual return to and mutual departure from the gate of our origin. It may be that the cost of this aspect of lesbian intensity is the loneliness Demeter experiences, the necessary time of bereavement and separation required to support an I-Thou relationship exposed to this mystery.

RAPE AND PATRIARCHAL VIOLATION

WHEREAS THE WOMEN whose work we have discussed thus far in this part of the book focus on the bond between Demeter and Persephone as the central clue to the meaning of the myth, others highlight Hades' disruption of that bond. Rather than seeing the myth primarily in terms of how it evokes images of a woman-centered matristic world, these writers view it in connection with the dominance of patriarchy. Rather than seeing it as celebrating the power of mother love, they see the myth as making painfully evident the vulnerability of the daughter and the disempowerment of the mother.

Mary Daly, for instance, believes the myth relates a "primordial mutilation," the ontological separation of mothers from daughters and sisters from sisters. She suggests that we tend to view the reunion of Demeter and Persephone much too sentimentally and bids us notice that when Zeus decides Persephone is to spend only part of each year with her mother, Demeter "sets aside her anger" and Hades now "possesses" the maiden. "The fact that the daughter was *allowed* to return for a 'period' of time says everything about patriarchy."[1]

In "Demeter Revisited," her introduction to *Women and Madness*, Phyllis Chesler retells the ancient myth in a way that highlights how the once inviolable bond between mother and daughter was changed forever by Hades' abduction of Persephone. Helios rebukes Demeter's angry response to her loss by asking, "Why mourn the natural fate of daughters?" Demeter tells him that if that is indeed the natural fate of daughters, "her inclination would be to let all mankind perish." But as the myth relates, that isn't what happens. What happens in Chesler's version is that all of Demeter's daughters, each a goddess in her own right, recognize her inability to protect them and each responds in a different way, by turning to a husband for the protection her mother can't provide, by denying her female origins and becoming a heroic male-identified woman, or by becoming a lesbian. Chesler begins her book with this myth because she wants us to see that "goddesses never die," that these same figures still live among us as the wounded women of patriarchy, as the women who fill the consulting rooms of psychotherapists and the wards of mental hospitals. In our time, as Jung, too, has said, the goddesses have become our pathologies.[2]

Annis Pratt, in an essay written for this volume, proclaims that what this myth most powerfully communicates is the image of female disempowerment in a male-dominated world. In a culture where rape is an everyday actual reality, Hades' rape of Persephone is read not just as a metaphor but as a reference to the very real vulnerability of women. Pratt is also sensitive to how women in patriarchy pass on their sense of their own victimization to their daughters, so that the image of woman-as-raped enters deeply into our consciousness. Patriarchy, the violent, dominating male energy represented by Hades, lives not only in the external culture but also within us as a complex set of internalized norms and expectations. Sadly, one of the results is that women end up blaming their mothers for their own failures and inadequacies. Pratt writes eloquently about archetypal disempowerment but is also concerned with the process whereby we women may discover archetypes of empowerment. This, she suggests, happens as, entering more deeply into the myth, we are able to forgive our mothers' limitations as due to their patriarchal fetters and then are able to recognize the gifts they have given us, and not only their limitations. It becomes possible then to shift from an exclusive focus on our personal mothers and set them in the larger and more empowering context of the generations of women in our families. What is most moving about this essay is its personal cast, Pratt's reflections on how this archetype in its negative and positive aspects has entered into her self-doubts and her accomplishments, her relationships with her mother and her daughters.

River Malcolm's poem "The Two Goddesses" communicates how powerfully the myth of Demeter and Persephone touches us when we read it as a story of rape, as a story that happens in our time, as a story about how daughters are raped and how the daughters feel betrayed not only by the rapist but also by their mothers' failure to protect them. In the poem, Persephone and Demeter, each in turn, speaks of how the rape has changed her life. Persephone communicates the terror of the god's violently wrenching her away from the world she has known, the physical horror of the rape, and her painful awareness that things can never be the same again. Again and again she asks, "And where was my mother when the earth swallowed my girlhood?" Demeter speaks not only of her loss and her grief but of her culpability. She knows she has failed her daughter, knows the daughter must hate her, knows things will never be the same, knows the daughter will never know how profoundly the mother who was not there when needed most loves her still. Here, in this poem, the mother (perhaps because she is a goddess) can do what our own mothers so rarely can, acknowledge her own guilt without expecting forgiveness, without expecting that that can erase what has happened. She is able to see what has happened to her daughter, not simply the external event but also what happened within that has changed her forever.

NOTES

1. Mary Daly, *Gyn/Ecology* (Boston: Beacon Press, 1978), 40–41.
2. Phyllis Chesler, "Demeter Revisited—An Introduction," *Women and Madness* (New York: Avon, 1972), xiv–xx.

Demeter, Persephone, and the Pedagogy of Archetypal Empowerment

ANNIS PRATT

IMAGINE A COLLEGE CLASSROOM full of eager students in their early twenties, most of them women at the paradoxical stage in psychological development when they most fiercely reject their mothers as life models but are most tempted to conform to patriarchal norms for women. But they have promised themselves to take a women's studies class, and there they sit, eagerly awaiting good news about being women from the professor, whom they intend to substitute for their mother as a role model. Well educated in the classics, she starts the class off by reading them the story of Demeter and Persephone based on the Homeric hymn: the version where Hades rapes Persephone and takes her away from her mother and their beloved fields to the underworld. She has done her classical research thoroughly, so she also tells them about cognate narratives in which Demeter had previously been raped by Poseidon, when, having turned herself into a mare in order to repel him, he overpowered her as a stallion; or other versions in which she was raped by Zeus while appealing to him against Poseidon, when she changed herself into a cow but was overpowered when he took the form of a bull.

These accounts make of Demeter's quest to rescue Persephone, the raped mother's attempt to save her raped daughter from the hands of her own rapist's brother. Not surprisingly, the outcome is mere compromise: mother and daughter suffered to live together under the constant threat of rupture and sexual violence. Imagine the bad news this denouement suggests to young women just setting forth on their quests for sexual and vocational identity. And what if the professor also brings to class, that first day, Phyllis Chesler's updating of these compromises, in which she depicts not only Demeter but also Psyche, Artemis, and Aphrodite encapsulated within a violent masculine culture with no hope for escape, merely reacting to a destructive and implicitly indestructible patriarchy? The psychological impact of being introduced to women's studies in these terms, as if patriarchal culture were absolute, with the only possibility a futile and compromised resistance, is devastating to women students, for whom it reaffirms their mothers' victimization and undermines their hopes for escape from the cycle of patriarchal denigration.

When I first developed my course in women's spirituality at the University of Wisconsin-Madison in the 1970s, these disempowering classical materials were the only ones available.

Soon, in the good company of many feminist archaeologists, theologians, and therapists who noticed how very transparent indeed were the Euro-patriarchal emperor's garments, I was able to assign more empowering archetypal narratives. In the very year of my first women's mythology course, Charlene Spretnak published a pre-Homeric Demeter/Kore narrative based on extensive research that said nothing about rape at all, an apatriarchal version of the Demeter/Persephone archetype that depicts mothers and daughters working through what separates them from empowering each other on a woman/woman rebirth into relationship with each other and with nature. Spretnak's re-visioned story tells about Persephone's desire to develop skills at aiding the dead, a career choice which Demeter at first opposes but later accepts as part of her daughter's maturation. Students recognize in this narrative that mothers can throw obstacles in the way of their psychological individuation, and they celebrate Persephone's persistence, which, unlike so many disagreements with mothers, leads to a new kind of relationship between them based on Persephone's unique skills and powers.

Jung recognized the specifically woman/woman empowerment of the mother/daughter transformational quest, although both he and his more orthodox disciples sometimes assume that maternal archetypes are contents within the psyche of the individual rather than crossing places for drives flowing between real people. I say this with especial pain, remembering myself as a vulnerable twenty-three-year-old bride in the early 1960s, visiting my first therapist. Unmothered, newly married, and shaken by an inchoate dread and anxiety which I did not know at the time emanated from my mother's physical abuse of me in childhood, I needed a therapist who could sort out my relationships with mother, father, and brother and then bring them into his office to mediate our dysfunctional relationship. I had at that time a dream I dreamed over and over, about a pathetic, thin little child whom I futilely tried to nourish. My therapist decided that what I needed was to develop my (internal) anima, and that, in his opinion, the best way to do that was to stop using birth control and become a mother myself.

I quickly conceived the first of my two daughters, whom I had to mother entirely on instinct, without any modeling of what real mothering could possibly entail. Only much later—in my midthirties and after a frightening nervous breakdown—did I find a developmental therapist who enabled me to complete the quest through my real mother-daughter history. My brother, also a Jungian therapist, once replied to my query about how he could treat his wife and daughters so badly if he was a feminist that "of course I am a good feminist—I come to terms with my anima every day." My mother died before I could effect any kind of familial reconciliation; and I often wonder if my brother's inability to get close to me has to do with his feeling that I am not his sister Annis but a mere vehicle for his anima or his shadow. Thus my own life strengthens my conviction that archetypes are neither transcendent absolutes nor facets of narcissistically subjective complexes but are psychological forces within an interactive field enabling real people to seek healthy relationship to each other.

My attempts to be a strong mother for my daughters were not always successful: I became an alcoholic (as my mother had been) while they were in their adolescence, frightening them with my hair-trigger temper and unstable emotional outbursts; only during their twenties did I model for them a strong, reliable, and sober mother as well as the witty, creative, and successful college professor I had been all along. I was more successful at the at-one-remove nurturing a teacher can provide, developing a pedagogy to enable students on their life journeys by absorbing the import of empowering archetypes, especially Aphrodite and Artemis. Shortly after the age of fifty, however, the energy propelling me as a successful wounded healer dried up abruptly. I took early retirement to renew a more relational, playful, and community-oriented life while giving range to my long-suppressed desire to write as an independent scholar, completing a long book about how men and women poets seek archetypal empowerment and starting a new book about my practice of transformational pedagogy.

My data for *Dancing with Goddesses* suggest to me a dialectical process in which we as daughters must bring to consciousness the full range of both our mothers' victimization and their hidden powers and qualities. This is a quest in which we must acknowledge and repudiate their patriarchal fetters, then absorb without letting it destroy us their rage against these limitations and, finally, assimilate into our personalities their positive qualities. The outcome is to negate, absorb, and transcend our mothers' personal lives in order to become new and separate personalities empowered by locating ourselves within the generations of women in our families.

My own quest started with acknowledging the Medusa archetype in my mother: when I looked at Medusa I saw the rage my mother had visited upon me. I found out after she died that my mother had renounced her birth name after suffering a trauma (I have never known what) at five years old, when she took to her bed, announcing she would never eat or breathe again until everyone called her a new name, after her father. So the unhappy, angry, but very real child remained undeveloped at the core of an ultra-"feminine" personality that she cultivated as an especially compliant daughter. Underneath this beautiful but dependent woman, beloved by many friends, there lurked the wild child she had repressed, for whom she named me.

After her death and the compassion and forgiveness that came from my location of the source of my mother's rage in her patriarchal self-victimization, I was freed in my forties to transcend her negative impact on my life and absorb the gifts she had given. Once I was absolutely clear about where her lost child left off and mine began, I took both wild children by the hand and walked with them through the pine woods she had loved best of all. It was then that I discovered that she had been a child columnist for a Boston newspaper, and I was able to absorb as my maternal heritage this forgotten career as writer along with her belief in the importance of women's education, her fierce spirituality, and her love of nature.

There is a fine line between a dangerous and parasitical lack of differentiation from the mother and a healthy mother/daughter empowerment. It seems much easier, especially for women in academe, to remain in a lifelong antagonism against their mothers while overidentifying either with their fathers or with academic norms in patriarchy. Academic institutions are structured upon masculine ideas of domination and competition, tempting even women professors who devote all their time and energy to women's studies to atrophy their emotional and relational qualities in a wan mimicry of its aggressions and competitions. I consider this (often unconscious) masculinization of the self responsible for the fierce resistance of many women's studies professors to archetypal and theological scholarship, which often leads to their dogmatic restriction of their syllabi to patriarchal abuses and resistance against them. Like the Homeric Demeter and Persephone, and like daughters of mothers who overidentify with patriarchy, both professors and students in such classrooms remain stuck in a cycle of victimization and reaction to it, bereft of pathways to genuine feminist empowerment.

Feminist pedagogical theory locates patriarchal critique and resistance as the second stage of feminist identity development: that of "revelation," characterized by questioning, anger, and guilt, with a tendency to blame men (or one's earlier passivity displaced onto less feminist women) for everything. My archetypal pedagogy, in contrast, engages students in the next stage of "embeddedness-emanation," when they affirm and strengthen their identity as women on the way to becoming effective activists in coalition with men and other groups working for common ethical goals in their communities.

Although an introduction to the mother/daughter archetype suffices to pack women students' knapsacks for their future mother-daughter reconciliations, in my own life I have come to the stage when I must absorb the import not only of Demeter and Kore but also the third goddess in the narrative, Hecate.

These elder archetypes round out the full range of feminine and feminist empowerment, from our wild acumen in girlhood, through joyous sensuality and social or biological motherhood, to a wisdom that draws upon the full range of our lived experiences. As good crones and elders we can become wonderful mothers to ourselves at last, insisting upon time to enjoy each other's jokes and creativity. Energized by the rebirth of buried aspects of our self as well as by postmenopausal zest, we may also find the strength to help our friends and relations and, eventually, ourselves on that final quest, for a death with dignity.

The Two Goddesses

RIVER MALCOLM

PERSEPHONE

At first it was only the lily
a kind of annunciation
as when Gabriel held it
singing birth birth birth
but that was another story.
     I bent to pick it, that lily,
and in that moment
was blessed: was at one
with the garland of girls
that danced in the meadow.
Softer than petals,
the blue up above,
the sun's bright caress.
Softer than petals,
the swirl of their skirts,
the brush of their maiden flesh.

     And then the earth opened.
Seized by a tremor of darkness
and wrenched from the world I'd known,
darkness forced into my mouth

and between my teeth,
darkness thrust down my throat,
darkness thrust through my nose,
darkness thrust through my ears,
darkness forced into my eyes,
a fist of darkness between my thighs
tearing my insides,
        and knowing
        I was forever changed
        forever different.
So it was Hades I wed,
King of Death,
God of the world below.

And where was my mother, oh goddess of all things that grow,
when his rough hands pulled me down to the root of it all?
Where was my mother and what was her power then,
when Hades took me like a calf or a dog or a bench
and made me a thing, a possession of his?
Where was my mother then and where the dance of her golden
   grains?
        Do not
        talk to me about life and the living.
I am the wife of Hades,
I am His Queen.
The shades salute him, and I,
seated on the cold gold throne at his side,
I too am saluted.
Before me, as before him,
the Underworld bows.
At my every word now,
the Nether World cringes
and scurries to obey.
Even Cerberus the fierce
whines when I approach, and begs
for a pat from his mistress's hand.

As for me, I do not think
of my mother's soft eyes,
her bosom, her arms,
they are part of a life I have left,
torn from me by the dark.
Where was she
when the earth opened up
and swallowed my girlhood?

And now I am Queen.
I have grown somewhat fond of my power.
Do not think I partake innocently.
Do not think I mistake these pomegranate seeds.
I know they're the food of the dead:
seeds of power, seeds of blood.
I who was torn from the world of my mother
I know these seeds.
Before that moment, there was no force in my world,
life danced in my mother's sweet circles
of flowers and fruits, growing and grains,
but now things are different.
I'm frankly intrigued by the taste of command
and savor the ruby red seeds slowly
crushing them knowingly
between strong teeth no longer innocent.
It is Hades, my husband, who bids me cease,
knowing,
as those of my father's generation
do know,
that Destiny must be obeyed
even by Gods.

And I go
as if I could be again the same girl I was,
soft skin   soft small bosom   soft eyes,
I, Queen of Death, Lady of Darkness,

I who rise from the earth
as the lily once did
as if to return to those innocent dances,
as if to rejoin that garland of girls,
as if my mother and I could be reunited,
as if the two goddesses could be made one.
She who blesses the earth with abundance,
she for whom flowers, grains, fruits grow once again,
she is my mother.
And I am her daughter, I,
in whom seeds of death are planted
and will sprout.

DEMETER

From the other side of the world child
I heard your scream
felt your abduction
in every pore of my skin
the stench of your violation,
the core of your sacred body defiled,
darkness forcing itself deep inside,
knowing I never prepared you for this.

Only the Sun would name the perpetrator,
but I should have known
who else could it be
but your father (his brother, what difference?):
male gods who long ago usurped
the power of our grandmothers,
those great ancient goddesses,
who being keepers of life
could not deny them their destiny.
I too, daughter, I am a keeper of life,
though while separate from you
I forget the world placed in my keeping.

And I mourn.
Nothing grows.
I reward small human kindnesses
and dream of giving immortality to a human child
as if somehow that would undo the harm
from which I could not preserve you.
But destiny, laughing, terrifies its mother
to intervene, and I a goddess
cannot do even this one small deed.
And I mourn.
Earth is barren, humans starve
baffled by this drama of the gods.

Daughter, do not imagine I deceive myself
or dream I can call you back as you were.
Nor do I dream of freeing you,
when you think of my absence, my failure,
from the hatred that hardens your eyes.
How can a goddess who makes the very grain to grow
allow her own child to be raped?

Do not be afraid: I know of your hate.
Even the goddesses, especially the goddesses
must dance with destiny, daughter.
Do not think I require you back as you were,
I know you are changed.
And I too, daughter, I also am changed,
oh flesh of my flesh,
these seeds of death within you,
they are seeds in my flesh.

I embrace all of you, daughter,
the change and the hate,
the longing to partake of your violator's power,
and I call you, I call you forth as you are
knowing you may not be able to love me now

in the face of my failed power,
power that seemed so great
to your child eyes.

You will never know Persephone
except as you rest your brow on my bosom
and remember a little
the girl you once were
and how we were whole
you will never know
the joy I feel in your being
no matter where you go
no matter what seeds of death sprout in you
no matter how pregnant with winter
oh my sweet flower of spring
you will never know
how my love for you makes the grains grow.

PUBERTY RITES

OTHER COMMENTATORS on the Eleusinian myth agree that the abduction is central—not as violation but as initiation.

Bruce Lincoln reads the Homeric hymn as a disguised account of a young woman's initiation into a male-dominated culture and proposes that the Eleusinian mysteries might have begun as female initiation rites marking the transition from maidenhood into adulthood, rites performed for women as they arrived at puberty in which the other members of the community, including the men, participated by taking on the roles of the other figures in the scenario described in the myth. With the transition to a more urban society, what may have originally been a tribal ritual mandatory for all young women became an elective mystery cult.

In his reading of the myth as an initiation scenario, Lincoln emphasizes Persephone's innocence and terror; he acknowledges the violence of the abduction and father Zeus's role in not only approving but instigating it. He interprets this as Zeus and Hades playing culturally approved roles designed to transform Persephone from child to woman. Initiations typically mark the transition from one life stage to another in dramatically violent ways and often involve a figurative death experience. Lincoln refers to other Greek myths in which rape, the forcible loss of virginity, is understood as initiatory as it often is in "male-centered, misogynistically inclined cultures. . . . Introduction to productive sexuality seems to be only a secondary motive for such practices, the real point being the forcible subjugation of women to male control." Lincoln notes that when Persephone returns, she returns to her mother and father, "toward whom there is no bitterness," as a new person, "whole, mature, fertile, and infinitely more complex."

Lincoln interprets the myth as the story of a young woman's initiation into a patriarchal world. Many women, however, read the myth as an initiatory scenario in which Hades serves to help Persephone make the transition to a more authentically female maturity. Women who look at the myth from a Jungian perspective seem particularly inclined to look at the female initiatory aspects of the myth not in order to discover the social function such rites might have played in the ancient world but rather to show how they illumine the inner experience of contemporary women. Thus Nor Hall, for example, writes that though the Eleusinian rites "no longer have visible structures, symbols, or spaces to manifest in," they "have turned inward" and are still lived as stages of psychic transformation.[1]

In accord with her interpretation, she transforms "abduction" into the more euphemistic concept of "seduction" and observes that "seduction is a kind of education":

> The event of first enrapturement seduces one out of one's childhood. One is snatched or seized by a totally unfamiliar attitude, caught against one's will it seems, by the recognition of something beyond the mother. . . .
>
> This captivation, being "taken" by another ("you can be taken without love")—seduced, raped, or enraptured—opens a door that was never there before, into a limitless and often terrifying basement. . . .
>
> There is no detaining the maiden's wending toward the death of what she has been. That imperative to move on, to create, pushes at us not only biologically, but psychically.[2]

Jennifer and Roger Woolger propose a similar understanding of the myth that, they believe, gives us a vision of the feminine life cycle that is "both spiritual and grounded in the body."[3] They see Persephone as the archetypal maiden, innocent and passive, accustomed to depend on others, her mother or her Olympian father, to protect and defend her. In their reading the Woolgers move back and forth between the Persephone of the myth and what they regard as "the Persephone woman," the woman caught in the role of the eternal maiden. (Jean Bolen also identifies Persephone as a "puella eterna" but tends to glide over precisely what fascinates the Woolgers, the difficult, resisted initiation through which Persephone is transformed; Bolen speaks of Persephone as simply "maturing" into her role as queen of the underworld.[4])

In the Woolgers' account Persephone's initiation begins as she becomes aware of the "earth opening up beneath her," an awareness that they see as directed at deep movements beginning "within her own body." That is, she begins to menstruate. Her first bleeding is the necessary prelude, the preparation for what happens next, the loss of her virginity. "The function of Hades is to carry her downward into a new consciousness of the inner movements of her body as a woman.[5] Hades helps her to know the self she is beginning to become.

"The wisdom of this extraordinary myth," as the Woolgers understand it, "is that the source of Persephone's transformation comes from beneath, from the lower depths of soul." Persephone's "true savior" is Hades, not Zeus. "The spirit in its Olympian form cannot initiate Persephone." A Persephone woman, they believe, often seeks to evade this initiation by turning to "spirituality" or by becoming what she has lost: the all-loving mother. But Demeter constellates Persephone. The all-giving woman who has not worked through her own neediness and dependence but, rather, sought to evade it will find herself surrounded by needy and clingingly dependent Persephone women.[6]

Persephone, the "eternal sacrificial victim," needs to get beyond her identification with her passivity and powerlessness and the sympathy and pity these elicit. Only a genuine encounter with Hades that brings the death of all attachment to innocence can free her. Thus the Woolgers understand Persephone's marriage to Hades as meaning the death of the maiden. "What must die in the maiden Persephone [is] precisely her maidenly innocence. . . . Too much light casts an enormous shadow, as Jung was constantly reminding us." The shadow of the all-innocent maiden is, in their interpretation, enormous rage and a lust for all-encompassing power, as the Orphics who called Persephone "Mother of the Furies" understood. The point of Persephone's initiation is to force her to come to terms with this dark side of herself, her Hecate aspect, "the witch and killer in herself."[7]

In her essay "Cycles of Becoming," Vera Bushe, who looks at the myth through the perspective of object relations theory and tries to take into account what such theorists as Margaret Mahler, Alice Miller, and Nancy Chodorow have written about female development, argues that the Persephone myth offers us the story of a *failed* initiation. In her view, that the myth, as it is available to us in the Homeric hymn, communicates patriarchal perspectives is part of its value. "Because modern women are products of patriarchy, patriarchal myths help us understand who we are." In Bushe's interpretation, Persephone refuses the initiatory experience offered to her in the underworld. She chooses not to participate in life during the period she spends there, chooses not to define herself. Persephone represents a woman with a "foreclosed identity," still wholly caught in the role of mother's daughter. This Bushe attributes to Demeter's narcissism; Demeter sees her daughter only as an extension of herself, and Persephone accepts being Demeter's daughter as her self-definition. Bushe sees Zeus's approval of Hades' abduction of his daughter as the god's attempt to help Persephone break free and expand her world. But the conclusion of the myth shows that he is unable to break the attachment between mother and daughter. Persephone is still to spend the major part of each year with Demeter. Bushe imagines that perhaps Persephone can use the one-third of each year she spends with Hades to begin developing a separate self and the time with Demeter to work consciously on developing a less symbiotic relation to her mother. But the myth as it stands gives no assurance of such an outcome. Bushe believes that we need a ritual for the transition from the role of daughter to that of mature woman and long for a myth that would correspond to such a ritual—but, alas, the Demeter and Persephone myth does not answer to this need and longing.

NOTES

1. Nor Hall, *The Moon and the Virgin* (New York: Harper and Row 1980), 85.

2. Ibid., 76–77, 84.

3. Jennifer Barker Woolger and Roger J. Woolger, *The Goddess Within* (New York: Fawcett Columbine, 1987), 285.

4. Jean Shinoda Bolen, *Goddesses in Everywoman* (San Francisco, Harper and Row, 1984), 209.

5. Woolger and Woolger, *Goddess*, 289.

6. Ibid., 242–43. (I have eliminated some italics.)

7. Ibid., 247–48.

The Rape of Persephone

BRUCE LINCOLN

THE WELL-KNOWN MYTH of Demeter and Persephone is
unquestionably the most important myth of classical antiquity to
focus on the lives of women, and it is thus possible that it may
have been tied to women's rites. At its heart is the bond of two
women, mother and daughter, a bond that is ruptured when Persephone is abducted by Hades, lord of the underworld, and reestablished when Demeter's mourning forces the gods to return her
daughter. It has been interpreted in many fashions, most often as
an allegory of the seasons or of the grain, but most convincingly, in
my opinion, by Henri Jeanmaire as the description of a woman's
initiation.[1]

This thesis has not gained wide acceptance in classical circles
and is today largely ignored. The reason for this, in large measure,
is that a view of the Persephone myth as a scenario of women's
initiation is not easily reconciled with the well-known fact that in
the mysteries of Eleusis, the most famous ritual associated with
the myth, men were initiated as well as women, the mysteries
being open to all who spoke Greek and who had not committed
homicide. I must emphasize that it was not Jeanmaire's intent, nor
is it mine, to offer an interpretation of the Eleusinian mysteries,
although certain details from the mysteries are of value to my
argument. My chief focus, like Jeanmaire's, is on the myth, for the

myth, in our opinion, preserves a state of affairs anterior to that apparent in the mysteries as historically reported.

It is our contention that a close reading of the texts in which the myth is recounted, especially the Homeric "Hymn to Demeter," reveals a scenario of a young woman's initiation. Beyond that, it is my hypothesis that at some point in prehistory, probably prior to the arrival of the Indo-Europeans in the Greek regions (ca. 1800 B.C.?), a ritual resembling that described in the myth was actually performed for some or all women in these regions upon their arriving at puberty. Other members of the society, including men, participated in the ritual by taking the roles of other characters in the myth.

Over the course of centuries, however, several major changes in Greek civilization resulted in modifications of this ritual pattern. The first of these was the advent of the Indo-Europeans, whose religious system emphasized male deities, ideologies, and rituals in contrast to the matri-centered religion of the Old European peoples who inhabited Greece before their coming. As a result, rituals that spoke directly to the lives of women must have declined in importance, disappeared entirely, or modified their form. Second, Greece changed from a predominantly tribal society to a predominantly urban one, and this, as Angelo Brelich argued, forced a change in the nature of initiatory rituals, whereby rites of passage that had been mandatory for all youths and that conveyed full membership and adult status in society, became impractical as population increased and as social roles became more differentiated. As a result, these tribal initiations were transformed, becoming elective cults into which individuals might be inducted and through which they would be promised salvation. In other words, puberty initiations became Mystery initiations— precisely the transformation I posit for the rites reflected in the Persephone myth. Third, numerous Greek city-states saw the evolution of democratic institutions and ideals. This was particularly true of Athens, the *polis* to which Eleusis was attached most closely. It is this process of democratization that may have resulted in the opening up of the Eleusinian Mysteries to all save barbarians and murderers.

That Persephone is a young girl on the verge of womanhood, and thus at an appropriate age for initiation, is clear from the texts in which her myth is related. Her by-name, *korē*, is virtually synonymous with Greek *parthenos*, "maiden, virgin," and the Latin sources regularly call her *virgo* or make reference to her *virginitas*. At the same time, the texts are equally insistent on the fact that the maiden has reached physical maturity and is thus of marriageable age. The Homeric "Hymn to Demeter," the oldest, most complete, and most important version of the Persephone myth, calls the maid *thalerē*, "nubile, ripened," (l. 79) and groups her with the "deep-breasted" (*bathukolpos*) Okeanids (l. 5). Other sources report that some of the gods had already asked for Persephone's hand, and artistic representations show a beautiful, full-breasted, teenage girl.

This girl, youthful and innocent, is suddenly and unexpectedly wrenched away from the world in which she has grown up. One day while gathering flowers with her playmates—an act that is still a ritual prelude to marriage in the Greek countryside—she is snatched up and whisked to the underworld, kicking and screaming all the way.

The verb used here, as in all Greek sources, to describe Hades' action is *harpazein* (ll. 3, 19, 56, and elsewhere), meaning "to seize, snatch, carry off," a term usually reserved for acts of war or thievery but always acts of violence. In Latin texts, another word connoting violence is found: *raptu*, meaning "abduction, seizure, rape."

The assault is thus violent, and the text emphasizes that Kore is *aekousan*, "unwilling" (ll. 19, 30, 72). She has been led into a trap. The beguiling narcissus was the bait, set forth by Gaia according to the instructions of Zeus (l. 8), and under Hades' powerful attack the maiden can only cry out, ironically calling to Zeus for assistance (l. 21).

Kore's companions—her age-mates, the Okeanids—take up

this cry, according to the Homeric hymn (l. 27), and the earliest known artistic representation of the myth, a painted wine cup from Phaistos dating from the middle Minoan period (just before 2000 BCE), shows two companions crying out while Kore disappears into the earth's chasm beside the "flower of deception". Other sources, however, place the goddesses Athene and Artemis beside Persephone and tell how these deities try to oppose Hades and protect their companion because, according to Claudian (*De Raptu Proserpine* 2.207f), "Their common virginity goads them to arms and makes them bitter at the crime of the wild ravisher." Their heroic defense is stopped, however, by Zeus with a blast of thunder.

Deceived by her father, abandoned by her companions, Kore looks to her mother for help. As soon as Demeter learns of her daughter's fate she runs to give aid, but by then it is too late and the girl has disappeared below the earth's surface. Demeter laments, grieving for Kore as if she were dead but searching for her nonetheless.

This heart-rending concern of Kore's mother stands in marked contrast to the attitude of the girl's father, Zeus, who planned the abduction himself and approved of it from the outset.

This set of circumstances, in which a father instigates the abduction of his daughter, against the wishes of the girl and her mother, has always posed a difficult problem for interpretation. Some scholars have been inclined to see a hidden enmity between the celestial father god Zeus and the terrestrial mother goddess Demeter, perhaps dating back to the opposition of Indo-European and pre–Indo-European, or of Olympian and Chthonic religious forms. Such a formulation, however, merely provides a possible historical background for what is a very live and important issue in the myth: Zeus and Demeter disagree violently as to what shall be the proper fate of their daughter. Although most texts seem to follow the Homeric hymn and sympathize with Demeter, there is no reason to view Zeus's actions as sinister or perverse. He is Kore's parent no less than Demeter, and since he is consistently pictured as a loving parent—witness the tears of blood he sheds at the death of his son, Sarpedon (*Iliad* 16.458–61)—it is fully possible that he has the girl's best interests at heart no less than her mother.

Zeus's view of what is good for Kore is quite different from that of Demeter, however, and to understand this we must confront a basic fact of Greek kinship ideology. The Greeks believed that there was a profound difference between mother and father, the former being seen as the biological parent, who gave birth, and the latter as the social parent, who gave and continues to give his children a place in the world throughout their lives. As part of this role, the Greek father arranged marriages, transferring daughters from his own household to that of another man, and from the status of daughter to that of wife.

On the strength of this, some scholars have interpreted the Persephone myth as the description of a marriage, but this is unlikely in view of the other family connections stated in the myth. Hades, Zeus, and Demeter are siblings, children of Cronos and Rhea (*Theogony*, 453–58; "Hymn to Demeter," ll. 85, 364). Persephone's abductor is thus both her maternal and paternal uncle (*mētrōs* and *patrōs*), and as such an unlikely mate; an uncle's chief role was to care for his niece or nephew in a protective way. To be sure, Demeter does not view Hades' action as protective or helpful, but from the standpoint of Zeus, Hades acts properly, undertaking the dangerous task of transforming Kore from child to woman.

When first we see Kore after her abduction she is in the underworld. In contrast to the detailed description of her capture, the sources offer little on what her existence is like in the subterranean realms, regularly referred to as "the murky gloom," *zophos ēeroeis* (ll. 80, 337, 402, 464). Those who favored a view of her myth as seasonal allegory interpreted her stay in the underworld as a mythopoeic description of winter, the time when the crops are underground. This view has fallen into disfavor, since Kore disappears while gathering flowers—thus in spring or early summer—and her absence cannot correspond to wintertime.

Another interpretation is possible, however. An initiand's time and place of seclusion may be referred to as "being in the underworld." Such terminology is probably used for a number of reasons. Often, the initiand is believed to experience literal or figurative death and rebirth through initiation. In other scenarios, a live initiand is expected to visit all or many of the cosmic realms, the underworld always being included in the tour. The underworld is thought to be a less well defined place than the land of the living—"hazy" or "murky," and thus well-suited to a person whose place in society is equally ill-defined. The initiand is a person in limbo, who has lost one status but not yet received another to take its place. Having lost her home, her parents, her playmates, indeed all the world she knew, Kore is in just such a position.

Kore suffers another loss in the "underworld," a loss that dramatically alters her status and even her name: the loss of her virginity. Kore's defloration changes her utterly. She has, in effect, been initiated by rape, a pattern found in a number of male-centered, misogynistically inclined cultures, and strongly suggested in numerous Greek myths. Introduction to productive sexuality seems to be only a secondary motive for such practices, the real point being the forcible subjugation of women to male control: Hades is no tender bridegroom who lovingly takes his bride to bed but, rather, is the male oppressor who forces his will upon a young girl for the first time, thus teaching her proper submission to all members of his sex.

Her virginity lost, Kore's name, which literally means "the maiden," becomes highly inappropriate, and she takes on a new name: Persephone. Such a change of name is a regular feature in the initiatory rites of innumerable peoples as a mark of the initiand's total transformation.

The rape of Persephone becomes a truly cosmic event. The famine plunges the world into a state of chaos and threatens the existence of men and gods alike. The crops disappear; the seasons turn topsy-turvy; the earth swallows but does not bring forth. All life hangs in the balance, and even Zeus cannot stand up under such pressure.

At first, Zeus dispatches messengers who attempt to dissuade Demeter from her anger, but when this proves impossible he decides to yield. He sends Hermes, guide of souls, to Hades, telling him to give up the girl, whom Hermes leads back to earth. Persephone's father—who instigated her initiation—thus calls it to a halt and restores her to the society that she left. This restoration is accomplished gradually, Persephone first coming to earth and rejoining Demeter, with whom she spends an entire day.

Persephone is thus restored to her mother, her father—toward whom there is no trace of bitterness—her home, and all she left; but she is no longer the same maiden who was taken from them. She will never be Kore, the maiden, again. She has matured, become sexualized, died, and been reborn.

NOTES

1. Henri Jeanmaire, *Couroi et Courètes* (Lille: Bibliothèque Universitaire, 1939), 269–79, 298–305. Similar ideas had already been presented by Otto Kern, *Die griechischen Mysterien der Klassischen Zeit* (Berlin: Weidmann, 1927), 25; Felix Speiser, "Die Eleusinischen Mysterien als primitive Initiation," *Zeitschrift für Ethnologie* 60 (1928): 362–72.

Cycles of Becoming

VERA BUSHE

"THE CONCEPT of elucidating the nature of the modern female psyche by drawing on the expressions of the female in myth is a creative and potentially profound approach."[1] Since patriarchy has been managing information for thirty-five hundred years, however, myths have generally been viewed from a patriarchal point of view and reflect development in patriarchal society. In fact, what we have is patriarchal mythology and patriarchal archetypes. It is Spretnak's view that we would have to go to ancient, pre-Olympian, matriarchal mythology to see the implications of patriarchal mythology. According to Spretnak, Jane Ellen Harrison found the pre-Olympian body of mythology to be different in many ways from the patriarchal Olympian system. While recognizing that the pre-Olympian body of myth exists, I have chosen a patriarchal myth to study because I believe that in order to understand ourselves in the world today we have to understand self in patriarchy. We live in a patriarchal world, and psychological theory comes out of human participation in that world. It seems appropriate to investigate the matriarchal myths for expansiveness, contrast, and understanding of evolution, but I don't agree with Spretnak that it is inadequate to look only at the patriarchal. Because modern women are products of patriarchy, patriarchal myths help us to understand who we are and how we react to living under patriarchy. For me, what is important about mythology is that it speaks to our inner subjective and collective experience as women in today's world.

"There are almost as many interpretations of myths as there are mythologists."[2] Not all daughters develop in the same way. Not all mothers are the same. This particular exploration of Homer's "Hymn to Demeter" is an expression of my consciousness. It comes out of my experience of trying to stand separate, with my own internal definitions and standards, in the presence of my mother without needing or wanting her approval or confirmation. When I read Alice Miller, I came to understand that the core issue I had been struggling with for twenty years was my mother's unhealthy narcissism and its impact on me as her daughter. I have never felt that my mother loved me for who I really am as a person. Miller states that every child has a legitimate narcissistic need to be noticed, understood, taken seriously, and respected by her mother. The narcissistic need I am speaking of is not the kind that places a premium on "appearance, surface, corporeal beauty, cosmetics."[3] I am speaking of the deeper issue of being seen and loved genuinely by another. In a narcissistic relationship, the mother projects aspects of herself onto the child and then loves the illusion she has created. Somehow, in the midst of projections, the child loses her soul to her mother. Stein states that with the loss of soul the child loses a sense of being able to direct her own life. As we will see later in the myth, Persephone is such a child. The myth creates a context for a psychological exploration of the narcissistic relationship between mother and daughter. Both the hymn, which I will refer to as a myth, and this paper focus on the unhealthy narcissistic mother. In exploring narcissism, I believe that I am coming closer to understanding the origins of loss of self for the love of another. It is my view that if we struggle with understanding our narcissistic attachments, we will come closer to the core of finding a separate self who can genuinely be in relationship with another.

INTERPRETING THE MYTH

Demeter's Narcissism

In this paper I am addressing the Demeter mother. A Demeter mother would lend a different flavor to managing her narcissism than, for example, an Artemis mother. Demeter is *the* maternal archetype. She is the most nurturing of the Greek goddesses. Her most important roles are to be mother of Persephone and provider of food (goddess of grain). Her relationship with Persephone was her most significant relationship. Demeter mothers have maternal persistence and feel that without a child "life is devoid of meaning and empty."[4] Demeter's attributes would guide her to mother more intensely and possessively than other mothers because of the importance of this relationship. It is her life, unlike Artemis, who has self-chosen goals that are separate from her children. According to Bolen, Artemis is a mother who fosters independence by teaching her children to fend for themselves in the world. "Artemis mothers do not look back with longing to when their children were babies or dependent toddlers."[5] Because she looks forward to her children's independence, an Artemis mother would act out her narcissism in such a way that her fulfillment comes out of seeing the separateness in her child. It is less likely that she would look upon her child as a part of herself whose interests are identical with her own. The Demeter mother is fulfilled in the maintaining of close attachment to her children and thus would be more likely not to see differences between herself and her child.

Alice Miller[6] suggests two ways to cope with narcissism: depression and grandiosity. Depression is a defense against experiencing the deep pain of loss of self. According to Fischer, "depressed mothers tended to express their depression by withdrawal, passively disengaging from emotional commitments."[7] We see Demeter's depression in her unwillingness to allow anything to flourish, her mourning for a year, her unwillingness to be active in any form other than aimless wandering for almost a year. She lives with her inability to find and bring back Persephone. Grandiosity is the defense against depression. We see Demeter's grandiosity both in having a huge temple built for the purpose of worshiping her and her mysteries and in the way she nourished and then abandoned Demophoon. Nobody asked for the child to be immortal. Was it not good enough for Demeter to nurse a mortal child? Why does she abandon Demophoon when her "immortalizing rituals" are disturbed? In disclosing who she really is, Demeter says, "I am Demeter the honored, the greatest benefit and joy to undying gods and mortals."[8] I don't hear humbleness in those words. According to Miller, grandiosity is connected to a sense of success. Demeter is ultimately able to force Zeus to arrange to bring her daughter back. For Demeter, that is a major success. In addition to the visible depression and grandiosity, Demeter's narcissism is seen throughout the myth. She does not consider the suggestion that this change in relationship might be good for Persephone. She never considers that her daughter may be ready for something different in her life. She does not support her daughter to take an independent step. She does not guide her daughter onto a separate path. She never waivers from wanting her daughter restored to her. She selfishly uses her powers to get her daughter back regardless of the consequences (famine) for others. All must suffer with her. She is her daughter's mother. According to Harding,[9] primitive people believed that women were impregnated by the moon and that the children were gifts of the moon. Coming out of a period of primitive traditions, Zeus's minimal role in his daughter's life may be understandable. Even when he tries to control Persephone's life, Demeter's power forces Zeus to have the daughter returned to her. Her energy is invested in her daughter, and she has difficulty separating herself from her loss of daughter. She spends her time "wasting away with longing for her daughter."[10] Demeter is also invested in the role of mother and the power that it has. This is demonstrated in how she takes over the nurturing of Metanira's child. She takes complete control of the child, and when the mother unwittingly interferes, Demeter, enraged, rejects the child and refuses to continue to bestow her immortal gifts upon him. Nobody, however, asked that the child be immortal. Specifically, Demophoon did not ask for immortality. According to Miller,[11] each mother can be empathic only to the extent she is free from her own childhood wounds. This situation demonstrates Balint's notion of "false empathy."[12] Demeter began to make Demophoon immortal because of her fantasy of what he needed. At some level she was gratifying her own needs.

Demeter and Persephone's Relationship

"Mothers experience daughters as one with themselves; their relationships to daughters are narcissistic."[13] If the mother is narcissistic, she creates, from the beginning of infancy, a narcissistic relationship with her daughter. The narcissistic quality of relationship is visible in the fact that both Demeter and Persephone are unwilling to continue their lives when separated from each other. Mother and daughter mirror each other. Both Demeter and Persephone are outraged. Both passively allow a year to go by until Zeus finally does something to resolve the problem. Neither Demeter nor Persephone made responsible choices for herself. Both of them resisted the influence of males (Zeus, Hades, and Helios). Both mother and daughter go into a grieving period. Both experience narcissistic depression from the loss of love-object availability. Both hope to be together again without considering other possible ways to be together. Both resist change. Both discard their roles. Persephone won't take on her role as queen of the underworld. Demeter won't take on her role as goddess of grain. Both refuse to function. Both are unwilling to eat. Both obey Zeus's decree. Both, in the end, take on their respective roles. Both mother and daughter shadow each other. According to Mahler, excessive shadowing is one sign that the awareness of separateness is causing great strain.[14] Also, these parallel behaviors are some measure of the quality of attachment and demonstrate Persephone as an extension of her mother. This is particularly visible in Persephone's unwillingness to admit that she reacted in a way that Demeter would not approve. Her inner censor tells her that she must avoid truth and blame Hades for her eating in the underworld instead of admitting that she ate the seeds without considering the consequences of her actions. Luke suggests Persephone "takes the pomegranate seed involuntarily, but voluntarily swallows it. In spite of her protests, she really has no intention of regressing to identification with her mother again."[15] Fischer states that censorship, which is in essence what Persephone chooses to do, is one path to differentiation. "The daughter quietly refuses to share certain of her feelings and experiences with her mother."[16] But I don't believe that censorship is an adequate form of separation. Because she is narcissisticly identified with her mother, her fear of separateness is debilitating, which causes her to censor her experience. Each time she censors her experience, she sinks deeper into trying to be what her mother wants her to be. Their situation echoes Deutsch's words about mothers and daughters: "Any separation between them will bring disaster to both."[17]

Luke describes Demeter and Persephone's narcissistic relationship in terms of possessiveness. She states that Demeter is wholly identified with her grief. Demeter is at "the beginning of the unspeakably painful struggle of a woman to separate from her possessive emotions."[18] She is desperately searching for what has been lost for the purposes of restoring it to exactly what it was before and doesn't come out of self-concern long enough to understand the situation or get help. The daughter is her extension and very much her mother's daughter. The mother possesses her daughter's infantile feminine aspect. For Luke, the myth demonstrates the fatality of the overprotective mother who tries to prevent growth and change, which every mother at some point must face. In reading the myth, I am left with a sense that the possessiveness and overprotectiveness come out of a sense of ownership.

Persephone is Demeter's love object, and Demeter is unwilling to give her up. The result is no growth for both mother and daughter.

Growth for Persephone

The myth demonstrates the continuity of preoedipal primary love and identification with mother. It also demonstrates how difficult it is for a girl to function separately if she is collusively bound to her mother. Demeter is not at all interested in letting go of her daughter. It is Zeus who intervenes in the relationship and imposes both separation and an additional triangular relationship in their lives. At this time in her life, when Persephone is being called to become a woman in the world, it is her father who authoritatively decides what her next step in life is to be. It is Zeus who attempts to expand her world by causing Persephone to be abducted from the innocence of prepubertal life and forced to confront heterosexual relations and social roles. "This confrontation emphasizes her tie and identification with her mother."[19] In the myth we see that Zeus is unable to break the attachment between mother and daughter. According to Chodorow, adolescent daughters may know on a cognitive level that they are differentiated and yet be overly attached, unindividuated, and without boundaries. Chodorow feels that these conflicts concern preoedipal issues that get replayed at a later time, taking into account development since the preoedipal period. It is my view that, in addition to the oedipal forces, daughters are narcissisticly tied to their mothers, and when they are stepping into the uncertainty of the future, feelings of dependence and attachment escalate.

What is the meaning of Persephone's spending two-thirds of her year with Demeter and one-third of her year with Hades? How does it serve Persephone to have this triangular relationship in this particular form? It would appear that since the first and most significant attachment in life is with mother, and because this relationship tends to be embedded in narcissism, the only path out of narcissistic identity would be to confront self in relation to the internalized and external mother over a period of time. It took years to create the narcissistic identity. Perhaps the figure of two-thirds is symbolic of just how much Persephone is tied to her mother both internally and externally. Letting go of narcissistic attachment and finding authentic self can't possibly happen overnight. In our culture, our mother is our initial source of identity, and there is a tendency to move out into the world carrying her with us. We step into heterosexual relations wanting our partners to be with us as we were with our mother. Chodorow's words, "Before she can fully develop extrafamilial commitments, therefore, a girl must confront her entanglement in familial relationships themselves," ring true.[20]

Kaplan states that relatedness requires a whole self and a whole other.[21] It is my view that there can be no true emotional relatedness if the individuals are bound up in narcissism. Persephone must confront her attachment to Demeter before she can begin to be fully present in her relationship with Hades and her role as queen of the underworld. The path toward authentic self has to come from rubbing up against the source of inherited self. Who am I if I am not being what my mother dreamed me to be? The mother molded her into being, particularly because of the distant father, and it is only in relation to her that Persephone can find herself. Perhaps that is why Persephone was destined to spend so much time with Demeter each year of her life. The time away from Demeter gives Persephone an opportunity to explore herself in a different environment. It gives her a chance to experience herself when not with her mother and potentially to see their differences. But she must spend the large portion of time finding herself in the presence of her mother. Unless she can do this, any separate self she does develop is a fragile one at best.

The Second Rapprochement

Before we reach adolescence, we develop a constant sense of self. Kaplan states that "every move into separate selfhood from birth until three years makes its distinctive contribution to constancy."[22] The child leaves rapprochement having struggled with the issue of separateness and developing a reliable inner mother. During the fourth subphase of the separation-individuation process, the child can take steps toward independence because she or he has gained a continuous sense of an inner mother. The task of this phase is to consolidate individuality and begin to develop emotional object constancy, which requires a reconciliation of oneness and separateness and creating a "unity out of disparate and often contradictory images of self and other."[23] The enduring inner conviction of being me and nobody else is the achievement of constancy. If the child has a positively cathected inner image of mother, she is able to form boundaries between self and other and function separately with mild discomfort. Kaplan suggests that what makes a child unique and sets her or him apart from others is how boundaries are reconciled.

According to Kaplan, when constancy prevails we are able to respect and value the separateness of others. If individuals have unforged constancy they have a very hard time coping with disappointment and strenuously resist new challenges. Demeter and Persephone's constancy is suspect because of their reaction to their separation from each other. They were both shattered and sank into despair. Given Demeter and Persephone's unwillingness to live separate lives and the strength and style of their resistance to change, I question the quality of their respective constancies. Does Persephone have an internal sense of who she is when she is not in the presence of her mother? Given her immobility in the underworld, it would be hard to say that constancy was not fragile. Her unwillingness to tackle the unfamiliar and integrate the experience into her sense of self does not suggest a strong sense of constancy. Does Demeter have an internal sense of herself when she is not mothering Persephone? It appears that she also struggles with constancy and her capacity to continue with her life, particularly in a different form. Both women refuse to nourish themselves when they are apart. This could be symbolic of their unwillingness to take anything into themselves that supports the continuation of life.

It makes sense that for mothers and daughters constancy would be an issue. It also makes sense that the issue would become clearly visible at adolescence. I agree with Jean Baker Miller[24] that girls have an internal sense of self and that interaction, based on emotional connection, is a vehicle for the development of the self. However, I question the authenticity of that "self." Because narcissistic attachment precedes constancy, it must impact the quality of constancy achieved in childhood, which subsequently influences adolescent constancy. I argue that the constancy that comes out of narcissistic attachment is more fragile. The more narcissisticly embedded a child is, the more difficult it is to work through the rapprochement crisis and then move into constancy authentically. The result is that the female adolescent identity is tremendously influenced by the relationship to the mother. The mother that was internalized during the first three years of life is inside her. Up until adolescence it is appropriate to have a sense of constancy that was forged from the relationship with the mother. Adolescence, however, is a time of expanding boundaries and creating a larger vision of who we might become in the world. The stable sense of who one is (constancy) is offered opportunities to enlarge. In my opinion, if original constancy was fragile, the newly available self-objects push daughters into a new "rapprochement crisis" in which they have to once again deal with an uncertain sense of self and separateness in the world. At adolescence, this crisis, in Western culture, is usually referred to as an identity crisis. The difference between the two crises is that the child struggles with the "I am" issue, whereas the adolescent struggles with the "Who am I?" issue. In essence they are both struggling with the same issue, which is existence as a person in the world.

CONCLUSION

Fleming states that "we have to build, quite consciously, a center within ourselves that will hold."[25] It is my view that the center we

build must be authentic. Persephone has an opportunity to discover and build an authentic identity by rubbing up against her
mother while she spends two-thirds of each year with her. For
Persephone, if she wants to come to an authentic identity, the
returning to mother each year will continue for many years to
come, because the more narcissisticly embedded one is the harder
it is to work your way out of narcissism and into authenticity. Also,
because she is a foreclosed personality, she probably doesn't have
the necessary exploration skills and experience to support her to
move out of the bind. As Mahler suggests, "the process of separation-individuation is always active and never finished."[26] There is
no point of arrival. We can only progressively, over the course of
life, come to own ourselves in the presence of our mother by
going out and having confirming experiences in the world and
seeing our differences and similarities. With each revisit of rapprochement crisis, instead of holding on to similarities as children
do, as adult women we need to seek out the differences. It is
through our differences that we can begin to have a sense of who
we are that is separate from our mother. This does not mean ig-
noring the sameness. If we ignore the sameness, we become inau-
thentic and our mother still owns us. The myth helps us recognize
the need to go back to the source of identity. Perhaps the greatest
tragedy in our culture is that we don't consciously deal with separation. We do not have rituals to support our movement away
from mothers. We do not have rituals to support mothers in letting go of their daughters. Nor do we have rituals for either mothers or daughters that support their definition of self as women in
the world.

NOTES

1. Charlene Spretnak, "Problems with Jungian Uses of Greek Goddess
   Mythology," *Anima* 6:30.

2. Ibid., 26.

3. M. Stein, "Narcissus," *Spring 1976,* 36.

4. Jean Shinoda Bolen, *Goddesses in Everywoman* (San Francisco: Harper and Row, 1984), 175.

5. Ibid., 64.

6. Alice Miller, *The Drama of the Gifted Child* (New York: Basic Books, 1981).

7. L. R. Fischer, *Linked Lives* (New York: Harper and Row, 1986), 160.

8. Apostolos N. Athanassakis, *The Homeric Hymns* (Baltimore: Johns Hopkins University, 1976), 9.

9. M. Esther Harding, *Woman's Mysteries* (New York: Harper and Row, 1971).

10. Charles Boer, *The Homeric Hymns* (Chicago: Swallow Press, 1970), 108.

11. Miller, *Drama of the Gifted Child.*

12. Nancy Chodorow, *The Reproduction of Mothering* (Berkeley: University of California Press, 1978), 101.

13. Ibid., 195.

14. Margaret Mahler, *Psychological Birth of a Human Infant* (New York: Basic Books, 1975).

15. Helen Luke, "The Mother-Daughter Mysteries," *Dromenon* 3, no. 3: 34.

16. Fischer, *Linked Lives,* 22.

17. As quoted in Chodorow, *Reproduction of Mothering,* 135.

18. Luke, "Mother-Daughter Mysteries," 31.

19. As quoted in Chodorow, *Reproduction of Mothering,* 137.

20. Ibid., 135.

21. L. J. Kaplan, *Oneness and Separateness: From Infant to Individual* (New York: Simon and Schuster, 1978).

22. Ibid., 35.

23. Ibid., 47.

24. Jean Baker Miller, "The Development of Women's Sense of Self," *Work in Progress*, 1984: 2–15.

25. P. C. Fleming, "Persephone's Search for Her Mother," *Psychological Perspectives* 15, no. 2: 139.

26. Mahler, *Psychological Birth*, 5.

MIDLIFE PASSAGE

W HEN THE EMPHASIS in our viewing of the myth falls on Persephone, we are likely to see the myth as representing a particular life passage, the one that leads from maidenhood to womanhood. If, however, our focal point is Demeter, then her passage beyond her identification with motherhood comes into view.

For the rape happens to Demeter, too. Indeed, the Homeric hymn concerns itself primarily with Demeter's, not her daughter's, response to Hades' abduction of Persephone, and this is what has most interested several commentators on the tale, including three represented in this volume: Helen Luke, Patricia Berry, and Polly Young-Eisendrath.

Luke begins her reading of the myth by noting the difference between Demeter and Gaia, who, so the hymn relates, actually came to Hades' aid. From the earth mother's perspective, neither rape nor death seems all that tragic, but from Demeter's they seem well-nigh unendurable. Demeter's task is to learn to come to terms with her loss, a loss that signifies not simply the loss of her daughter but more profoundly the loss of her own daughterly aspect: the youthfulness to which she still unconsciously clings represents her resistance to taking on the challenges of the second half of life. The grief is real and appropriate; this is a painful and difficult transition but a necessary one. Demeter's nine-day search symbolizes that after Persephone's disappearance she is pregnant with herself, with the self she must now become. Persephone may return, but she will not return to her daughterly role, not regress to an identification with her mother, for Luke believes that Persephone swallowed the pomegranate seeds voluntarily, signaling that she is ready to assimilate her underworld experience. Because, for Luke, Persephone represents an aspect of Demeter, this means that Demeter, too, has now come to terms with what this passage requires of her.

Patricia Berry is less sanguine. She, too, sees the rape as at the heart of the myth. She suggests that Gaia not only condones and aids the rape but understands it as a necessary experience for Demeter to undergo. "At Eleusis," Berry says, "rape was elevated to the state of a mystery." This does not mean, as James Hillman makes explicit, that rape is always necessary. There is a particular style of consciousness, Persephone's exaggerated innocence, Demeter's denial of all but upper-world reality, that resists other modes of descent to underworld experience and so constellates rape, the forced descent.[1]

Like Luke, Berry understands Persephone as an aspect of Demeter, but not as Demeter's daughterly or maidenly aspect, not as the youthfulness and innocence she still clings to, but precisely as her "in the underworld" aspect. What Persephone's rape means, in terms of Demeter's perspective, is precisely Demeter's suffering. Demeter needs the underworld experience into which Persephone initiates her—that is what she is seeking as she engages in her search for Persephone. Her suffering over the loss, her extravagant grief and rage, are, as Berry understands them, an expression of her "compromise" with the rape, her both experiencing it and refusing it. Her immersion in her suffering is psychopathology, soul-suffering, expressed as profound depression and in destructive behavior. Her involvement with the household and nursery in the Eleusinian palace represents a way of evading "the needs of her own deepening."

Berry seems unsure that the reunion of Demeter and Persephone at the end of the myth represents that full entering into loss for which Demeter's soul seems to long. Deep suffering in itself does not guarantee transformation. Demeter could stay stuck in her neurosis forever. It is not clear that she has really let go of the perspective that grants reality and value only to the upper world and continues to resist descent. Berry hopes to help us see that the archetype has both a psychopathogical and a normal aspect; the pathology and its therapy lie in the same archetypal pattern. Demeter's pathology is her suffering; psychotherapy, attending to her soul, would require her to enter ever more deeply into that suffering.

Polly Young-Eisendrath also reads the myth in terms of its relevance to the central task of midlife, which she views as the acceptance of experiences of loss and limitation as inescapable and transformative. To understand the myth rightly, we must see that, contra Kerenyi, it is *not* about cyclical renewal, not about raging and grieving and then getting everything back again, but about irretrievable loss, inexpungeable change. Young-Eisendrath focuses her whole analysis on one episode in the myth, Demeter's attempt to make Metanira's infant son Demophoon immortal, which Young-Eisendrath regards as an attempt to evade the reality of her loss of Persephone. This is Demeter's folly: the attempt to make time stand still, the refusal to accept that her wish to undo the abduction represents an impossible wish. As Young-Eisendrath understands it, one becomes a *person* when one has learned to renounce such impossible wishes and come to terms with finitude, with one's status as mortal, not god. Some losses can be recovered, but some, and this is what the myth teaches, must be suffered. Metanira here becomes the initiator, the one who knows that loss cannot be evaded or erased. But Demeter shows us all the immature ways in which we are likely to respond to grief and loss, she participates in all the stages of mourning that modern psychology has so carefully delineated. Young-Eisendrath focuses particularly on how, in her anger at Hades, Demeter identifies with the aggressor, trying to abduct Demophoon from his mother as ruthlessly as Hades had abducted Persephone. Metanira's anger frees Demeter from her identification and enables her to complete the process of mourning. This completion is expressed through the creative activity Demeter now turns to: the institution of the mysteries. Demeter herself is the first initiate. The mysteries are designed to teach what she has learned; the mysteries grant not immortality but a different understanding of loss and death.

My own "Persephone and Hades" understands the meaning of the myth in similar ways, though in my experience it was Persephone herself who led me to this new understanding of the meaning of loss and death, for at midlife I found myself required to confront Persephone not as maiden, not as Demeter's daughter, but as the dread goddess of the underworld.

I have also included an excerpt from my *Journey through Menopause*, which explores the relevance of some of the figures in the myth to the third and last phase of a woman's life. As Persephone may represent the maiden and the initiation she must suffer and Demeter the mature woman experiencing the transitions of midlife, so Hecate, Rhea, and Baubo may serve to give body to our images of the crone.

NOTES

1. See James Hillman, *Dreams and the Underworld* (New York: Harper and Row, 1979), 49.

Mother and Daughter Mysteries

HELEN LUKE

IN ANCIENT GREECE the Eleusinian mysteries of Demeter bear witness to the overwhelming need of woman in her already growing separation from the natural pattern of the primitive feminine—the need for the Goddess to teach her the *meaning* of the deep transformation of her being from daughter to mother to daughter again. How much greater is that need today, when so often the woman lives almost like a man in the outer world and must find the whole meaning of her motherhood inwardly instead of physically, and when so many of those who do bear children are simply playing at "mothers and babies," never having allowed themselves to experience consciously the violent end of their daughter identification.

Persephone is playing with her companions in the eternal spring, completely contained in her carefree belief that nothing can change this happy state of youth and beauty. Underneath, however, the urge to consciousness is stirring, and "the maiden not to be named" strays away from her fellows, and, intoxicated by the scent of a narcissus, she stoops to pick it and in so doing opens the door through which the lord of the underworld rushes up to seize her. We may notice here that Gaia, mother earth, is clearly distinguished from Demeter in this myth. She is Zeus's fellow conspirator as it were! Kerenyi says, "From the Earth

Mother's point of view, neither seduction nor death is the least bit tragic or even dramatic."

The moment of breakthrough for a woman is always symbolically a rape—a necessity—something which takes hold with overmastering power and brooks no resistance.

Persephone cries out in fear and protest as the cord of her tie to her mother, to her unconscious youthfulness, is violently cut, and Demeter, the mother, hears and knows that the daughter is lost but not how. For nine days she wanders over the earth in fear and sorrow, searching for her daughter but not *understanding*. She is wholly identified with her grief, swallowed by it, even her body forgotten so that she does not eat or wash. It is the beginning of the unspeakably painful struggle of a woman to separate from her possessive emotions, the struggle which alone can give birth to love. As Demeter sank into her grief, so every time we are shocked out of some happy identification with another, which we have fondly imagined to be an unbreakable state, we are beset by the temptation to this surrender, to this despairing search for that which has been lost, demanding that it be restored to us exactly as it was, without any effort to discover the meaning of the experience. If we imagine we have succeeded in restoring the status quo, then the whole story will begin again and repeat itself endlessly and pointlessly until we can follow the goddess to the next step—the dawning of her attempt to *understand*. This cut, this loss, must be experienced by every woman both as daughter and as mother or, especially in later years, as *both* at the same time, for in every relationship between two women the mother and the daughter archetypes are constellated; each may mother the other, each may depend on the other and ask to be mothered—the balance weighted now one way, now the other.

At this point we will look at the specific experience of the loss of the daughter in older women. It is the loss of the young and carefree part of oneself, the opportunity for the discoveries of meaning which are the task of the second half of life: it is the change from the life of outer projection to the detachment, the turning inward, which leads to the "immediate experience of being outside time," in Jung's words. In the language of this myth, death rises up and takes away the woman's belief in everlasting spring. The great majority of women today, having no contact at all with the Demeter mystery, have extreme difficulty in giving up this unconscious clinging to youth, their partial identification with man's anima image, the unraped Persephone eternally picking flowers in blissful unconsciousness of the dark world below her. To such women the menopause brings long-drawn-out disturbances of the body and the psyche as the conflict grows more acute and remains unresolved.

Kerenyi has written, "To enter into the figure of Demeter means to be pursued, to be robbed, to be raped" (as Persephone), "to rage and grieve, to fail to understand" (as Demeter), "and then to get everything back and be born again" (as Demeter and Persephone—the twofold single reality of Demeter-Kore). There can be no shortcuts in this experience. All through her nine-day search (the symbolic nine of pregnancy), in her conscious abandonment to grief the goddess has nevertheless carried burning torches in her hand, symbol perhaps of that small fire of attention which must be kept burning through the darkness of our journey when all meaning seems to have left us. On the tenth day Hecate, the hitherto dormant intuition, comes, also bearing a torch, and tells Demeter that her daughter has been ravished away, though she does not know who the ravisher may be. Demeter's moon nature brings the first rift in the isolation her absorbing personal grief has created. The stricken mother begins to intuit, to hear for the first time a voice which leads her to reflect upon that which has brought about her loss. She emerges enough from her self-concern to seek the aid of conscious reason. Together the two goddesses approach and question Helios, the sun, and he tells Demeter what has happened—that Zeus himself has arranged this marriage for her daughter and that this should be accepted as a good, a happy fate. But although her conscious mind has seen and understood, she cannot accept this reasonable answer. "She fails to understand" with her essential being and continues "to rage and to grieve."

Strangely enough, a woman is certainly right to reject this all-too-easy rational solution. "Let us be sensible," we say, "our loss is good for us." Our grief was nothing but a childish reaction, and so on. Nevertheless, the sun's calm reasoning has affected us. We must go on living. We must emerge from this totally self-centered, self-pitying sorrow and be awake to other people. We must work, we must relate, but we must not deny our grief. And so Demeter comes to the well of the maidens at Eleusis—the place where the woman consciously draws the water up from the depths—and listens to the wisdom of the unconscious. There sitting under an olive tree she meets the king's daughters and offers to work as nurse to a child or at any menial task. No longer obsessed with *her* child, she can look again on the beautiful daughters of others and respond.

Demeter here appears as a woman past childbearing—she has lost her own child; she can never bear another in the flesh. Even the partial acceptance of this means that she can now give of her wisdom to the children of others. Demeter, being a goddess, has the power to bestow immortality, and she feeds the child of the king and queen with inner wisdom, and at night she thrusts him like a brand into the fire which burns but does not consume.

What is the meaning of this incident for us? It can perhaps be seen from two opposite angles. The fear and the protest of the human mother is on the one hand a warning of how fatal to a child's inner life is the overprotective possessiveness of mother love that tries to prevent all suffering and danger from touching the beloved son. But from another angle, on another level, the human mother's instinct is surely right. This is a human baby and must grow up into a human being, subject to death. If he is to reach immortality, he must reach it on the hard road of human experience and the battle for consciousness—not be given immunity and deprived of the suffering and dignity of manhood by a goddess. To feed the infant the food of divine wisdom is well, but to thrust him into the fire of premature transformation is to deprive him of his choice as a human being. The woman's experience of the dark is so often expressed in myth by the descent of the child, daughter or, more often, son, into hell. It is a more terrible experience for the feminine psyche than her own descent.

It is the failure of this attempt to play the goddess and use her powers on the human child that recalls her to her true goddess nature. She remembers who she is, reveals herself, and immediately begins to prepare for the passing on of her vision, her essence, on an altogether different level—the symbolic level of the mysteries.

So the goddess remembers herself and builds her temple, within which she now encloses herself, and in which she sits down again in a grief more terrible than before. It is not regression; it is her cave of introversion. Whereas at first she had simply surrendered to her sorrow, she now enters consciously into it. She is in a ritual, holy place, contained. She does not yet know the solution, but she herself must accept the dark, and inner death, if her daughter is ever to return to the light of day. And as the goddess withdrew, so the earth dried up and withered, the sap of growth departed, and the land lay dying. The wasteland around the Fisher King in the Grail legend carries the same meaning—when it is time for a transformation of the whole personality, the birth of a totally new attitude, everything dries up inwardly and outwardly and life becomes more and more sterile until the *conscious* mind is forced to recognize the gravity of the situation, is compelled to accept the validity of the unconscious.

The gods now become frantic at what is happening on earth— pretty soon there will be no more men to worship the mighty gods of reason! As always happens, they get busy *bribing* Demeter to emerge from her temple and her sorrow—urging her to settle for a pleasant life of peace and honor on Olympus and to forget about her daughter down below, who can be left to keep the dark powers happy and prevent them from bothering the upper gods. So does reason and the fear of the dark speak to us. "Even if my greatest value does stay buried forever, it is foolish and arrogant of me to make so much fuss about it. I must conquer my misery, stop thinking about it, make the best of things as they are. Surely the great god Zeus must know best, and he is offering me ease and a position of great importance." But Demeter does not for a moment yield to good-sense arguments. There can be no halfway solution, no stopping at the state of separation of the opposites. She is deaf to all the entreaties and appeals of every god in turn.

The gods give in to Demeter, of course, and at last the conscious and the unconscious, the masculine and the feminine, begin to pull together. It seems at first simply a capitulation of consciousness to the regressive longing of the mother. Zeus sends Hermes to tell Hades he must give Persephone back and restore the status quo, for Zeus himself cannot produce the solution which reconciles the opposites. Only when Hades, the lord of death, Zeus's dark brother, will cooperate can the answer come. It is he who gives Persephone the seed of the pomegranate to eat—and she, who has hitherto rejected all food (refused to assimilate the experience), now in the moment when she is full of joy at the thought of not having to accept it, takes the pomegranate seed involuntarily, but voluntarily swallows it. In spite of her protests, she really has no intention of regressing to identification with her mother again. This is an image of how the saving thing can happen in the unconscious before the conscious mind can grasp at all what is going on. There are many dreams in which the dreamer tries to return to an old thing or situation but finds, for example, the doors barred or the telephone broken. The ego still yearns for the status quo, but further down the price has been paid, and we *can't* go back. Hence the great value of dreams in making us aware of these movements below. Even Demeter in her conscious planning still half yearns for her daughter to return as before, but her questioning is quite perfunctory. As soon as she knows the seed has been eaten, there is no more said on the subject—all is joy. Persephone has eaten the food of Hades, has taken the seed of the dark into herself and can now give birth to her own new personality. So also can her mother. They have both passed through death to the renewal of a new spring—the inward renewal which age need never lose—and have accepted the equal necessity of winter and life in the darkness of the underworld.

The Rape of Demeter/ Persephone and Neurosis

PATRICIA BERRY

DEMETER IS AN EXAMPLE of a mythic figure evidencing neurotic behavior. In approaching this figure and this myth, however, I shall not be doing an "interpretation"; I shall not be dealing with the events in the story step by step, making them coherent and "fitting" as a narrative or case history. Rather, I shall read the story as a mythical image, as though there were no beginning, no end—as though it all went on at once, and forever.

Demeter consciousness has to do with "life," the life of the seasons, the growth of the grain, agricultural vegetation. She is an earth mother, but in one important sense a limited one: she suffers an extreme loss within her very motherhood, the rape and abduction of her daughter Persephone. Moreover, this loss is aided by the greater, older earth mother, Gaia (who grows the seductive flower for Hades)—as though nature at the Gaia level understands the rape as necessary.

It is one of those curiosities about archetypes that they appear just as easily pathologically (abnormally) as they do normally. This normality/abnormality of the archetype is a very useful idea for neuroses and their therapy, for the idea implies that in one and the same archetypal pattern lie both the pathology and its therapy. If we take seriously the traditional maxim of "like cures like," then once we recognize an archetypal pattern, we know a great deal about curing it. That is, we treat it with itself—by deepening it, expanding it (so that it is no longer so narrowly fixated), and by giving it substance, body (so that it can now begin to carry what it is trying to express). But the difficulty with any neurotic symptom is that not only does it express something (its telos, intentional purpose, or finality, as Jung would call it), it also tries to make certain that that goal is never reached (as Adler might have said).

For an explanation of this "self-defeating" situation we might remember Freud's description of the symptom as a compromise solution. The symptom actually expresses the repressed content. But this expression is partial, a kind of token to unconscious forces, which makes possible their containment by or in the symptom. Total repression would risk total collapse, but this partial repression allows the safety of a compromise, neurotic containment. Thus the symptom acts as a safety valve, allowing the continued existence of the repressed. So the real stigma of a neurosis is that it uses itself to defend against itself, superficially using its own contents to defend against any deeper entry into those contents. We might invert the maxim of "like cures like" to read also, "like *defends* against like."

In the Demeter style of the psyche how might such defenses appear? To begin with, her very suffering may manifest neurotically. It may take on that "suffering for the sake of suffering" quality, or that misery to avoid deeper pain.

But we must be careful, because this need to suffer is also quite genuine. There is a teleological reason for it. Demeter *needs* her underworld daughter, and it is through the suffering of the mother that this need is symptomatically expressed. Her suffering is her compromise with the rape—her manner of experiencing it and refusing it. To put it another way, Persephone's rape is experienced as Demeter's neurosis. And this neurosis is continually present within the archetype. Since myths are eternal and never fully resolved in life, we may expect certain parts of our personalities to be in perpetual enactment of some rather disagreeable mythic kinks. When in tune with Demeter and receiving her gifts,

I must also expect some of the accompanying difficulties and unconscious tendencies of that archetype. Then, too, my need will
be always to deepen teleologically in the direction of Hades, my
daughter's realm. Thus I suffer, and yet thus I also resist—for that
too is part of my mythic pattern. There is no way *out* of a myth—
only a way more deeply into it.

We have mentioned suffering as itself a defensive measure. We
might enlarge that to include the phenomenon which Freud describes as mourning. Freud sees mourning as aggression against
the lost object, now turned inward. Thus I punish myself, and I
would add, others by means of displacement (for example, the
mourner or depressive who punishes others, or poisons the atmo-
sphere with his or her mood).

When we view Freud's mechanism of internalized aggression
in a more Jungian way, we immediately see that the introverted
aggression accomplishes quite the same thing as would Freud's
extraverted idea of aggression. For what is punished is the archetypal component, the daughter Persephone, wherever that happens to appear, externally or internally. A mourning Demeter who
has lost the daughter, therefore hates the daughter, and all that
underworld business the daughter now represents. Neurotically,
Demeter's consciousness clings all the more fervently (and de-
structively) to the upper world, adamantly denying underworld
attributes—such as precision (the house becomes a mess), dis-
crimination (one thing is as good as another—all feelings, all sensations of equal value, and thus of no value), sense of essence
(things become of value for their superficial, rather than under-
worldly, attributes), sense of significance (the ordinary loses its
link with the gods, the archetypal, and is therefore "nothing but").

Demeter consciousness becomes depressed, and within this depression we can see many classically psychiatric attributes: she
ceases to bathe, ceases to eat, disguises her beauty, denies the
future (her possibilities of rejuvenation and productivity), re-
gresses to menial tasks beneath her ability (or sees her tasks as
menial), becomes narcissistic and self-concerned, sees (and actu-

ally engenders) worldwide catastrophe, and incessantly weeps. The depression of Demeter consciousness manifests itself with a certain dry asceticism (no bathing, no eating, no sensuality) and self-denial. But alongside this dryness, she weeps with "vain and insatiate anger." So her wetness is in effect dry, an excess of tears that neither moistens nor makes for flow or connection. There is no anima in this wetness. It is a kind of continuous downpour that erodes rather than replenishes the soil, making it ever more dry and less fertile.

Another peculiarity of Demeter depression is her tendency to seek refuge among man, the social world, the city. She doesn't go off alone into the woods as might Artemis, or try to prove her self-sufficiency as might Hera, or rush into a love affair as might Aphrodite. Rather, she breaks her connection with the Gods and seeks refuge in the polis, the world of everyday events, "reality." Thus she may defend herself from the needs of her own deepening with "reality excuses." It becomes "impractical" to tend to her soul. She has no time. It is not her business. She must take care of the children and the household (which, chances are, she is doing inadequately, with only the surface of herself, anyway). Indeed, then the needs of Demeter's soul begin to cast themselves in ways that actually *are* impractical and antisocial. She perhaps expresses these needs in suicide attempts (literalizing death as Hades), in religious conversion (portraying her need for spirit), or by leaving her family, breaking her marriage, and living out in desperation some fling or affair (in a displaced enactment of her daughter Persephone).

As it is Persephone's narcissism (the flower narcissus), in the Homeric tale, which brings Hades rushing up upon her, so Demeter's narcissism helps connect, and yet depotentiate, underworld forces. One way we see this is in the ceaseless self-indulgence of much of her suffering. Her dry tears erode the soil, her suffering engenders suffering for all the world, her mourning, mourning. On and on, as though her suffering fed upon itself— and yet where is the sustenance for such feeding, since everyday life gets worse and worse? It is as though this repetition were mimetic of another underworld characteristic—the endless cycle by which essence is expressed (for example, Ixion on the wheel, Sisyphus and his stone, and so forth). In the upper world this endless, cyclical essence is expressed as repetition. Apparently meaningless emotions are compelled to repeat again and again fruitlessly as though to connect to the essence beneath themselves, the Hades realm.

Since Demeter's depression takes her toward the realm of man, rather than away from it, her kind of regression takes her into nearness, neglecting her connections with the divine. By losing connection with what she is, a Goddess, she demeans the personal, so that life's little messes become of great value. The significance in the small becomes the small inflated with significance. Demeter's closeness has become actually a defense against the divine depths and results in a proximity that is petty, mean, and overly personal. A witchiness appears, and the personal becomes self-important as Demeter sits in her "sumptuous" temple, smothering in mundane events, cut off from Olympus.

Since she is dissociated from both Olympus and Hades, this neurotic pattern may become very destructive indeed. Demeter's earthiness now becomes the weight which smothers every living potential. She conceals the seeds in the ground. Not only does she sever herself from Olympus, but now all connection between man and the Gods is threatened. Consciousness is leveled to the grassland, the horizontal, and spirit lies fallow, beneath the earth. Existence grows barren and fruitless. As Demeter is split from Hades, she now enacts his deathliness—but in her own way, for it is earth she kills with. To find and reunite with her spirited daughter becomes a matter of psychic survival.

But what brings this reunion about? Or, therapeutically speaking, what are its necessary preconditions? Just because Demeter suffers deeply, and causes suffering for others, does not guarantee change for the future. Excluding grace, or spontaneous remission, she could go on like that in her neurosis forever. Of course, another archetype might constellate, giving her relief in that way. But this kind of relief would be more the sort deriving from a "rest cure" or a "change of scene" and would avoid delving the depths of her own particular archetype. The kind of movement we are really interested in would be one from within her own archetype, within her own substance. For this, it would seem first necessary that her compromise container fail. The suffering of Demeter consciousness must become unbearable to that which carries it, her neurosis. The underworld intentionality of her symptoms must become too much for its surface containment.

Now what would such a failure feel like to Demeter consciousness? It might very well feel like rape. It might very well feel like something happening *to* her—since it is the last thing she feels she wants and precisely what she is defending herself against. So the phallic force bursts up from beneath, through the ground of her awareness, her earthy defenses, and takes the maiden cherished within motherly folds, life's innocence.

Indeed, Demeter consciousness tends to draw rape and violence upon itself. We know of two stories in which Demeter herself is raped. In one, fleeing the advances of Poseidon, she turns herself into a mare—a peculiar transformative choice in that now the rape can be consumated quite naturally: Poseidon in his horse form and she, obligingly, a mare. The second tale is one that Demeter fabricates to explain her unfortunate circumstances to the daughters of Celeus. And like all lies, this one contains some psychological truth. In it, she spins an elaborate fantasy of how she has been raped by pirates and carried far away from her homeland. We might certainly say that, via the rape of her daughter, Demeter was raped from her natural grounding; but it is interesting that *she* construes this as horizontal movement (from Crete to Thoricos) instead of as the vertical movement that more accurately describes her daughter's rape. Again, Demeter consciousness views events as above and across the earth's surface, in lieu of the radical, the fearful shift of perspective that would view these same events as beneath, in depth.

And yet to accept our own rape, downward into the underworld, is no easy matter, since by definition it must happen *to* us,
and to that part of us most inviolate—the virgin. Let me qualify
this: it is not just any virgin who constellates or necessitates rape
but primarily Persephone, whose devastating innocence and half-
conscious teasing lead anyway into underworld realms, whatever
they may be. For other virginal figures, like the Goddesses Artemis and Athene, rape would be an archetypal monstrosity, an
actual destruction of the archetype instead of a deepening
through it. Practically, we might put in this way: rape is a horror;
but when it is constellated, in one way or another, if it connects to
the Demeter/Persephone archetype, then the violation is not only
possible but absolutely essential.

We mentioned how for Demeter consciousness the rape must
be unbearable. We might add now a second condition: that it be
"ununderstandable." When the rape happens to Demeter's Persephone, she can have no footing beneath it. She cannot understand (stand beneath). As "Demeter Green Verdure" she deals
with the vegetation of the horizontal world. With the rape, her
perspective shifts toward the vertical as well—now taking on the
depths and heights, and the route of spirit. Without the vertical
sense, Demeter cannot "stand beneath." She cannot move in
terms of depths or levels. Not only depth as "the unconscious" but
depth potential as a seed in each moment of life, its metaphorical
implications below its apparent sense. But this limitation is a natural and necessary one. Any sort of pseudounderstanding, helping
to explain away her state or rationalizing it into containment, giving her a too easy verticality, would block her participation in the
archetype and its profound possibilities.

This has bearing on our treatment of underworld anxieties and
dream motifs. When such threats are constellated, the worst possible interpretation, in light of the Demeter-Persephone myth,
would be to make the value judgment of "destructive animus" or
"negative shadow" concerning these figures. In fact such an attitude would lock the dreamer within her virginal state and further

her confinement within a superficial, upper-world rationale. Of course, when we make such interpretations, it is because we assume the dark pursuer is out to destroy the dreamer's femininity. Our intentions are really humanitarian and, we think, all in favor of the feminine. But we overlook the deeper layers of the myth, which would support the threats as precisely the mode of initiation. The "rapist" may be constellated in response to the dreamer's too narrow virginity, and his purpose may be to escort her physically into that deeper body which lies beneath all surfaces, the psychic realm.

Often in rape dreams the dreamer appears to flee entirely the Persephone/Demeter constellation and turns instead to another: fleeing toward the light, calling the police, rushing to her husband, locking the car doors, and so on. The variety and desperateness of the defense to rape situations attest to just how unbearable this archetypal constellation is for collective consciousness. It is not that these situations cannot also be reflected from the Demeter/ Persephone perspective. Rather it is that these moves become attempts to get out altogether from this archetypal pattern and the necessity of its rape.

Much more fashionable nowadays is holding one's ground, standing for one's right—all of which is understandable in the light of contemporary events. But the accompanying difficulty is that by pushing ourselves forward as subjects, we then lose touch with the possibility of experiencing ourselves back and downward as objects. We forget that to be raped into consciousness is also a way.

Even if the occasion of psychic rape is not foreign to us, we haven't known where to put it. And so we have had to fight off the experience all the more blindly. A working archetypal model for these overpowering, backward, downward movements is given by the Demeter/Persephone myth, in which rape was, after all, elevated to the status of a mystery in ancient Greece. Because we have lost these rites, rape is now even more threatening, and therefore we have a great deal of difficulty experiencing Demeter/

Persephone consciousness in any but the most superficial, defensive, and neurotic ways. So, in order to deepen this archetypal consciousness, a more trenchant and effective analysis of our Demeter defenses is needed. Beyond this analysis, and ultimately, however, it is perhaps only our love for the daughter, and therefore for the underworld, the telos of our symptoms, that makes certain our movement down and into depth.

Demeter's Folly

Experiencing Loss in Middle Life

POLLY YOUNG-EISENDRATH

THE DISTINCTION between immortals and mortals was paramount for the Greeks. Even the name given to the species of humanity indicated that we were the "ones who would die." In our society, we seem to have all but forgotten the problem of differentiating between goddesses or gods and humans. The conflict between our finite humanity and our wish for divinity is everywhere in evidence as people face middle life and death with feelings of despair and meaninglessness. It is the confrontation with loss, usually experienced for the first time as a "shocking loss" in middle life, that propels many people into a middle-age crisis and a renewal of the impossible wishes of childhood—to be perfect, immortal, and totally loved.

Middle life is a time of readjustment of one's sense of self and personal meaning to include experiences of loss and limitation as part of being a person. The shock of repeated and unpredictable losses in middle and later life is a condition for which few of us are prepared. Loss through death, desertion, illness, or separation comes over us like a rape of ordinary consciousness, in a way entirely different from the earlier typical losses of childhood and adolescence which were more predictable and shared by our peers. The unpredictable nature of loss in later life can partially

206

explain the sense of helplessness that pervades in common complaints of depression in people over thirty-five.

The story of Demeter and Persephone offers a rich array of imagery to illuminate the psychological experience of our response to sudden loss. The story begins with the rape of a maiden and ends with the creation of a new meaning system, the Eleusinian mysteries, or rites. It teaches us about the opportunity for development following an experience presented initially as loss. The story, as I will interpret it here, lends us a new perspective on the conflict between humanity and divinity in ourselves.

The essence of uniquely human existence, according to Jung, is conflict. This story is about the conflict between attachment and separation. We feel an eternal bonding with each other and with the earth itself, but we recognize our eventual separation from them, and we experience this separation as loss. If we are tempted to think of ourselves as immortal, we have abandoned the project of our own development.

The most important lesson I have learned from the story of Demeter and Persephone is to distinguish between two types of loss, each one being prominent in middle and later life. The first I call loss due to immutable fate and connect it with the archetypal realm of emotion, instinct, darkness, and death. This is the type of loss which we must accept and integrate, learn from its meaning. The other type I call loss due to abuse of freedom. This is a loss of consciousness of ourselves as finite persons, as mortals, and we experience this type of loss when we think and act as if we are goddesses or gods.

DEMETER'S FOLLY AND "COMPLEX" TERMINOLOGY

Interpretations of the Demeter and Persephone story, such as Carl Kerenyi's, often stress the nature of cyclical renewal and restoration. For example, Kerenyi says that Demeter shows us what "it means to be pursued, to be robbed, raped, to fail to understand, to rage and grieve, but *then to get everything back* and be born again" (italics added). The idea that we can get everything back is the assumption of restoration or cyclical renewal of natural life (for example, even as the leaves fall, the seeds sprout). This kind of restoration appears to belong to nature rather than humanity; it is the character of the subhuman or the suprahuman to be restored and renewed, rather than the character of human life.

The distinction between immortal or archetypal and mortal or personal realities seems to be central to the process of individuation in the second half of life. Individuation is defined here from Jung's psychology as the successive integrations of part-personalities or "complexes" into personal awareness and identity over the life span. In the second half of life, we are involved especially with acknowledging complexes which concern loss and separation. The goal of integrating these complexes appears to be relativizing our experience of personal responsibility and establishing renewed commitment to a larger meaning context, such as a spiritual context or the larger human community.

Archetypal reality in human life, patterned around our deepest emotional experiences, is quite distinct from personal reality, which is organized sequentially and narratively as a lifetime. Recognition of the finitude of personal reality, the awareness of our own death, is a distinct characteristic of being human. Demeter's folly, as I have learned about it from the story, is the confusion between archetypal or divine and personal or human reality. When Demeter attempts to transform a human child, Demophoon, into a god, she is attempting to make time stand still. But standstill in human life is death. Rather than mourn the loss of Persephone, Demeter grabbed for a quick substitution, and if she were to have had her way, nothing would have changed on Olympos. That is, if Demeter had simply replaced Persephone she would not have influenced Zeus, Hermes would not have activated the release of Persephone, and the Eleusinian rites would not have been founded. Only through the angry recognition by the human mother, Metanira, is development restored.

All of us commit Demeter's folly from time to time when we are too eager to hand over our development to unconscious images and moods that seem more meaningful and moving than ordinary consciousness. As a Jungian psychologist and analyst in training, I find myself tempted to flirt with the divine most often in the face of a client's depression. From a Jungian perspective, I may be too quick to stress the archetypal meaning and see the restorative aspect of unconscious reality. I can become prone to "Jungian folly" and swim around in the world of archetypal imagery in which things turn into their opposites and cyclical time rules. Sometimes I apply a Freudian interpretation to my archetypal tendencies: that they are flirtations with divine illusions. When I confront my Jungian follies from this perspective, I find myself face to face with the impossible wishes of childhood and the adult recognition that individuals are finite and vulnerable.

Individuation is a lifelong struggle for unity in the personality. At any moment it is a striving for coherence in the experience of being a person, and it seems to require an ability to accept the immutable while focusing on its meaning. To me, this kind of focusing includes a constant recognition of the limitation and vulnerability of individual human life. If we slip into stressing the restorative or cyclical nature of unconscious cognitions, over and above what we know of the finitude of human reality, I believe that we are *wishing* that every end were really a beginning and that human life were indeed divine.

The confrontation with loss in middle life can be called a crisis in two different ways: (1) usually it is sudden, like a rape of consciousness, and (2) it is critical for further development, for individuation beyond the heroic-nurturant phase of early adulthood.

The Demeter-Persephone story presents a paradigm regarding human loss. The story suggests that it is imperative to distinguish between two types of loss and to respond to each differently. One is the type of loss, such as aging and separation through death, that must be accepted and cannot be changed. This is loss due to the fate of being human. The second type of loss, due to an abuse of human freedom, can be made good through the recovery of an aspect of oneself that has been lost, buried or underdeveloped.

I have found the hymn most astonishing as a detailed psychological account of the mourning process. It is a poem dated no later than 650 BCE but was surely told countless times before it was recorded. Demeter's actions and responses to her daughter's disappearance are a psychological lesson as modern as a recent summary of research conducted on the process of human grief.

From the outset I would like to emphasize Metanira's sentiment as the human or personal perspective on the problem of loss. She says that "we who are human have to endure gifts from the gods, though hard."[1] The most difficult gift is love. We feel an eternal bonding to people, things, and the earth itself. Demeter, I believe, represents archetypal attachment in the image of the Great Mother, and her adventure in the poem can be understood as the universal experience of grieving that each of us encounters when we recognize that, though our bond feels eternal, we are finite and separation is inevitable. Human life, from the point of view of consciousness, is limited, finite, and individual. From the point of view of Demeter, or the archetypal experience of attachment, we seek reparation and restoration quickly in response to the shock of loss.

The first phase of recognizing a loss, shock, and alarm, is movingly represented by Demeter's response to her daughter's disappearance. The despair of the grieving person often leads directly to a search to replace the lost object (that is, a person, a body part, an idea, or whatever). If the replacement occurs too quickly and a superficial *status quo* is reestablished in identity, we talk about denial of grief and the subsequent depression, physical complaints, and diminished self-esteem that result.

Searching may lead to substitution, as it does with Demeter. Hasty substitution can result in increased vulnerability and repeated occurrences of loss, as with people who lose possessions—

for example, their cars are stolen or wallets misplaced—when they are involved in a frantic search to replace a loved one from whom they have been separated. The path from substitution to a true restitution and a new meaning system involves containing and working through the loss rather than denying it. Hence, it is important that the grieving person express the ambivalence and anger felt about going on and examine closely any commitments made through action during the period of shock and searching.

Here we can look at Demeter's promise to nurse Demophoon, her substitution for the lost Persephone. She addresses Metanira, who has eagerly agreed to pay a goodly wage to the old nurse in whom Metanira has recognized "majesty, a grace, as if of kings." Demeter's statement, touching and commonplace, belies her urgent desire to bewitch and transform a human baby into a divine child.

In Demeter's bargaining and threats to Zeus, in her desire to withdraw from the company of gods while seeking human companionship (ambivalence of the bereaved in seeking companionship), in her weeping and yearning, she displays many of the signs of the second phase of acute mourning and grief. But it is her hasty substitution of Demophoon for Persephone that so distinctively teaches us the difference between a loss due to immutable fate and a loss due to abuse of human freedom. From the point of view of consciousness, of Metanira, the wish for divinity is an abuse. Not to be contained in the workings of time, to escape the human life cycle, is not to be human at all. The Homeric poet describes both the inhuman transformation of Demophoon (roasting in fire) and the human wishes to transcend limitation. Taken together, the unconscious tendency to repeat and the half-conscious impulse to wish result in stagnation, not individuation. Metanira colludes with Demeter's repetition compulsion when Metanira hastily hands over her only son, born late, to be nursed by an apparent divinity.

Giving over a sense of control typically involves anger, and for most people, a genuine response to loss includes anger. Unrecognized anger in loss can result in a "tragic identification with the aggressor," one of the most ironic defenses against grief. Identification with the aggressor involves unconsciously repeating toward another what was experienced as aggression against oneself. In the story, Demeter seizes Demophoon away from Metanira just as Hades had abducted Persephone. The poet must have intended this meaning, for he refers to Demophoon as "a new flower" after referring to Persephone as "that flower, glorious in her beauty."

It is Metanira's angry recognition of this situation that finally frees Demeter from her identification. In my estimation, Metanira's realization of her loss is one of the great dramatic moments in the hymn:

> She screamed
> and she beat her thighs,
> frightened
> for her child,
> and completely
> outraged
> in her heart
> and she spoke
> these words,
> wailing:
> "Baby Demophoon,
> the stranger
> hides you in all that fire
> and makes me weep
> and brings me bitter pain."

Everyone is vulnerable to identification with the aggressor when confronted with a situation of loss in which one is at the mercy of another or a group. As Demeter felt helpless to move Zeus with her initial anger, the grieving person may feel not only helpless but also abused. One can imagine that, if Demeter had carried her plan forward, her identification with the abductor might have resulted only in another cycle of loss, to be interpreted as depression and characterological problems with conscience.

Instead, Demeter is freed by Metanira's anger. Not all anger in grief is expressed as openly as Metanira's, but apparently its expression is essential in the resolution of a grief reaction.

The conscious recognition of anger, in the hymn, provides the transforming element so that a new development can take place. Demophoon is returned to his humanity, and Demeter is freed to behave as a goddess again. She thus completes the process of mourning and restores her self-esteem by having a temple built and retreating there to contain and accept the reality of her loss. Even at the moment of her fury at Metanira's "stupidity," Demeter alludes to the creation of a new meaning system that is the eventual outcome of working through the grief of loss:

> I am the honorable
> Demeter,
> producer of
> the greatest blessing,
> the greatest joy,
> for man
> and god
> alike.
> But come now,
> have all the people
> build for me
> a huge temple
> and an altar
> beneath it,
> below the acropolis
> and its high wall . . .
> And I myself
> will inaugurate
> the mysteries,
> so that
> in doing them

piously
you will please
my heart.

At this, Demeter transforms herself, throwing away her agedness and becoming the astonishingly beautiful goddess. The truthful recognition of loss here, initially from the side of human consciousness, reestablishes order and permits the archetypal world to evolve symbolically to a new state at the same time the personal world of meaning is also reestablished.

The pain of Demeter's grief for her loss is now experienced directly for the first time, and she enters into a period of despair accompanied by a rage at humankind for having deprived her of her substitution. This full experience of grieving is what leads to further development and to affecting Zeus in remote Olympos. I think that Demeter's pain, represented in her bringing famine to the earth, is a moving depiction of what one suffers emotionally in response to traumatic loss.

> The earth
> did not take seed
> that year,
> for Demeter
> in her beautiful crown
> concealed it . . .
> And in fact
> she would have wiped out
> the whole race
> of talking men
> with a painful famine,
> and deprived
> those who live on Olympos
> of the glorious honor
> of offerings and sacrifices,
> if Zeus
> hadn't noticed it,

and thought about it
in his heart.

The painful catharsis of active grieving paves the way to a completion of the mourning process. The felt anger, hurt, disappointment, and sadness that accompany repeated attempts at recovery
eventually help to break the tie of attachment to what was lost.

This is not the completion of the process, however, in regard to
individuation. Restitution of meaning and coherence of self comprise the final step in a successful completion. Although restitution may take many forms, from a new relationship to a creative
act, the hymn represents it as the establishing of a new meaning
system. Even Zeus, in his distant temple, thinks about the pain
"in his heart." He is moved to begin the process of restitution,
and Demeter completes it. The restorative aspect of Persephone's
return must be interpreted, from my point of view, as a restoration
of meaning and not merely as the return of what has been lost.
The poet of the hymn dedicates but a few lines to account for her
actual reunion and then gives us more than a hundred lines of
Persephone *telling the story* of the rape and her sojourn in Hades.
This narrative becomes the focus of the reunion itself and leads
into the initiation of the Eleusinian ritual. This marks the establishment of a new order, leading to enthronement of Persephone
as Queen of the Underworld, the return of Demeter to Olympos,
and the initiation of agricultural rites connected with a Great
Mother goddess in Greece. An initiate in the Eleusinian mysteries
did not obtain immortality but apprehended the meaning of life
and death differently than before initiation.

What is divine in the story of Demeter and Persephone develops from a less differentiated to a more differentiated state: Demeter as ineffectual victim of Zeus's plot to powerful earth
goddess; Persephone as adolescent daughter to queen of the underworld. What is human (the civilization of Eleusis, represented
by Demophoon and Metanira) also develops in terms of new cultural modes of agriculture and initiation.

From the point of view of the archetypal world, then, restitution is made when a new meaning is achieved. Even in Olympos, things *have* changed; restitution is not repetition. From the point of view of the archetypal world, Persephone is no longer merely daughter; she is no longer residing only at Olympus, and Zeus is no longer immune to Demeter's threats.

Remarkable is Demeter's progression through all of the distinct emotional phases of grief investigated by modern researchers and only recently "discovered." Demeter shows us much about human attachment and loss, about our fate in love and death. She and Persephone depict a cyclical existence, but not a repetition. They portray the timelessness of human bonding and the famine of human grief. They seem to represent the archetypal or emotional-instinctual patterning of the experience of attachment and loss. They do not, however, depict the personal experience of loss through death and aging.

The work of immutable fate, the loss of another or a part of oneself, is a time of standstill and disruption. At just such a moment, we can be seized by an unconscious complex and overtaken by a wish. We are beside ourselves with feelings of shock and fear. In the face of loss in middle life, especially in the loss of vitality and beauty, one may give way to childish wishes and dreams of perfect fulfillment. In terms of Metanira's wish to make her son divine, were she to have completely handed over his humanity, he would have been lost entirely—dead. Thinking in terms of the story, her crisis is a crisis of consciousness (she was not watching). The crisis is resolved in a moment of conscious recognition followed by anger, often a transforming emotion.

There is something ironic, poignant, paradoxical in the extreme, about the moment at which Metanira saves her son's humanity while losing his immortality. At the moment of crisis or shock, we are indeed "stupid people, brainless" who "don't even know" if fate is bringing us something good or something bad, as Demeter says. Metanira acts in favor of retrieving the finitude and vulnerability of human life, of becoming aware of limitation in the face of her wish for divinity. This is the lesson I have learned from the poem, one which I find congruent with the struggle of people in resolving loss in middle life.

The individual who gives over to the desire to be immortal, who denies, through behavior, substitution, repression, or whatever, the finitude of human life, can only give over to a cyclical depression, an alternation of inflation and deflation, of the maiden Persephone and the abducted Persephone.

At the level of consciousness we may convince ourselves that nothing is wrong in the face of loss, but at the level of the archetypal our emotions speak through our bodies and our disclaimed actions. We remain heroically in control at the price of depression, anxiety, confusion, and illness.

To return to Metanira, what does she show us about the human response to loss? I believe that she shows the necessity of maintaining a clear awareness of our finitude and limitation while we embrace our emotional life. We admit the goddess into our household and simultaneously hold onto our humanity and consciousness. The specific nature of human life, from the point of view of individuation as the story renders it, is the necessity of maintaining unification in the face of dissolution. Integrity and self-consistency, in the recognition and integration of loss, result in a new meaning system or a new point of view that transcends the personal but does not reduce or deny it.

Said another way, loss comes to be recognized as the very essence of human relationship. It intensifies the value of the individual in that the individual is transient. The story seems to say, "Find a way through your own personal awareness and identity to discover a deeper meaning in human loss than a simple ending. Build a temple, practice a ritual, embrace many possibilities and you will apprehend a new perspective on human life and death."

To interpret the "Hymn to Demeter" as primarily a saga of loss and restoration is itself wishful thinking, I believe. Part of the reason I find this story so compelling is that it highlights the realization that human loss is meaningful. The gods and the humans are not equals, but in fact, the turning point of the drama is Metanira's angry recognition. Perhaps consciousness of human vulnerability and limitation is at the forefront of change. And confrontation with the impossible wishes, the wishes for perfection in oneself and others, provides the royal road to further development in later life.

NOTE

1. All quotations from the hymn are from the translation by Charles Boer, *The Homeric Hymns* (Irving, Tex.: Spring Publications, 1979).

Persephone in Hades

CHRISTINE DOWNING

As far back as I can remember there have been several mythic patterns with which I have felt myself to be closely identified. Nevertheless, Persephone has a special place. From her I learned a relation to myth different from that which all these other identifications, and all my familiarity with many mythological traditions and with much of the scholarly writing about mythology, had taught me. From my lifelong involvement with this particular myth I discovered how the apprehension of a mythic pattern teaches one that there may be symbolically meaningful connections between events that otherwise might seem isolated moments or stages. There is an inner bond between what one does and what apparently happens to one.

Often, in ways that continue to surprise, I have found that there are correlates in hitherto unnoticed parts of the Persephone myth to apparently isolated fragments or accidents of my life—and then I am less sure those personal experiences are adventitious after all.

I have come to understand, also, through my involvement with this myth, the difference between relating to a myth and relating to a mythological figure. It seems vitally important no longer to identify with only one character in the myth, Persephone, nor to focus on one episode within the story, Persephone's forced abduction by Hades. This transformation was not something at which I deliberately aimed. There was, rather, a gradual and seemingly inevitable discovery of how all the elements of the myth necessarily belong together, so that I now see that the myth is the *mythos,* the plot, the action, not the figure abstracted from it. Persephone *is* the one about whom this story, with all its ramifications, is told.

In ways that I am still discovering, her story is my story. "Always," as far back as I can remember, I have been Persephone. I am spring's child, born on the first day of spring; Persephone is the goddess of spring. My mother loves myths and fairy tales and loves to tell them. Her own children and now grandchildren, too, have outgrown having such stories told to them, and so she tells them instead to the children of strangers in parks and libraries. Probably it was from her that I first learned I was Persephone. I do not know. I cannot remember a time when it was not so.

Yet in many ways it seemed that it was only because of having been born on a particular day that I happened to be *this* maiden among the many other possibilities. Persephone is at first simply one among many maidens with no clear differentiation from the others; this is indicated in the Homeric "Hymn to Demeter," the most richly detailed ancient account of her abduction, by presenting her playing

> *With those big-breasted*
> *daughters of oceanos,*
> *picking flowers,*
> *roses*
> *and crocus*
> *and beautiful violets,*
> *in lush meadow,*
> *and iris,*
> *and hyacinth,*
> *narcissus even*[1]

This scene calls vividly to mind a dream I had some twenty years ago:

In this dream I am one among a group of young women of the tribe, hardly conscious of myself as more than just one of them, until the handsome young chief of our people calls me to dance with him and thus signals his choice of me as his bride. Through this choice, through his recognition of me, I become aware of myself, and through the warmth of his love and its sensitivity I become more and more someone worthy of it, someone able to receive and in time to return. Then there is a drought and our people must go elsewhere in search of water. I am left behind alone, with the unborn son, their future leader, in my womb as token of their hope to return. I have become one who can wait alone and in peace for the birth of this son who now represents the future of my people.

At that time I was indeed a young woman of the tribe, hardly conscious of myself as more than just one of them. Hardly conscious, either, as I have said, of Persephone as more than just one of the many maiden goddesses, though I did feel an identification with the rhythms of her life: the summers of ripeness and the winters of separation and loss, and the always unexpected (though always dreamed of) rescue by the messenger god. There were many parts of the myth that seemed less relevant, like the parts of a dream that one is not yet prepared to understand.

In the years of my own budding womanhood, just before my marriage, Persephone was preeminently spring and the beauty of spring.

Before I could appreciate the Hades part of the story, I needed first to understand more clearly what the Homeric hymn assumes to be the starting point of the Persephone story: "Demeter, that awesome goddess, with her beautiful hair."

In my early twenties I began to discover my relation to her, to Persephone's mother, and to apprehend why this myth is the basis for the "cult of the two goddesses," the Eleusinian mysteries. It is the relation to Demeter that makes Persephone different from the other maidens, the other anima figures, whose mothers are an insignificant and often wholly disregarded aspect of their lives.

Persephone is the maiden who has a mother. Indeed, as the title "Hymn to Demeter" indicates, our most important source for the Persephone myth is one that views it from Demeter's perspective. That perspective was one I began to understand sometime during the years when I was literally becoming a mother myself. In losing my own maidenhood, I experienced what it is to lose one's dearly loved maiden daughter. I had indeed lost her, my own maidenness—not just in losing my biological virginity but also in losing that in-oneselfness that Esther Harding has helped us to recognize is the essence of virginity. There was part of me that mourned the end of the period of introspective self-enclosure that had characterized the earlier years, as another part of me rejoiced in motherhood and an existence primarily given over to relationships, to giving birth and nurturing.

Were it not for my dreams, I might not know how deeply being a mother enters into my ways of being in the world. The dreams reveal the centrality of mother/child imagery to my way of perceiving even situations that have little to do with biological relationships. The many times I appear in my dreams as a mother have served to make me realize that I am as much mother as daughter, as much Demeter as Persephone.

As Persephone is not just any maiden, so Demeter is not just any mother. There are many incarnations of the Great Mother who gives and devours—and most of them represent the mother as the hero-son relates to her. Demeter, on the other hand, exemplifies the mother's own experience of motherhood. How different that perspective is. From the maternal side we are brought in touch with how much of motherhood is loss. Demeter, as this myth shows her to us, is the grieving mother. She experiences the loss of the other, the loss of her child, as the loss of self (which as Freud taught us is what deep mourning always feels like). All of us who are mothers know the truth of this, know how intimately the cutting fear of loss, the searing pain of loss, are interwoven with our mothering. To let go of a child—to death, to another, to madness, to simply going its own way—is more than we can bear and yet we must. The extravagance of Demeter's grief is something we can well understand. I feel in it her suspicion that in some way the loss is due to her own neglect (wholly irrespective of whether that is objectively so or not). Though my own expressions of mourning are muted and muffled in comparison with hers, I can nevertheless identify with how entirely she allows herself to be taken over by her anger and sorrow, how ready she is to let everything else fall apart and simply *be* grief. Only a goddess could mourn so extravagantly.

I am struck, too, by how Demeter in the course of her disconsolate wandering ended up mothering again after all, serving as nurse to another woman's child—intent, this time, on raising a child who would escape death and the fates. This hope, too, had to be surrendered.

Carl Kerenyi has understood well what it is to enter into the figure of Demeter: it "means to be pursued, to be robbed, raped, to fail to understand, to rage and grieve, but then to get everything back and be born again."[2] The hymn to Demeter is *her* hymn, as the open part of the Eleusinian rites seems to have been devoted to her. As long as the focus is on the mother/daughter aspect of the Persephone mythologem, the mother does have the more important role. As long as the focus is here, the Persephone mythologem is clearly more directly pertinent to women than to men. In classical Athens, the most important Demetrian cultic event was the Thesmophoria, a woman's ritual that took the shape of an imitation of Demeter's grief. This representation of the basic emotions of woman's life as divine provided solace and encouragement.

Demeter's story ends in a reunion with her daughter, a reunion beautifully described in the hymn: "Their hearts had relief from their griefs while each took and gave back joyousness." Kerenyi's reading of this reunion rings true. It shows, he suggests, that the two, mother and maiden, are one. (This is represented in the mythological traditions about Persephone and Demeter by "doubling"—Demeter, too, is raped; Persephone, too, becomes a mother.) Motherhood and maidenhood are two phases of a woman's life, endlessly repeating: the maiden becomes a mother, the mother gives birth to the maiden, who becomes a mother, who. . . . To recognize one's participation in this ongoing pattern is to be given access to a kind of immortality, an immortality very different from the hero's self-perpetuation. It seems also to mean that being a mother does not, after all, have to mean *not* being the maiden. One can be experienced *and* innocent, turned toward others *and* in oneself. Demeter and Persephone are distinguished in the myth and rite, but precisely in order to insist on their unity. They are the two goddesses who share one cult. Of the two, Demeter is the more accessible, the more human and kindly, the one more concerned with the practical needs of human life. (Within the Olympian pantheon, Demeter's sphere is not as all-embracing as that of the ancient mother-goddess; she is goddess of the grain, of that which grows to human benefit, not goddess of all that grows.) Most important, nothing connected with Demeter is secret.

However, there is another part to the myth that we have thus far neglected: Persephone's experience in Hades and her relation to its dark god. For a long while when I attended to this part of the story I did so from the perspective of the upper world, understood it as Demeter does and as does that part of Persephone that longs to return. I knew that her joy in the reunion was as great as Demeter's, for I know how deep in me is the longing to be mothered—and I do not expect there will ever be a time when my mother-longing will be entirely assuaged. I am the abandoned child in my dreams as well as the neglecting and grieving mother.

I felt I knew all too well what it is to be pulled into the underworld. I related time spent in the underworld to times of depression and separation, times when I felt I had lost my ego independence, times when I felt taken over by something outside myself. During such times, I wanted only and desperately to "get back"—and knew only a messenger from the gods could make that happen. I could not bring it about myself. Being back meant health and innocence, wholeness and happiness.

I could understand Persephone's abduction in another sense as well, as initiation into sexual experience (and beyond that into motherhood). The sexual symbolism is obvious—the radiantly awesome flower that Persephone reaches out to pluck as the earth opens up and Hades appears is clearly a phallus; the red-juice-dripping, seed-filled pomegranate she eats in Hades clearly suggests the womb. (Ovid reports that Aphrodite induced Eros to inflame Hades with love because she was jealous of Persephone's seeming determination to remain a virgin. Ovid also has Persephone eat of the pomegranate out of her own careless innocence rather than at Hades' deceitful urging.) The oedipal element is also apparent—Hades, who is sometimes spoken of as the chthonic Zeus, is here brother to Zeus and has Zeus's paternal permission to seize Persephone. Indeed, the sun, only witness to the abduction, tells Demeter, "There is no other god responsible but Zeus." And in the Orphic tradition it is Zeus himself, in the form of a serpent, who seduces Persephone.

The myth captures the ambivalence of the maiden's relation to sexuality as I myself remember it—she reaches out *and* is taken, the lover is deeply familiar *and* a stranger, she is still the person she was (Demeter's daughter) *and* so changed that she will never be the same again. This "being taken" is in part being taken over by one's own capacity for passion; it is sexual ecstasy. The male as rapist, the male as chance agent of self-discovery—both are true. Thus for a long while Hades meant two quite different things between which I perceived no connection: he took me from myself (by pulling me into times of depression and inertia); he gave me to myself (through a sexual initiation experienced as a self-discovery in which the male's participation was almost incidental). My sense of this is that I still understood Hades in terms of his influence on Persephone's relation to Demeter. I did not discern that Persephone's relation to Hades had an integral meaning of its own. Hades was what, or more appropriately *who* (for the personification of these energies is integral to mythology's value to a deep psychological understanding), separated Persephone from Demeter, an experience that was at the same time loss of mother and gain of self.

Only recently have I come to see that the relation to Hades is just as central a part of Persephone as her relation to Demeter. In the National Museum at Athens there is an important relief depicting two scenes: in one Demeter and Persephone are seated at a banquet, in the other Persephone is seated with Hades. The two parts of the story are equally important and belong together. This is further confirmed by there being a temple dedicated to Hades at Eleusis (set, most appropriately, in a natural cave within the rocky side of the hill—the *temenos,* the threshold, of the world). Only as we understand Hades' role in the myth and what it means that Persephone should stay with him as goddess of the underworld can we appreciate how the Eleusinian cult could become the most important mystery in late classical and Hellenistic times for men as well as women. It then becomes evident why Persephone is the focus of the secret part of the cult, as Demeter is the focus of its exoteric side—and why it is that the secret cult, the mystery, is the one that matters in the Hellenistic period, as Demeter's cult may have dominated in an earlier agricultural period. Later, Demeter is important not so much because of her relation to grain but because she is the first initiate, the first to understand what has happened to her daughter. Persephone is regarded as the secret, hidden, ineffable goddess, related to things beyond, not even to be named except as *Thea.* She is, as Freud called her, the silent goddess of death.

I have had an entirely different relationship to this long-familiar myth since I have begun to see Persephone in Hades as its center. When one begins there and sees that the whole story is told about a figure who first and foremost is goddess of the underworld, one understands very differently what it means to say that she is also goddess of spring and renewal. To start with death, with the underworld, as a given is to see life in an entirely different way.

To be Persephone, to be *this* goddess, Persephone *must* be raped. Nor can the rape any longer be understood as necessary only as prelude to the joy-filled reunion with Demeter. That reunion is part of the public happenings—it is not the secret. The secret has to do with Persephone's relation to the secret world, the hidden world, the underworld. Persephone gives herself to Hades; she becomes his consort. All the stories that are told about her (other than Demeter's hymn) refer to her in this role. There are no myths that tell of someone arriving in Hades and finding her absent. As goddess of the underworld she is always there. It seems important that she does not bear Hades any children (though in some traditions she and Zeus are the parents of Dionysos). The queen of the underworld is not the Great Mother. She is not the source of literal, physical life.

For a long while I understood Persephone as the innocent victim of Hades' rape, just as Freud allowed his early patients to convince him they all had been infantile victims of parental seduction. I laid all the blame for Persephone's being in Hades on the apparent abductor—and saw it as a bad experience, saw it as meaning bad experiences, from which one could, of course, learn and from which one would, one hoped, eventually recover. Then I began to see Hades as meaning not "bad" but "deep"—and to recognize how much in me, although not quite consciously, yearned for the depths that Hades represents. I also see now why being taken to those depths is always an abduction. For we—or, at least, I—never feel quite whole enough, quite courageous enough, quite mature enough to go *there* on our own. We are always still virginal before the really transformative (killing) experiences.

I now understand Hades' realm, the underworld, the depths, to mean the realm of souls rather than of egos, the realm where experience is perceived symbolically. In the *Odyssey*, Hades is next to the house of dreams. The Greek underworld is not terrible and horrifying, full of punishments and tortures, but, simply, beyond life. Hades is not only the god of the underworld but the god of wealth, hidden wealth. I now see Hades very differently than I had previously. Earlier I had welcomed Hermes as the guide *out* of the underworld; now I have come to welcome Hades as the guide *into* it. I feel I understand now how Persephone moves from defense against Hades to love for him. When Orpheus comes to beg for Eurydice's release, he appeals to Hades and Persephone, "If there is any truth in the story of long ago, then you yourselves were brought together by love." James Hillman helps me say it: "Life becomes relieved of having to be a vast defensive arrangement against psychic realities."³ I now understand those times of confusion and hopelessness, which once were so self-evidently "away from myself" experiences, as times of being pulled *to* myself. I had been accustomed to look at Hades from the perspective of everyday life, from the perspective of Demeter when she resents Hades, rejects Olympus, and lives in "the cities of men." I can still remember a period about ten years ago during which I felt propelled, as though by outward circumstances, into a kind of death.

It was a time during which there was no hoping or dreaming left in me at all. I knew a despair utterly different from any confusion or depression I had ever experienced earlier. I discovered that I could not extricate myself. There did not seem to be any way out of having to be in this apart-from-myself kind of place. There was no way of forcing my way out and no way of cheating my way out or pretending that things were different than they were. One of the things that was most difficult about this time for me was that it was a time when I really could not imagine that things would ever be different, because I could not even imagine what being different might be like. Among the most painful aspects of this experience was that during this time I did not seem to be dreaming at all. I was not in touch with the part of me that dreams. That was difficult because dreams would have given me a sense that, somewhere, there was something that was still alive in me, but I had no contact with that vital core at all. I knew there was no choice: this had to be lived. That is all there was to it. In a literal, outward, practical way I functioned well through all this, but none of that functioning seemed to have anything to do with me in ways that mattered at all. I thought that to be alive again would be to be back in the daylight world feeling it to be real, to love another again, to be involved with others and with my work. But I knew that for the time being at least, all I could do was simply stay with how things were. Eventually I discovered that there is indeed a natural healing process. There is an end to an experience like this that we do not make happen but that comes. In my particular situation this came when I finally had a dream. It was a frightening dream in which I died. But that dying was the first sign of life I had had; that dying was the beginning of a gradual emergence back to health.

That experience taught me some important things. I learned that things can be *that* bad, which I had not known before, and that one is a different person after having lived through something so powerful. I learned that one recovers, and that being here in this world of others in an ordinary, simple kind of way is a gift. But I was still very much caught (as I look at it from where I am now) in an ego relationship to the experience. I looked on it from the perspective of the consciousness of the daylight world, in relation to the image of heroic endurance. I was aware of having come through something and now, thank God, being on the other side of it. I believed that having had such an experience was something important, something to be grateful for, but I was also very grateful to have it behind me. At this time I felt most closely connected to that moment in Persephone's myth when Persephone is reunited with her mother. I felt the joy of being back from the underworld, of the reconnection between those two halves of myself, the abducted half and the grieving half. That there *is* joy in such returns I would not even now deny. But I do now understand the time *in* the underworld differently.

This changed understanding of Hades came not from meditating on the myth but from a personal experience that I only afterward saw as connected to the Persephone mythologem.

A few years ago, I participated in a visionary experience in which I felt myself pulled to my own dissolution. I felt myself being pulled toward death or to a state that was indistinguishably death or madness and I felt very powerfully my fear of that—and particularly my fear of my fear. I discovered that night how afraid I was (and have always been) of being anxious, fearful, weak, helpless. But somehow I let myself fear and I let myself go mad and I let myself die—because I realized that not to let myself die would be a much worse death. I felt, and I think this is part of what provoked the fear, that this dying that I felt happening to me was a kind of unending fall into nothingness, nothingness, nothingness. But I discovered that the more I allowed myself to fall, the less it felt like that. I discovered that I had never really believed that there is a center at the center. And that there is. It was not at all a case of overcoming my fear, of overcoming my fragmentation or my hurts—but precisely a discovery that such overcoming is beside the point. The fear, the pain, the incompleteness, the woundedness, the dying were there. They were my pain and my fear and my fragmentation, but I had come to a kind of objective relation to them. The fear was no longer fearsome; I could just let it be, rather than trying to run away from it. I saw then that wholeness did not mean not being in parts, that health did not mean not hurting.

During that night I relinquished my negative view of illness, suffering, and mourning. I no longer saw these as things to get over, to put behind or deny. I now see that night as a night spent in Hades.

The Persephone of the Eleusinian rites, the Persephone who is Hades' bride, enables us to confront the most formidable moments of our lives as integral to them, as occasions for a deep seeing. The mysteries were showings and seeings. Some scholars believe that the climax of the rite was an announcement of the birth of a divine child, Brimos, and that this might be an alternative name for Dionysos, who in the Orphic tradition is indeed held to be the son of Zeus and Persephone.

The secret of the Eleusinian rites seems to be that they give one a happy arrival in the underworld. "Thrice happy are those of mortals, who having seen these rites depart for Hades; for to them alone is it granted to have found life there; to the rest all there is evil," cries Sophocles, and Pindar tells us: "Happy is he who having seen these rites goes below the hollow earth; for he knows the end of life and he knows its god-sent beginnings." The Eleusinian initiation provides an entrance now (not just after death) to this realm where the perspective is in a sense postmortem: transpersonal and imaginal. But time spent in Hades that is not spent trying desperately to get out also leads to the discovery of the power and beauty of the dark moments in our life, the real confusions and desolations. Fear is so different when one does not have to fear fear but can simply *fear;* incompleteness and hurt are also different when one sees them not as something to get beyond but as something to live. I think of the beauty box that Psyche had to obtain from Persephone—clearly the beauty it provides is very different from any Aphrodite might have power to bestow. I think also of Sophocles' *Oedipus at Colonus.* Because Oedipus had so fully lived his years of harried exile and blind wandering, his death on the outskirts of Eleusis is itself a mystery, a nonritualistic but nevertheless blessed initiation into Persephone's realm:

> *the underworld*
> *Opened in love the unlit door of earth.*
> *For he was taken without lamentation,*
> *Illness or suffering; indeed his end*
> *was wonderful if mortal's ever was.*[4]

As I try to consider again the whole mythologem and what I have thus far discovered in it and through it, I realize how important it is that Persephone does and does not return from Hades. Though from the point of view of the cult, Persephone is always there, she does not belong only with Hades but also with Demeter, not only in the underworld but also here on earth. I understand too that I am and am not Persephone. Even today it is the maiden Persephone with whom I identify; the goddess of the underworld is still a deep mystery to me. I am pulled to the underworld and return. She remains.

NOTES

1. Charles Boer, trans., *The Homeric Hymns* (Chicago: Swallow Press, 1970), 91.

2. C. G. Jung and C. Kerenyi, *Essays on a Science of Mythology* (Princeton: Princeton University Press, 1969), 123.

3. James Hillman, *ReVisioning Psychology* (New York: Harper and Row, 1975), 208.

4. Sophocles, *Oedipus at Colonus,* lines 1662–65, translated by Robert Fitzgerald in *The Complete Greek Tragedies,* edited by David Grene and Richmond Lattimore, vol. 2 (Chicago: University of Chicago Press, 1959), 150.

Hekate, Rhea, and Baubo

Perspectives on Menopause

CHRISTINE DOWNING

BECAUSE THERE IS LITTLE in our culture to support a symbolic understanding of menopausal dream and symptom, I found myself looking once again to Greek mythology, hoping it might provide some guidance. My search for menopausal rituals yielded little; fortunately, however, there are myths that can help us to an appreciation of the symbolic significance of the passage. The major Olympian goddesses are associated primarily with earlier life phases, with youth and fulfilled maturity, though both Artemis and Demeter are relevant to the self-understanding of menopausal women. Artemis, through her sacralizing of all the physiological mysteries peculiar to feminine life—menstruation, childbirth, menopause, death—and through her modeling of a self-sufficient womanhood in no way dependent on the exercise of reproductive capacity or on participation in heterosexual relationships, represents the blessings that may be available to the postmenopausal woman. In her raging grief at the loss of her daughter, Persephone, and thus at the loss of her mother function, Demeter displays a quite different aspect. Her reunion with her daughter and with her own capacity for fruitful activity comes at the cost of accepting the reality of underworld experience, for the separation will recur for a third of each year. (One thinks of Prospero's "Every third thought shall be my grave.") Yet there are minor goddesses that more clearly illuminate the polymorphous meaning of menopause: Hekate, Rhea, and Baubo. (We might note, however, that each of these three is involved in helping Demeter accept the loss of her motherhood: Baubo is the first to coax her at least momentarily out of her self-devouring grief, Rhea proposes the arrangement whereby Demeter might be reconnected with her daughter on a new basis, Hekate presides over the reunion.)

The association of menopause with fearful and despicable dreams is given powerful recognition in the traditions about Hekate. In Greek mythology nightmares come from Hekate, who is herself a postmenopausal goddess. Hekate is closely associated with Persephone and Demeter; in the triad of maiden/mother/crone she is the crone, the hag, the wise and dread old woman.

In Hesiod's *Theogony,* Hekate is the goddess whom Zeus honors above all, who has a share of the earth, the sea, and the starry heaven. She is a great mother goddess associated with fair judgment and with victory in battle and game, with the fruitfulness of the sea, the flocks, and the human family. But elsewhere she is much more restrictedly defined as an underworld goddess. In the Homeric "Hymn to Demeter" it is Hekate who hears Persephone's cry as Hades pulls her down into the underworld and Hekate who lights the maiden's way back to earth and promises to see to it that the agreement whereby Persephone spends part of each year below and part above is kept. Thus three-faced Hekate is the goddess of the threshold between the underworld and earth, perhaps once identical with three-headed Cerberus, the dog who guards the entrance to Hades. She is preeminently the goddess of the threshold and the crossroad; her image stands at the entrance to every house and at intersections; the key is her emblem. Hermes, another chthonic divinity associated with entrances and highways, makes crossings seem deceptively simple; Hekate represents the seriousness and precariousness of all transitions. Like Circe (a Hekate by-form), who directs Odysseus to the underworld but does not accompany him, Hekate watches at the gates.

As guardian of the entrance to the inner world, we may also imagine her as watching over all that passes in and out of the woman's body: menstrual blood, seminal emissions, the newborn child.

In popular religion Hekate is the goddess of witchcraft and sorcery who roams the earth on moonless nights in the company of howling dogs and hungry ghosts. It is those ghosts we meet in our nightmares. Not all the dead appear as haunting spirits, only those who died too early, were murdered, or did not receive appropriate burial rites. Ghosts are souls who find no rest in death; sacrifices to Hekate are designed to appease the anger of the dead who were not ready to die. Hekate is present at those moments when souls connect with and leave bodies, at childbirth and at death. Her eerie following consists of those for whom this connection or separation was not properly accomplished; she is queen of those souls who are still fast bound to the upper world. Thus menopausal nightmares may come from what is not ready to die yet, from that in our souls not yet prepared to leave the body of a premenopausal woman. (Another common "symptom" of menopause is insomnia. I wonder if it might reflect a fear of those same nightmares, a reluctance to cross the threshold into sleep, sensing its connection to the threshold into death.)

Esther Harding speaks of the "importune ghosts" that come forward at the time of the menopausal transition, demanding a more fundamental confrontation with the dark side, our shadow, than was possible earlier.[1] This is a time for honoring our pathology, for acknowledging that in us that remains incomplete, fearful, and wounded. We need now, as Irene Claremont de Castillejo puts it, to "weep the tears which are still unshed."[2] The ghosts that follow Hekate ask only that they be openly mourned, ritually buried. Under her tutelage I see my dreams as providing me with the opportunity for understanding what my fantasies of pregnancy, metamorphosis, dismemberment, madness, disease, and death most deeply portend and what they promise.

Helene Deutsch describes how often menopause stimulates "a strong urge to become pregnant and to re-experience motherhood." In some this is literalized, so that "often even against their conscious will, they give life to one or two lateborn children—before the closing of the gates, so to speak. One has the impression that even if sterility has already set in, it may yield to the woman's passionate wish still to be capable of reproduction."[3] Or the intense longing may be expressed in a hysterical pregnancy where the woman is fully persuaded she is carrying a child, or in dreams like mine that I carried with me into waking life.

The desperate yearning for a child is represented by several of the nightmare figures associated with Hekate, by Gello and Lamia, who kidnap children, and by Mormo, who has lost her own child and so devours the children of others. Dreams of infanticide seem to express the same refusal to accept the loss of one's capacity to have a child. Thus Hecuba (in Greek, Hekabe), a recognized by-form of Hekate, after losing her many children during the Trojan War, comes to reject her passive role as the grieving mother. She becomes a vengeful agent of horror who blinds Polymnestor and murders his infant sons. Soon thereafter she is transformed into one of the fiery-eyed dogs who follow Hekate. Medea, who invokes Hekate as her patron goddess, kills her own young sons when she feels herself rejected as woman, wife, and mother.

More often, however, the continued attachment to childbearing is expressed in myths or dreams about the miraculous impregnation of a long-sterile or clearly postmenopausal woman. The child born of such a conception is typically a divine child or one dedicated to a god, indicating that the birth is not an ordinary, literal birth. The most familiar such tale is probably that of the biblical Sarah, promised a child when it had long ceased "to be with her after the manner of women." This ancient story explicitly admits that there is something ludicrous, laughter provoking, about the longing of a menopausal woman to bear a child and yet suggests that the yearning refers not to the realm of repetition and regression, the past, but to the genuinely new, the promised future. The transition from literal mothering may not be easy; it may be experienced as violently imposed. Before we are ready for a divine conception, we may first have to endure dreams in which our mothering (or our children) are murdered. Some anachronistic self-identification with our motherhood, some reluctance to accept the inevitable incompleteness of our mothering, our failures, our guilts, or our regret at never having had children, may haunt us in nightmare form. But the dream of a miraculous impregnation signifies precisely our release from the literal dimensions of childbearing, our birth into the new possibilities of postmenopausal feminine existence.

Even Deutsch admits that "after motherhood has ceased to serve the species, it goes on serving the individual experience." Old age, she says, adds a new phase of motherhood: grandmotherhood.[4] The difference between mothering and grandmothering is suggested by some of the Greek traditions about Rhea. What distinguishes Rhea from Gaia, the original creatrix in Greek mythology, and from Demeter, the goddess associated with the grain and with intensely personal motherly devotion, is that Rhea is the always sympathetic and majestic "mother of the gods." She is mother to the adult divinities who comprise the Olympian pantheon and thus grandmother to their children, especially Dionysos and Persephone. After the Titans have dismembered Zeus's son, Rhea gathers up the pieces and boils them in a magic stew; thus she re-members Dionysos. When Persephone is abducted by Hades, it is Rhea who comes up with the fertile compromise whereby Persephone may spend two-thirds of the year with her grief-struck mother and one-third in the underworld. It is also Rhea who persuades Demeter, still wholly immersed in her personal drama even after the reunion with Persephone, to make the fields productive again.

In the triad of Persephone, Demeter, and Rhea, Rhea is clearly the grandmother, purified of the possessiveness and the demands for heroic achievement that too often contaminate the love of mothers for their daughters or their sons. But as is true of all goddesses, the many phases of her life coexist simultaneously. Rhea is not only grandmother; she is at the same time the young daughter of Gaia and Ouranos kept captive in her mother's body and also the sister-spouse of Kronos, cunningly scheming to thwart her husband's attempt to contain his children within his own belly. She is maiden and mother as well as grandmother.

Deutsch notes that "women who are good observers of themselves report that, confronted with the climacterium, they experience a kind of depersonalization, a split in which they feel simultaneously young and old." The mythological correlate suggests that this feeling should not too easily be dismissed as an illusion. Indeed, it may be when maiden and crone are *not* both present that the real danger occurs. It is Hekate's hearing Persephone's cry and later bringing her back to earth that assures Persephone's benign transition into womanhood and her reconciliation with motherhood (that is, her reunion with Demeter, the mother). Hekate does not try to prevent the necessary Hades experience, as Demeter would have. Just as important, it is precisely in relation to Persephone that Hekate appears as something other than a fearful, destructive demon. Maiden and crone need each other as surely as do *puer* and *senex,* youth and old man, though the polarities are not identical. Where the senex represents rigidity, perfection, and order and is sorely in need of the narcissistic, inquisitive inspiration of the puer, Hekate the crone embodies a raging, roaming, unbound energy that finds its balance in maiden Persephone's self-enclosed passivity. Kronos as senex represents the unchanging; Hekate is associated with thresholds and crossroads, with transitions and transformations.

To literalize the sense of one's continued youthfulness may issue in ludicrous (though perhaps sometimes necessary) behavior, but to deny it is to rob our aging self of something it needs.

A quite different symbol of the new life that menopause brings is the outrageously flamboyant female sexuality of Baubo. Deutsch names as among the "regressive elements" that often accompany "the progressive movement toward biologic withering" an "increase of sexual excitation" and "heightened sexual interest." She sketches a rather cruel portrait of the outwardly comical self-presentation of the woman involved in such a "second puberty": her ridiculously overpainted face and too youthful clothes, the clearly inferior admirers with whom she surrounds herself. Deutsch also observes that, just as in puberty, this resurgence of libido may be accompanied by a vigorous struggle against these sensations, which leads to the sexual yearnings appearing as rape fantasies. Such fantasies and nightmares were long ago recognized as included in Hekate's repertoire. Among her grim, uncanny attendants are the Incubae, orgiastic nightmares that stifle and outrage sleeping women, and the Empusae, filthy demons so hungry for love that they devour their lovers. In Greek mythology there are also other nightmare figures, the twin brothers Ephialtes and Otus, who seek to outrage Hera, the faithful wife, and Artemis, the self-contained virgin—as though women too long devoted to fidelity or chastity will inevitably at the approach of menopause suddenly long for a sexuality that they can only imagine as being forced on them. When femininity is closely identified with reproductive capacity, the end of that capacity may well trigger a fear that one is losing one's sexuality.

But the newly released sexuality may represent not the denial of that fear but rather the genuine discovery of a sexuality that transcends wifely obligation or motherly potential, that is truly one's own. The traditions about Baubo suggest that the Greeks were capable of greeting her self-indulgent, proud display of feminine sexuality with veneration rather than satire. When grief-stricken Demeter arrives at Eleusis, still in fruitless search of her daughter, she is entertained by the ancient dry nurse, Baubo. As Baubo swirls about in an obscene dance in which she ostentatiously displays her vulva, Demeter cannot restrain her laughter. Baubo *is* the vulva, as she is also the wise old woman who is often given Hekate's place in the Eleusinian triad: Persephone/ Demeter/Baubo. The myth suggests that the old woman can represent feminine sexuality in its essence more fully and more awesomely than can the reticent virgin or the reproductively oriented mother. It is too simple to dismiss the aging woman's heightened sexuality as only pathology or illusion. Baubo's spreading of her legs is regarded as a ritual act. She is often represented seated on a pig, legs outspread, holding a ladder upright in her hand; she connects us to the divine. The terra-cotta figurines that shape a vulva as though one could there find a face, indeed a whole body, suggest the radical autonomy of feminine sexuality—its fearfulness and its sacrality. (It is only fair to acknowledge that this obscenely sexual old woman is sometimes also represented as displaying not just pudenda but her most truly secret genital parts, her womb itself, and within it a male child. Thus, here the very epitome of female sexuality is represented by an image that implies that it contains a masculine element.) Baubo's vulgarity and Rhea's grandmotherly serenity may at first seem polar opposites, but the inner connection between these aspects of female maturity must have been apparent to those Greeks who identified Rhea with Kybele, the fearsome, sexually potent Oriental mother goddess, and worshiped her with orgiastic rituals.

The new, more insistent affirmation of one's female sexuality as self-validating, as complete in itself, as sacred, may also show itself in dreams or fantasies (or literal realizations) of homosexual passion in women who have hitherto consciously regarded themselves as entirely heterosexual. Deutsch speaks of how menopause may affect a woman's relation to her own sex. "Friendships previously loyal and harmless begin to be troubled; well-sublimated homosexuality is subjected to the same tests as sometimes in puberty: the sublimation is no longer sufficient." The woman may succumb to her long-repressed homosexuality or, even more frequently, to a homophobic panic that destroys long-treasured old friendships. How much more gently Harding puts this when she speaks of the "autumn" of a woman's life as a time when a woman who has devoted herself to the life of a wife and mother can at last give attention to her relationships with women, which have until now probably been left "in an exceedingly undifferentiated state." The pull toward deeper relationships with women (or toward a more conscious realization of the importance such relationships have had all along) is, indeed, something many of us experience at this time in our lives, as we tend to yearn more for the intensification that same-sex friendships can bring than for the complement usually sought in relationships with men. The deep bonding possible among women is suggested by the joy that Persephone and Demeter give to and receive from each other when they are reunited and in which they so naturally include Hekate. Hekate's close association with Artemis suggests that the old woman's love participates in that respectful honoring of the other's in-oneselfness that Artemis expects and gives, a loving purged of possessiveness.

All this suggests that after menopause the polymorphousness of our sexuality reappears; one may rediscover the continued presence of desires one has not lived. Deutsch refers to the reemergence of incestuous fantasies, now more likely directed toward one's children than, as in childhood, toward one's parents. I remember a dream of making passionate love to my daughter, kissing her lips, her breasts, her clitoris, and then being gently restrained by her from entering her with my tongue. I found the dream beautiful, not frightening. It spoke to me of my love for her and myself, my love for woman-ness, my joy in being part of the continuing cycle of love represented by women giving birth to daughters who will in turn have daughters. The dream acknowledges also that there are limits to our union.

The acceptance of limits, of separateness, of finitude, is clearly itself a central task of menopause. Something *is* over; someday we *will* die. Full coming to terms with our death is probably the task of the far side of this period into which menopause initiates us, not of its beginning. Nevertheless, from now on, "death and distance" are in the mix.

NOTES

1. M. Esther Harding, *The Way of All Women* (New York: Harper and Row, 1975), 254–55.

2. Irene Claremont de Castillejo, *Knowing Woman* (New York: Harper and Row, 1973), 157.

3. Helene Deutsch, *The Psychology of Women: Motherhood* (New York: Bantam, 1973), 478.

4. Ibid., 504.

GLIMPSES OF A POSTPATRIARCHAL WORLD

ALTHOUGH MOST of the contemporary perspectives on the myth that we have considered thus far read it in relation to the psychology of women, the myth is not just about women but also about gender issues, not just about mothers and daughters but also about the relations between women and men. Of course there are aspects that are particularly relevant to women's lives, as the all-women's ritual, the Thesmophoria, makes evident. But the Eleusinian mysteries were open to all, men and women, slave and free.

Carl Kerenyi, noting that all initiates took names with feminine endings, says that all entered into the figure of Demeter, the first initiate, as though understanding that the release from the fear of death that the mysteries provide requires entrance into a female perspective.

Catherine Keller, too, believes that the ritual made it possible for what seems like an exclusively female experience, the connection between mothers and daughters, to provide all who participated in it a glimpse of what relationships that honor both intimacy and independence might be like. The Mysteries seem to have presented the mother-daughter bond in a way that communicated to both men and women an affirmation that reconnection can triumph even over the deadening force of a rapacious separation. The Mysteries, she believes, suggested that the mother-daughter relationship can be redemptive for all, can extend and transform the otherwise shattered or repressed original continuum from which we all emerge. Reflection on them can teach us that maturation means the gradual differentiation and modulation of the empathic continuum, in a way that leaves us neither bound to parent figures nor severed from them.[1] Persephone, as Ovid tells us, still longed for Demeter while in the underworld, but she also enjoyed her power as its queen; she rejoices in her reunion with her mother, but she does not return unchanged nor to stay. She is still connected while separated, still separate when reconnected; relatedness and autonomy are not necessarily discrete developments.

Thus the myth may today be profoundly relevant to the experiences of both women and men, as the Mysteries were felt to be in the ancient world. To allow the myth to speak fully today means, I believe, not trying to hold on to it as just ours, as speaking only about women, only to women.

I believe the myth of Demeter and Persephone might help to imagine forward to a possible postpatriarchal world, not by interpreting what the myth meant *then* but by reimagining it. As we have seen, many women have found in this myth resources for the imaginal re-creation of a prepatriarchal matristic world. But like Dorothy Dinnerstein I see a danger in our being transfixed by the dream of a conflict-free world ruled by an all-giving and all-powerful mother.[2] Polly Young-Eisendrath, in the essay included in the immediately preceding section of this book, and Naomi Goldenberg, in the essay included here (both of whom also seem to agree with Dinnerstein), draw our attention to elements in the myth that might help us get beyond the myth of female innocence and perfect love. They remind us that not all the aggression in the story is male, remind us of what they see as Demeter's tyrannical hold on her daughter and of her trying to steal Metanira's child, dipping him into the fire and violently throwing him to the floor when caught. They note how fearfully everyone then runs around desperately seeking to soothe the goddess's wrath. They ask us to remember how Demeter threatens to starve the whole human race and how every god and goddess tries without avail to persuade her to relent.

Turning to the myth as a resource to support our hopes that women and men might discover forms of relationship based on our together having moved beyond the distorted and destructive forms characteristic of patriarchal society involves the kind of critical examination of the female actors in the myth that Goldenberg's essay provides. It also involves getting past a focus on the mother's or the daughter's, Demeter's or Persephone's perspective as representing the only possible female perspectives—and, beyond that, calls upon us to listen to what we might learn from the male figures in the myth.

As I look at the male figures in the myth—Zeus, Hades, Helios, Demophoon, Hermes, Triptolemus, Brimo/Dionysos—I am struck by how many of them there are and what varied roles they play. I have come to sense that to understand the myth fully would entail a patient exploration of how each enters the tale, how it might look from his perspective, and then perhaps discovering that these so-called male perspectives are perspectives in which I participate—familiar, not alien; integral, not extraneous.

I have always felt that Hades abducted me along with Persephone—abducted me into the underworld of Greek mythology, into the world of the goddesses, and into those times of deep reflection on my own life that have been part of that immersion. The "Hymn to Demeter" depicts Hades only as the dreadful god whom Demeter experiences as an intruder and despoiler; it gives us no sense of what this episode means to him, of his motives, his feelings. Ovid (though with Ovid, scholars never seem to agree about when he is being ironic and when not) writes that Hades came for Persephone after having first seen and fallen in love with her and then having received permission from her father. I am struck by how many of the gods seek to force themselves upon one woman after another and that Hades reaches only for this one—and even the hymn acknowledges the kindliness with which he sends Persephone back to her mother.

I have come to see Hades as representing the impossibility of an all-female world forever immune to intrusion by the male. Demeter had sought to keep her daughter with her forever, to protect her from all contact with the masculine. Persephone *reaches* for the narcissus as she later reaches for the pomegranate. There is some spark essential to her becoming herself, becoming the goddess of the underworld and not just Demeter's daughter, that the relation to Hades makes possible. His temple is outside the sacred precincts, his power in the underworld becomes subordinate to hers, his role is in some ways minor—and yet essential. He helps get something started that might otherwise remain barren.

In her novel based on the ancient myth, *The Goddess Letters,* Carol Orlock shows Persephone trying to understand what their relation means from Hades' perspective. She imagines that during the nearly two thousand years that they were worshipped at Eleusis, Demeter and Persephone are engaged in a lively correspondence; the novel consists of their letters to one another. During this long, long period of time, both goddesses come to understand the meaning of their separation ever more profoundly, and gradually Persephone comes to love her underworld consort. She writes her mother about all that Hades does to make her feel at home in his realm; she writes of how he confides in her how he would in the beginning have preferred Zeus's kingdom to the one assigned to him. She writes about asking him why he had abducted her and his answering, "I thought you'd see the beauty here. With you here I thought it could be known not simply as a place of death but as life-giving." Persephone tells her mother that she chose to eat the pomegranate seed because for an instant, at least, she believed that Hades loved her and couldn't bear the thought of her leaving him forever.[3]

I have included John Daughter's witty but serious account, "Hades Speaks," in this volume because truly to look at this story from a male perspective would seem to require allowing a man to tell us what Hades' version of the whole story might be!

Of course, each of the other male figures also plays an essential role in the story: Helios is the only one to *see* what happened when Persephone disappeared; Zeus comes to recognize that Demeter's claim cannot be ignored; Hermes leads Persephone back up from the underworld; the birth of Iacchus marks the climax of the mysteries. It may give us pause to recognize that in the hymn great-grandmother Gaia seems to side with Zeus and Hades against Demeter, that Hekate can witness the abduction without feeling she should interfere, that Baubo can tease Demeter about how seriously she is taking what has happened, that grandmother Rhea is the one who comes up with the fertile compromise by which Demeter, Persephone, and Hades are given their due.

A postpatriarchal imagining of the myth onward would, I believe, entail our moving to take on earth's perspective, Gaia's perspective, moving beyond our identification with male or female perspectives. I am persuaded that as we retell, reimagine, the myth of Demeter and Persephone, as we honor the diversity of female and male perspectives within the myth and on the myth, we have the possibility of transforming our relationships with one another and with Gaia.

Notes

1. Catherine Keller, *From a Broken Web* (Boston: Beacon Press, 1986), 153–154.

2. Dorothy Dinnerstein, *The Mermaid and the Minotaur* (New York: Harper and Row, 1977), 204.

3. Carol Orlock, *The Goddess Letters* (New York: St. Martin's Press, 1987), 38, 89, 90, 93.

Sightings of Maternal Rage and Paternal Love in the Homeric "Hymn to Demeter"

NAOMI R. GOLDENBERG

MUCH OF THE PSYCHOLOGICAL RICHNESS of Greek mythology lies in its depiction of deities as complex personalities with positive and negative qualities. In contrast, contemporary monotheistic traditions—such as Judaism, Christianity, and Islam—often display an inability to tolerate contradictions in the images of their divinities. Idealization of deity has become the norm in the dominant Western religions.

Perhaps this prevailing convention of seeing God as morally consistent, all-good, or all-just has influenced current feminist thinking about the Homeric "Hymn to Demeter." In many interpretations of the poem, Demeter is seen as a deity who is a perfect parent. She is described as a thoroughly reliable mother who is able to love her daughter without selfishness or ambivalence. Any discord in the story is generally viewed as arising from the acts and desires of Zeus and Hades, the most prominent male actors in the hymn. Even Philip Slater, whose work generally offers insight into the subject of familial hostility in Greek myth, writes that "the Demeter-Kore myth . . . is unique in having parental affection as its primary motivational theme."[1] While I do not disagree that love between mother and child is an important theme, I think that our psychological understanding of the myth can be deepened if we do not focus exclusively on Demeter's love for her daughter.

In her relationship to children other than Persephone, Demeter appears ambivalent. When she agrees to care for Demophoon, the son of Celeus and Metanira, she promises to nourish the baby and protect him from "woeful witchcraft." By day, she keeps her word. The child thrives "like some immortal being" because "Demeter anoints him with ambrosia as if he were the offspring of a god and breathes sweetly upon him as she holds him to her bosom."[2] But at night the goddess treats Demophoon differently. She places the child in flames, "hid[ing] him like a brand in the heart of the fire, unknown to his dear parents."[3]

When Metanira, the child's mother, discovers Demeter's nightly ritual, she is horrified. "Demophoon, my son," she screams, "the strange woman buries you deep in fire and works grief and bitter sorrow for me."[4] Although the goddess rationalizes her actions by explaining it as a rite to make the baby immortal— "I would have made your dear son deathless and unaging all his days and would have bestowed on him everlasting honour"[5]—we should be suspicious of her explanation. Perhaps Metanira has correctly discerned the vestiges of infant sacrifice within the rite. In the hymn, the mortal mother and the divine mother may well represent a split image of one mother who can act both to harm and to protect her child.

An enraged Demeter throws the baby on the ground when Metanira interrupts her fire ritual. It is surprising that the goddess who is often seen as the epitome of maternal concern has no appreciation for another mother's vigilance and worry about her child's welfare. After all, if Demeter had kept such close watch on Persephone, she might have been able to prevent her daughter's abduction. Instead of showing compassion for Metanira, she is furious with her.

Perhaps Demeter's possessiveness of Demophoon could be paralleled with her unwillingness to share Persephone with

Hades. In the beginning of the hymn, when Helios tells Demeter that it is Zeus who gave Hades permission to run off with Persephone, he urges her to moderate her grief and rage. He points out that Hades is a good match for her daughter: "Yet, goddess, cease your loud lament and keep not vain anger unrelentingly: Aidoneus, the Ruler of Many, is no unfitting husband among the deathless gods for your child, being your own brother and born of the same stock: also, for honour, he has that third share which he received when division was made at the first, and is appointed lord of those among whom he dwells."[6]

Helios's argument does not convince Demeter to accept Hades as Persephone's mate. His words only serve to fuel her rage. The poet tells us that after the sun god speaks to the goddess "grief yet more terrible and savage came into the heart of Demeter, and thereafter she was so angered with the dark-clouded Son of Cronos that she avoided the gathering of the gods and high Olympus."[7] Could Demeter's rage at Zeus be explained in part by her refusal to share authority over Persephone with him? Although Hades' abduction of her daughter is surely the prime cause of Demeter's anger and depression, the possessive quality of the goddess's love for Persephone ought not to be overlooked, given the jealousy she displays over Metanira's involvement with her son.

After her authority over Demophoon is questioned, Demeter curses the Eleusinians with a dire prophecy: "As the years move round and when he is in his prime, the sons of the Eleusinians shall ever wage war and dread strife with one another continually."[8] She then demands that they pay tribute to her by building a large temple in which they will perform rites in her honor. In this way, she says, the Eleusinians will "win the favour of my heart."[9] When she departs, she leaves the women of Celeus's household quaking with fear throughout the night.

The Eleusinians waste no time in trying to appease the goddess's wrath. At Celeus's command they begin to work on a temple and altar at once. But Demeter is unmoved by their efforts.

In her grief and anger, she causes famine to spread over the earth and threatens the whole human race with starvation. When this threat of starvation is considered alongside the goddess's fury at the Eleusinians and her suspicious treatment of Demophoon, Demeter's capacity for violence becomes apparent.

Our desire for loving goddesses and loving mothers ought not to bias our reading of the hymn so that Demeter's hostility to children other than her daughter is invisible to us. Perhaps the myth splits the image of the child into the one whom the mother cherishes, Persephone, and the ones whom she menaces, Demophoon, the Eleusinians, and all other mortal beings.

Once we see Demeter in a less idealized manner, we can notice something interesting about Hades. In the hymn it is he who feeds Persephone. He replaces the earth mother as the parent who feeds and by doing so wins the right to have Persephone with him for a third of the year. In order to see Hades as a parent, it is necessary to treat Hades and Zeus as a combined image of father and lover. I feel that such a reading is justified, since we know that Zeus is both brother to Hades and father to Persephone and that he plays a major role in the abduction of his daughter.

Remember, the hymn opens with a scene of Persephone at play "apart from Demeter."[10] The myth thus places estrangement from the mother in a causal relation to the attraction to the father as a source of nourishment. Of course, the attraction is also a seduction; the food, consisting of that famous pomegranate seed, is associated with semen. Nevertheless, the fantasy of receiving food from the father is present amid the imagery of rape: "He secretly put in my mouth sweet food, a pomegranate seed," Persephone says, "and forced me to taste against my will."[11]

I see Persephone's attraction to Hades symbolized in the hymn by her desire to pluck "a marvellous, radiant flower" that Zeus causes to grow as "a snare for the bloomlike girl."[12] The exaggerated, overblown terms used to describe this flower can be read as reminiscent of the romantic fantasies that girls often have about their fathers: "It was a thing of awe whether for deathless gods or mortal men to see: from its root grew a hundred blooms and it smelled most sweetly, so that all wide heaven above and the whole earth and the sea's salt swell laughed for joy. And the girl was amazed and reached out with both hands to take the lovely toy."[13]

Perhaps one reason Persephone turns to Hades is that she fears her mother might be an unreliable provider of food. (Demeter does prove herself capable of letting mortal children go hungry.) Melanie Klein believes that at the time of weaning, a child often turns away from the mother in frustration and sees the father as the preferable parent. She thinks that the child then imagines the father's penis as a more dependable source of oral satisfaction than the mother's breast. "In a number of children's analyses," writes Klein, "I discovered that the little girl's choice of the father as love-object ensued on weaning. This deprivation . . . loosens the bond to the mother and brings into operation the heterosexual attraction, reinforced by the father's caresses, which are now construed as a seduction. As a love-object the father, too, subserves in the first instance the purpose of oral gratification."[14]

In such cases Klein believes that the child soon becomes disappointed with the father's imperfect capacity to nurture and looks again to the mother. But once the initial estrangement from the mother occurs, childhood may be lived in alternate phases of preferring each parent in turn. This part of Kleinian psychoanalytic theory can, perhaps, shed some light on why Persephone must shuttle between Demeter and Hades after she swallows the seed.

The Homeric "Hymn to Demeter" may well illustrate the vacillation between the different kinds of love and fear that a daughter can have for both parents. The mother could be feared and hated when she refuses to give food. Winter (when Demeter and Persephone are separated and mortal children worry about having enough to eat) might then be imagined as a punishing mother's angry absence. Likewise, the father could be feared and hated for his seductiveness. A desire to be fed by him might then be felt as synonymous with wanting sex with him and incurring the mother's wrath.

The wish to maintain unambivalent feelings toward one parent might be another reason why interpreters have tended to overlook Demeter's imperfections and disregard the feeding Hades does. However, if the hymn is read closely, I believe that maternal rage emerges as a theme that is just as important as maternal love, and wishes and fears about paternal affection become visible.

NOTES

1. Philip E. Slater, *The Glory of Her* (Boston, Beacon Press, 1968), 29.

2. "To Demeter," lines 230–37, in *Hesiod: The Homeric Hymns and Homerica*, translated by Hugh G. Evelyn-White (Cambridge: Harvard University Press, 1970), 305–7.

3. Ibid., 307, line 239.

4. Ibid., lines 248–49.

5. Ibid., lines 260–61.

6. Ibid., 295, lines 82–87.

7. Ibid., lines 90–93.

8. Ibid., 309, lines 265–67.

9. Ibid., line 274.

10. Ibid., 289, line 5.

11. Ibid., 319, lines 411–13.

12. Ibid., 289, lines 9–11.

13. Ibid., lines 10–16.

14. Melanie Klein, "The Psychological Principles of Early Analysis," in *Love, Guilt, and Reparation and Other Works 1921–1945* (New York: Delacorte Press, 1975), 129n.

Hades Speaks

JOHN DAUGHTERS

T HAT WOMAN has been spreading her own version of the
story for long enough. Everyone on Olympus knew what was
going on, and I just figured that I was better off staying above it,
so to speak. Times have changed. The gods aren't honored like in
the old days, and her version has been accepted by the masses for
lack of the truth. This is the real story.

I'd been watching her for some time. It's not easy finding a wife
when you're a god. Sure, you can get all the mortals you want, but
you always have to replace them. They don't last. I didn't have
time for it. I'm a busy man, and I wanted something for eternity.
It had to be a goddess.

I talked to my brother about it, what did he think and all. Zeus
was all for it. Of course, he's for almost anything when it comes to
women. His concern wasn't about the girl, but on the other hand,
it never is. His first reaction was "watch out for her mother." He
should know, it was their affair that produced the girl in the first
place.

His second bit of advice was to run off with the girl and let the
mother know later. That's why I had been watching. That woman
NEVER let her out of her sight! Talk about super-mom! "Watch
out for this, dear, watch out for that, be nice, and oh, you're such
a good little girl!" It was disgusting! She was never going to let

her grow up! I could see her in a few thousand years, still being a good girl and taking care of mommy. She deserved better.

I was a little worried about her weight, too. Too thin. A woman needs to look like a woman, not a child. That's her mother's thing. Keep her thin and girlish so she doesn't catch anyone's eye. I saw right through it.

I sensed there was going to be trouble, but I was fascinated! She was so bright, she glowed as if filled with light. She sparkled when she smiled and danced like the wind in the meadow. I felt good just watching her. So refreshing! So different from my work world.

I've got a lot of responsibility and it keeps getting bigger, although I did reduce some of the paperwork when I figured out what to do with the complaints. I give them to Hephaestus to burn in his forge! This *isn't* a democracy. I've got souls to reward, souls to punish, some to keep forever, and some to send back to the upper world. Recycling isn't something new, you know. The toughest part is keeping everyone in their place. If all those souls got loose there would be Hell to pay!

I manage to keep things under control pretty well, thank you. And speaking of thank yous, I don't get very many. This line of work isn't all sweetness and light, if you know what I mean. I stay busy and keep a low profile. That's what my name means, the unseen one.

Anyway, it's a demanding job and I needed some joy in my life. And joy she has! She laughed, danced, and wove flowers in her hair. That's where I got the idea to get her away from her mother. Just pop up a beautiful narcissus at the far end of the meadow when her mother wasn't looking and she'd go for it. Simple, subtle, and effective. I liked it.

She went for it. It was almost too easy. It's amazing, how far you can get with flowers.

We had some problems at first. Everyone does. She was afraid her mother would miss her and "I really ought to be going" and "What are you doing?" and all that. She got over it. In fact, she sort of liked the idea of being carried away. It removes all the guilt, I suppose. She likes being a queen, too. There is a part of her that really gets into the power of it all. She took to it like a mare in heat. Things settled down and I thought we had it made. Wrong. Let me read from my journal.

"Hermes stopped in today." I didn't even know he was in town. That kid is fast! "He brought bad news. That woman is creating an uproar up above. She went to Zeus and complained that her daughter had been abducted." Abducted? She's never heard of marriage? I think she's been in a snit ever since Zeus left her for another woman. Zeus was cool. He told her he didn't know anything about it and she should forget it. She didn't buy it. She had asked Helios, the sun god, what he had seen and he said he had seen me capture Persephone and she put the pressure on Zeus. "After all, she's your daughter too." Wrong approach. Guilt doesn't work with Zeus. He's not into it. You don't get where he is by second-guessing yourself. He told her she was lucky. Not every girl does so well. What was she doing, saving her for a doctor or something? He did his best, but it didn't work. She got ugly, started moping around and refused to do her job. Nothing was growing and people were getting worried and complaints were pouring in from all over. It was tempting to tell him how I handle complaints, but I thought better of it.

Hermes said perhaps I ought to send her back. Persephone set him straight on that one! He then suggested a little visit, just to assure her mother she was all right. She really lit up. Her mother may be a little touched, but she loves her. She is loving, tolerant, and forgiving. That's what makes her so special.

She wanted me to go with her to visit her mother, but I put my foot down. I could see it and I didn't like it. Her mother would fuss over her and then say something like "Your friend can sleep in the guest room as long as he disappears when I have the girls over." Forget it! I told her to go until her mother was strong enough to go back to work but count me out! I've got plenty to do around here. You don't catch me laying down on the job!

I enjoyed Hermes. He appreciated the subtlety of the flower to get Persephone. He said a "lot of people would have used jewels or gold. Overkill. You got the most return from the least investment." Of course, I agreed. I didn't become the wealthiest god by giving it away. He's clever. I could use someone like him around here. Then I could take a real vacation. I was going to bring it up over dinner, but he was gone. Too bad. That kid could really go places if he would ever settle down.

The visit home went as expected. A *big* fuss when she got there. "Oh, you poor baby! Are you all right? You aren't hurt, are you? Why didn't you scream?" I liked that one. She screamed all right. Enough to wake the dead, if you know what I mean. Her mother bored in. "What did he do to you?" Persephone lied and said "He forced me!" I can tell you *that* produced hysteria. "What did he force you to do?" "Eat, mother, he forced me to eat." That wasn't totally untrue. I have been concerned about her weight and did encourage her to eat a little more. "What did he force you to eat?" The grilling was getting intense and Persephone had a stroke of genius. "Pomegranate seeds! I ate some pomegranate seeds!" "After all," she told me later, "I could have said 'forbidden fruit,' but there are some things you just don't tell your mother." Especially, I thought, when your mother is a manic-depressive in a hysterical phase! But I didn't say anything. She loves her mother and I wanted to stay out of it.

I did get involved once. Her mother had gotten a job taking care of a baby that had taken her fancy. That was OK by me; fussing over a baby is what she does best, and she left us alone. The thing was, she got this idea to make him immortal by putting him in the fireplace. First of all, there are easier ways, and second, what's the use of being immortal if you are going to spend eternity being a mama's boy! *Somebody* had to wake the parents up! Well, there was a scene, the parents paid her off and sent her packing. To hear her tell it, they were awed by the presence of a goddess and gave her offerings in atonement. Severance pay and a chariot out of town, if you ask me.

It's interesting how she got the job. She concocted some cock and bull story about how she was an escapee from some pirates who had abducted her from Crete. There's that word again. Wishful thinking as far as I'm concerned. This isn't the first time she has said something like this. She once said that Poseidon had desired her and she changed into a mare to get away but he changed into a stallion and raped her. I can imagine what triggered that little fantasy! Poseidon's my brother and I checked it out. He denied it . . . but he was certainly intrigued with the idea. My brothers are a little kinky, that way.

Do you know what my fantasy is? Just once, I wish that woman would give me a little credit for being a good provider and a loyal loving husband. Now there's a real fantasy!

Anyway, her mother went back to work and the crops flourished. Everyone was thanking Zeus and he was lapping it up. Zeus thanked me in private. I told him to thank Persephone, she's the one who agreed to stick it out until the crops were in, but Zeus got all the glory. He acknowledged Hermes for bringing her back, but he only did it to build a little loyalty in the family and to look modest to the masses. I think Hermes had a hand in that. That kid has a gift for public relations. I really wish he had stayed for dinner. We could use some good PR around here.

We finally got her mother out of our hair. We set her up in a little temple by the mountain in Eleusis. It was a mystery to everyone what she did there, but she had a few fellow man-haters as followers and she wasn't causing us any trouble. I really didn't know if they were all man-haters, but I do know you had to sacrifice a pig to join. The place was pretty, but no god I know ever made a guest appearance there!

In spite of everything, she has never liked me. One of her rituals was to "conquer the fear of death." Sure. Even the gods are nervous around me, and mortals are terrified. It's not that I'm a bad person, it's just that I like to keep people in the dark, so to speak. A little fear and trepidation makes this place a lot easier to manage.

I talked to Hephaestus one day. He wondered in a casual sort of way if I was worried about Persephone being gone so long. Ha! With that woman as a chaperone no one would even get close! I sure understand his concern, though. He can't leave work without his wife stepping out. It's hard to love someone who doesn't return it. Actually, I don't think that Aphrodite doesn't love him, it's just that she loves all men.

Do I love Persephone? Oh yes! I love her vitality, the flowers in her hair, her joy and the light she brings to my life. I love her loyalty, her devotion, and her ability to care. I *need* her! Does Persephone love me? Aaaaaaah . . . beyond a shadow of a doubt! I understand why her mother doesn't like sharing her with anyone. She loves so intensely, so openly, so completely. And she needs me too. She needs my power, my dark side, my earthiness. With me, she can be all that she isn't up above.

We need each other. It's a perfect match.

CONCERN FOR THE EARTH

A S I REFLECT on the many re-visionings of this myth with which I am familiar, I find myself especially challenged by Helen Luke's reading, which emphasizes the importance for women of fully experiencing their emancipation from the role of daughter—because it helped me see that in my insistent disavowal of Demeter's perspective I had been caught in an identification with Persephone's. I began to see that as a sixty-year-old crone it might be well past time for me to move beyond the perspectives of either Demeter or Persephone and see the myth instead from the perspectives of Gaia and Rhea, time to take seriously again the often discredited sense in which this myth is about fertility, about the renewal of the earth. For, although we may never know exactly what the mysteries revealed that served to free those who participated from their fear of death, we do know that it was integrally connected to their apprehending an analogy between the soul's journey to the underworld and the display of a ripened ear of corn.

Unlike Demeter, Gaia is not the personal mother nor the goddess of cultivated grain but rather goddess of the earth, of all that grows, goddess of generativity, of ever-renewing and changing life. In the myth she comes to Hades' aid, grows the narcissus whose plucking opens the path to the underworld; she sees what happens as part of the necessary order of things. Rhea, the mother of Demeter but also of both Hades and Zeus, appears after Persephone's return and persuades Demeter that it is time to let go of her anger at Zeus and bring an end to the barrenness that has made this the most terrible year on earth. And at the end Demeter does seem to forgive—and straightway the fat furrows of the soil are heavy with corn, and dread Hades reappears as wealth-giving Ploutos.

A postpatriarchal imagining of the myth onward involves, as I have already suggested, moving to take on earth's perspective, Gaia's perspective, moving beyond our identification with male or female perspectives. Let me be clear. I am not saying that if only we were able to do this, the continuance of life would be assured, the renewal of earth established—but unless we do this, the future looks bleak indeed.

Gloria Orenstein's reading of the myth from an "ecofeminist" perspective, from the perspective of a woman deeply committed to the conviction that feminism *means* concern for the earth and all that lives upon it, finds the myth as recounted to us in the Homeric hymn to be permeated with the patriarchal attitudes toward women and the earth that have helped shape our presently bleak situation. Her critical rereading of the myth issues in a passionately prophetic call to participate in the creation of new myths that might restore power to women and fertility to the earth. It is an upsetting piece; many of us may disagree with some of her points while applauding her overall thesis. Indeed, I was urged to edit it, to make it more palatable, more easily accepted. I choose to include it as it was written precisely to indicate the wide range of interpretations to which the myth may give rise, to suggest how not all feminisms are easily reconciled with one another. If this interpretation of the myth disturbs, that is, after all, one of the functions of myth—to challenge as well as undergird accepted perspectives.

An Ecofeminist Perspective on the Demeter-Persephone Myth

Gloria Feman Orenstein

WHEN I LOOK at the Demeter-Persephone myth, I cannot fail to note the fact that Persephone was attracted by a beautiful narcissus as part of the snare that Zeus had connived in order that she be abducted and married off to Hades (the king of the underworld, often known as hell), against both her will and that of her mother. I have also read that "the narcissus is a member of the amaryllis family and is named from the Greek *narke*, 'a drugged stupor.' The bulb is very poisonous."[1] Thus, I see that Persephone was drugged/poisoned, abducted (bride rape), sacrificed to the god of the underworld, and raped (of course, since this all took place contrary to her will). I also see that the plot to abduct her was hatched by a sky father-god, Zeus, in collaboration with the ruler of the underworld, Hades. Persephone's amnesias were induced by a drug, and it was the drugged state that facilitated carrying out the violence, the violation, and ultimately the disempowerment of two goddesses, Demeter and Persephone.

I have also been told that this myth is about an agricultural fertility cycle, and I have read that "for nine days and nights, Demeter roamed all of Greece seeking her daughter or news of her whereabouts. . . . In all Demeter wandered for a whole year, during which time she turned her back on the Olympians and neglected her duties as Earth Mother; the land turned barren, animals and human beings alike lost interest in reproduction, and slowly the earth was dying."[2]

At this point I would like us to imagine that we are living in a world in which we are told the Demeter-Persephone myth in order to explain both the death of nature and the rape of women. What do I see? First of all I notice that the male god of the dead deceived Persephone, disguising himself as an image of fertility, a narcissus, but one that was spectacular, more wondrous than regular flowers produced by the great Earth Mother herself (like modern reproductive and fertility technology)—but one that was also *poisonous*. Then I submit this observation to a commonsense interpretation of what is happening to the planet today. With the advent of the new reproductive technologies, the "technodocs" of the scientific establishment are disguising the death of nature as a new technology for fertility. Women who find themselves infertile must often submit to in vitro fertilization or to any number of other new "fertility technologies" created by men. While very attractive, like the narcissus, and purporting to create life in the absence of fertility, they also offer the narcotic of forgetting the very reason for the increase in infertility both in women and on the planet, in general. The cause of this increased infertility is that the earth is being poisoned as a result of the same scientific technologies that are now being used to invent an artificial fertility. Yet these are the kinds of technologies that purport to heal the death of nature that they, themselves, have induced.

Attributing the decrease in the fertility of the earth to the sorrow and anger of Demeter lamenting the drugging, abduction, and rape of her daughter by the Lord of the Underworld, as well as to her neglect of her duties as Goddess of Fertility, is, to my mind, another instance of "making the victim guilty." If Demeter and Persephone are, indeed, actually one, mother and daughter, mature fruit and seed, then Demeter's seed, her own fertility, (Persephone) has been stolen, and the death of nature has been caused *not* by Demeter's denying the earth her powers of fertility but rather because her seed has been purloined by the patriarchs, and all memory of the Mother Age has been erased via narcosis. The myth attempts to make us believe that the cause of the death of nature was Demeter's neglect of her duties, when actually the cause of the death of nature was the violation of Demeter's fertility, the stealing of her seed, and the male plot to divest her of her power by sacrificing the fruit of her womb to the Lord of the Underworld. As we see in this myth, patriarchal attempts at matricide and goddess murder result in transforming the fertile earth into a wasteland.

Indeed, the abduction of Persephone is similar to a vampiristic withdrawal of blood or life force from the Goddess of Agriculture by the spirits of hell.

Persephone's disappearance into the underworld as the wife of Hades is not, to my mind, symbolic either of a winter season or of any phase in a fertility cycle in which the seed thrives underground. This I construe as another mind binding for women. Were we to apply this myth to our current ecocrisis, we might be led to believe that we are merely living through a dark night of winter, one phase of a larger cosmic or historical fertility cycle, and that this phase has come to be known as the patriarchal period, a winter cycle in which women and nature were simultaneously exploited and raped, a dark cycle in which male gods were considered to be superior to female goddesses, male humans to female humans, and humans were posited as superior to nature. But this is no fertility cycle we are living through. This *is* the death of nature! Riane Eisler, in *The Chalice and the Blade*,[3] has argued convincingly that when we see the patriarchal period of history within the larger context of some preceding thousands of millennia of goddess-centered civilizations, we realize that this is merely a temporary detour in history, one that can be changed by reclaiming a partnership model—nonhierarchical, nondominator, and nondualist, inspired by the goddess civilizations dating as far back as the Upper Paleolithic.

One could easily have been convinced by this reasoning, as I was, but the caveat is that we have seriously failed to make important distinctions. If you dilute a small amount of poison in a larger solution of pure liquid, you might not see its danger quite as clearly. Nevertheless, if it is a lethal substance, even if diluted, it can still kill. The death of nature that has taken place under the aegis of patriarchal civilization—its weapons of war, its technologies of death, and so on—seems to be irreversible. The mythic question for our era is: once you have irreparably damaged the seed (Persephone), can you restore nature (healthy agriculture/ Demeter)?

The representation of Demeter as a goddess who would choose to let nature die as her response to the rape of her daughter appears to me to be more slanderous than empowering of women, as well as an example of the inversion of agency. The myth attributes the actions causing the death of nature to Demeter rather than to its true cause, the plot hatched and carried out by Zeus and Hades.

The myth is a "myth" precisely because it denies the truth of the interconnected web of life. It does this by attributing a death-dealing agency to Demeter, when it was actually the abduction of Persephone by Hades that deprived Demeter of her *creative* agency. For her agency was one that creates fertility, and this is precisely what was taken from her when her seed was stolen.

I have also read, regarding the conclusion of the myth, that Demeter's "daughter, tricked by Hades into eating a seed of the red juicy pomegranate, must spend one-third of the year underground with him and the remaining two-thirds above with her mother." We learn that this "returns to the structural analogy between the cycle of the seasonal grain and the cycle of human life."4

Once more I submit this to a test of common sense. Why would the red pomegranate, the symbol of life, of the womb, and of fertility ("pomegranates were eaten by souls in the underworld to bring about rebirth"5) be the cause of Persephone's guaranteed continual return to Hades?

I have also read that at the Thesmophoria, the mysteries at

Eleusis held in honor of Demeter and Persephone, "certain women who have purified themselves for three days and who bear the name of "Drawers Up" bring up the rotten portions of the swine that have been cast into the megara. And they descend into the inner sanctuaries and having brought up [the remains] they place them on the altars, and they hold that whoever takes of the remains and mixes it with his seed will have a good crop. And they say that in and about the chasms are snakes that consume the most part of what is thrown in."[6] Each year women who were sexually abstinent sacrificed pigs into deep chasms in the earth that were filled with snakes. These chasms were called megara. The snakes would eat the pigs, and the following year the women would descend into the earth and remove the uneaten remains of the pigs sacrificed the previous year. They would then place these remains upon altars, as described above, and offer them up, as well as mix them with their seed to ensure an abundant crop.

Once more I ask myself what it means to offer up on an alter the wastes and decayed remains of a sacrifice? Aren't offerings usually the best of what one possesses—not the garbage? How can the mixing of these remains with one's seed produce a good crop? Once again we have an altering of the fertile seed by mixing it with putrefaction from the underworld. What deities would accept such an offering? This act also corresponds mythically to Persephone's eating of the pomegranate—feeding death to a deity of the upper world in the guise of offering that deity a symbol of fertility. We are led to believe that something poisonous, something representing death, decay, and the underworld (in this case the decayed remains of the pigs), is really a sign of fertility. Yet, on the contrary, this mixing of the seed with the sacrificial remains probably ensures that death and decay will enter into the agricultural cycle, and rather than producing a good crop will actually contribute to bringing about the death of nature as well as the return of all Persephones to the land of the dead. And since the myth came into existence after the rites, I see the pomegranate, like the narcissus, as a disguise in which death masquerades as life. Here death appears as a pomegranate, the fruit of the womb of rebirth. Actually, the pomegranate was from Hades, and eating its seeds caused Persephone to return to the underworld for one-third of every year. So she was tricked into eating what looked like a symbol of fertility but was, in actuality, a fruit of death. These offerings of fruits and flowers as disguises for poison and abduction to hell remind me of the poisoned apple in the fairy tale of Snow White.

The myth, as it comes down to us, actually offers us a poisoned apple for our own psychic consumption. Contemporary feminists have been lured or seduced into a reclamation of this myth, both because of the strong mother-daughter bond and because Demeter's anger seemed powerful, since the myth relates that she withheld all fertility from the earth as a result of her anger. But this individuation of Demeter creates a false separation, or a split, between Demeter and Persephone, who are really one—two aspects of the same thing—the principle of fertility. "In fact, the bond between mother and maiden is imagined so closely and so ideally that their union suggests, rather, a union of principles, that is, one figure in two guises. Is this, then, the one great goddess in her dual form as mother and maiden, the older and younger aspect of the one figure, mother of the living and the dead?"[7] When Persephone is abducted, Demeter is raped as well. When the seed is stolen, the earth begins to die. This myth inverts the agency of the cause of the death of nature, attributing the act to Demeter instead of to Zeus and Hades. It omits the male agency of death dealing twice. Feminists have naively bought into the pomegranate as a simple symbol of rebirth. Actually it is used as a lure, a disguise, and a deception that results in linking Persephone to Hades forever. Extending the symbolism to our contemporary crisis, young women are lured by the promise of fertility in the guise of the new reproductive technologies into forgetting that their own infertility was caused by the very ideology that produced the kinds of technologies that poison the earth and cause infertility in the first place. Thus, women who avail themselves of them are captured by the patriarchy, abused and exploited, and guaranteed a life in hell. These contemporary Persephones can, also, only be released from hell on a part-time basis, that is, if they let themselves be nourished by the poisoned fruits (pomegranate) of the patriarchy—if they do not rebel or revolt, but simply work part-time in institutions that, while appearing to be related to the powers of Demeter, are always ultimately linked to the powers of Hades.

In the story as it comes down to us, both Demeter and Persephone are disempowered. While it is moving that the mother of fertility mourns the loss of her daughter, I see that motif as a trick to ensnare modern Persephones (contemporary women), and lure us into a modern connivance with the spirits of the underworld and its ideology of violence coupled with its history of war. Contemporary women should not be seduced by the Demeter-Persephone mythologem into believing that this is one myth in which female deities regain their power. On the contrary, both mother and daughter (who are really two aspects of one fertility principle) are disempowered. Women are tricked into believing that symbols of fertility represent real fertility, when they have been used and abused by the patriarchal or (demonic) principle as disguises to seduce powerful women into death and disempowerment. I see the Demeter-Persephone myth as a myth of matricide, gynocide, and goddess murder, which, as Mary Daly has shown in *Gyn/Ecology,* can be found at the center of patriarchal ideology. This is the meaning of the false fruit of rebirth. Like a test-tube baby, Persephone, poisoned by the pomegranate, is merely a simulacrum of spring. She does not represent true fertility. She represents a kind of male motherhood, the rebirth of Hades via the deceit of the poisoned pomegranate.

The Demeter-Persephone myth teaches us that matricide, gynocide, and goddess murder produce a wasteland. It also alerts women to be suspicious of the lure of fertility when produced by patriarchal technologies and cut off from the natural, organic life cycles. The myth deploys many techniques of deception, ranging from disguising death as life to the inversion of agency whereby Demeter is made to seem responsible for the death of nature, and Zeus and Hades, who conspired and hatched the plot of the lure and rape of Persephone, ultimately appear as reasonable men with whom one can negotiate Persephone's return.

Ecofeminism sees the interconnectedness between the death of nature and the rape of women. The Demeter-Persephone myth shows us precisely how the fates of women and nature are entwined within patriarchal ideology and praxis and, finally, leads us to taking mythic stories more seriously. What constitutes the myth of the myth is not so much the fact that the protagonists are deities—as it is the fact that the actions and their consequences may be real, but we are deluded into thinking they are not, because we live in a civilization whose technologies have induced precisely those amnesias that prevent us from believing that a goddess civilization once existed in which women were powerful and in charge of agriculture, that humans are a part of nature, not above or outside of nature, and that beings in a spirit world might not only interact with beings on earth but also be damaged by the ways in which humans conduct our affairs on earth. And for those who prefer to think in more scientific terms, the entire cosmos—all planets, solar systems, and so on—will surely be affected by the extinction of planet Earth. For me, the value of the ancient myths is that they correctly contextualize the dramas they narrate. They situate the affairs of humans and earthly concerns within the parameters of the universe and its mysteries—life and death.

A source of hope for us today is that ecofeminist artists and writers have begun to create new cosmic scenarios in which the earth can be saved and women can be restored to their original powers. When these stories are disseminated (seeded), they can bear fruits which may restore fertility to women and nature again. This is our creative offering to the unknown powers/deities/mysteries—our plea/prayer for rebirth and regeneration. It is our task to begin to remove the lethal elements from all the fruits of our offerings. If we continue to produce and offer up poison, can we ever hope to regain favor with the deity(ies)/god(s)/goddess(es)— the larger will of the universe?

NOTES

1. Barbara G. Walker, *The Woman's Dictionary of Symbols and Sacred Objects* (New York: Harper and Row, 1988), 430.

2. Barbara Smith, "Greece: Section I: Cosmogony, Theogony, and Pantheon" in *The Feminist Companion to Mythology*, edited by Carolyne Larrington (London: Pandora Press, 1992), 69.

3. Riane Eisler, *The Chalice and the Blade: Our History, Our Future* (San Francisco: Harper and Row, 1987).

4. Anne Baring and Jules Cashford, *The Myth of the Goddess: Evolution of an Image* (London: Viking, Arkana, 1991), 369.

5. Walker, *The Woman's Dictionary*, 806. Robert Graves, *The Greek Myths*, vol. 1 (Baltimore: Penguin Books, 1955), 91.

6. Quote from Jane Harrison, *Prolegomena to the Study of Greek Religion* in Baring and Cashford, 375.

7. Baring and Cashford, 368.

A NEW TELLING OF THE MYTH

W HAT FOLLOWS is a retelling of the myth of Demeter and Persephone by Laura Simms. It seemed self-evident to me that a book that celebrates the power of a myth to continue to engender new interpretations and new tellings, to inspire new mythmaking, should end as it began, with the *story,* for that, after all, is what myths most essentially are: stories.

Laura Simms is a storyteller; she tells her tales directly to her audience so as to make the event more ritual than entertainment. In her performance the words are not memorized but spring forth spontaneously in relationship to her listeners and her sense of what is happening in the room. She says, "I tell the stories so that they can open my heart and mind and that of my audience. So the myth is real in the telling and not limited to an idea or literal explanation." What you will read is an attempt to create a written version of what she does on stage. Because we have so little understanding of mythic perspective, she has sought to help us recover the feel of mythic process by interspersing material drawn from her own life and descriptions of the process of creating the performance piece into her retelling of the ancient myth. The written version does that also, but in a somewhat more abbreviated form.

Simms says that her passionate involvement with the story

began at a time when she felt paralyzed and knew that to heal herself she needed to experience her dark side, her rage, her bliss, and her body—and to understand the potency of the female mysteries in the present.

Her telling makes that potency visibly present. The myth of Demeter and Persephone and the rituals celebrated in their honor at Eleusis still speak, still have the power to help us bring our lives to speech.

Long Journey Home

A Retelling of the Myth of Demeter and Persephone

LAURA SIMS

SUPPLICATION

I honor the Great Mother
all pervasive space itself
the source of life.
Beyond death and birth,
masculine and feminine,
pain and pleasure,
dark and light.
To her, the essence of co-emergence
I offer this wedding song
of earth and sky, of body and mind,
of myth and self.
I offer it for the benefit of the earth.
May the ancient tale breathe new life into life.

INNER OFFERING

My mother died on August 3, 1969. I wrote a letter to a friend:
"Today my mother died. It is the saddest day of my life, and the

most peaceful. I have a feeling of joy. Death is the most certain experience I have known."

What I knew then at the moment of her death, I kept forgetting. It has been a long journey home.

Narrator: For years after my mother's death, I dreamed repeatedly that she was still alive, living somewhere near the ocean, still crippled. She refused to see me. Sometimes I would phone my father, who informed me that he was remarried and didn't want to find my mother. I would awake, depressed.

In the autumn of 1986 three things happened on the same day: My boyfriend called. His father had died a few days before and he was making a trip with his high-school sweetheart that we had planned together. An hour later I received a box with his father's ashes from her address, asking me in her handwriting to save the ashes on my shrine until he returned.

Second, in the late afternoon a girlfriend visited me. "You look like a hag," she said. "I think you're undergoing a descent. Don't be too depressed. Women who undergo this ritual are lucky. When it's over you'll be a changed person." "How long does it last?" I asked. "It could be years." She left me a list of books and hurried off. I was not encouraged.

The third event occurred later in the afternoon after my second bath in scalding-hot water, weeping. I came into the kitchen and felt myself thrown up against the wall. My feet were off the ground. I had a vision. The earth opened in my kitchen floor. I saw a violent war. Up out of the chaos, blood, and death rose a female deity. I said, out loud, "She is rising up." The floor closed. My feet were on the ground. I made a gesture as if in prayer. "She is returning. The masculine backlash will be awful. I will serve Her." I slept for five hours. That night I gave in to falling apart. I canceled work. I began rereading the myth of Demeter and Persephone. I bought a new journal. My best friends were story, nightmares, and hot baths.

I decided to work with the myth of Demeter and Persephone

in order to heal myself. Although I am a storyteller, it was not my intention to tell the story in performance but to explore the relationship between true life events and myth. I chose the tale because it was a female story of descent and ascent, and because it was the myth that informed the pre-Hellenic mysteries at Eleusis for two thousand years before Christianity.

I made an odd plan to create a one-woman show using only my true-life and other narratives. I used the myth secretly, as an unspoken structure underlying the piece. I quickly discovered that most people didn't know the story and that I was escaping from the truth and potency of the myth myself. I began again. This time I incorporated sections of the myth, woven in and out of stories. The more I worked in this way, the more I was guided, disturbed, and penetrated by the images in the myth. No other story that I have ever told has had the effect on me or my audiences, female and male.

As I worked I made important discoveries. A myth is like an ecosystem. It is more than the sum of its parts, and no single event stands without the relatedness of all other parts of the story. It exists on all levels at once, material, spiritual, ecological, personal, and physical. The myth, when spoken or enacted, has meaning and potency only in the present. It takes shape according to who is telling it, when it is being told, who is hearing it, and the environment or season in which the performance takes place. No matter how carefully it is studied, analyzed, and understood, the very nature of myth undoes any fixed meaning or analysis. The myth is alive—more close to truth than fact—and must be approached like wilderness, on its own terms, to be experienced fully.

The story is an initiation, holding within it obvious and secret instructions about becoming fully alive within one's body, on the earth, and in the universe. I had to surrender to the reality that what it may have meant in the past is somewhat unknowable to me, for I am living in the present. However, within the images, like seeds that have preserved their origins within the husk, inspiration can be summoned that stimulates authentic awakening and growth toward a greater sense of interdependence and bliss in this world.

Myth: I sing to Demeter, the holy mother, the goddess of the barley and the wheat, the thick-haired one, the joyful, all-nourishing mother. The sorrowing woman, the wrathful deity. I sing to her and her trim-ankled child, the daughter, the virgin, the silent one, the speechless one, the queen of the underworld, the dangerous one—Persephone—who was taken away against her will to the underworld by Hades. Hades, the faceless one, the all-inviting, the lord of the underworld, brother of her father Zeus. And to Hecate, the three-faced goddess who once ruled the dark realm, the old one now banished to the gates of the entrance to hell. To them I sing and to you.

It was always summer. Static. Ceaseless, like the humming of crickets in green grass. A moment between time. A respite between breaths. Demeter, dethroned by the god Zeus, raped, betrayed, is alone with her daughter in the Rarian fields, safe from his treachery. Her child, the trim-ankled maiden, golden-haired and virgin, gathers flowers with her lovely playmates, the big-breasted daughters of Oceanus.

In the distance, Zeus, back turned to the earth, rules from Olympus surrounded by his retinue of gods and goddesses.

Mortals make animal offerings to Zeus. They have long forgotten their obeisance to the goddess. Long forgotten their origins. The air is thick with the foul smell of burning flesh.

At the crossroads between death and life, Hecate sits with her dogs at the mouth of the cave to hell. She is an old hag, like a madwoman. She reigns over the cries of women giving birth and the torturous moans of dying. Like Demeter, she does not dwell on Olympus.

Beneath the earth, dry, angry, ignorant, and alone, Hades rules the underworld devoid of spirit. He is filled with frustration and longing. He seeks solace from Zeus. Zeus, his mind devoid of soul, offers his daughter in marriage, to be taken by force. Rape is the only communication he knows.

Because Zeus does not have the power to make things grow, he goes to Gaia and requests that she place a hundred-petaled narcissus on the earth to allure his daughter.

She, who knows the past, present, and future, sets our tale in motion when she plants a flower so lovely and irresistible that the young Persephone, drawn by the smell, the beauty, the form, and the color, cannot resist and plucks it from the earth.

Narrator: We can assume all of this from the beginning of the tale and what we know of the deities. The characteristics of genuine mythic deities are multifaceted and nondual. Within each one are contained their opposing energies. They are not to be seen literally. They are internal energies. They are separate, defined with singular characteristics only in narrative. Also, all are part of one great deity, the mother of bliss, Gaia. Demeter, Persephone, and Hera are one. Zeus, Poseidon, and Hades are one. Also, in order to tell this tale, I had to surrender up my personal likes and dislikes, conceptions, and information about history and look at what the story presented.

Myth: Persephone was drawn to the flower. She heard the SOUND OF HOOVES beneath the earth. She ignored the sound. The flower was too beautiful. She pulled it loose by its roots, and the earth broke open. Up out of the chasm rose a faceless man riding a chariot with four black horses. He grabbed her against her will and carried her around the earth. As long as she could see the sky and smell the ocean, she thought she would be safe, but as he dragged her down beneath the ground, it grew dark. She screamed for her mother. She knew her life would never be the same.

Narrator: When she was eleven years old in summer camp, her only wish was that when she returned home her mother would go with her to buy tampons at the pharmacy. On parent's day, her mother and father arrived late. Her mother looked messy and overweight. The girl was angry. When they left, her mother wrote a letter saying how awful her daughter was. The mother complained of a ceaseless headache. The girl tried to call to apologize. For four nights no one was home. Then she got her father on the phone. He said, "Mommy had such a bad headache she went into the hospital. She'll be home soon." Two days later she got a four-page letter. One word on each page, scrawled. It read, "I" "Love" "You," "Mommy."

The last day of summer camp the children were brought to a theater where they walked across a stage alone. Happy parents claimed their children. She went across the stage three times. She was the last child. At last she saw her father and her brother at the back of the theater. She saw them walk toward her through a thin tunnel of light. She knew her life would never be the same. "Where is Mommy?" she asked. "Mommy is in the hospital. She had a stroke" answers the father while turning to walk away. She follows and asks her brother, "What is a stroke?" He answers back to her, "She is crippled on the left side. She will never walk again." In the back of the car she watches as if in a dream as they enter the Jewish Disease Hospital garden. Disabled people. It is an underworld of the maimed. Then she saw a strange nurse pushing a wheelchair holding a white-haired woman, accompanied by her father and brother. It was her mother. Her auburn hair had turned white. Her mouth twisted to one side.

Filled with compassion, blazing with kindness, she went to embrace her mother. Her mother reached out, nearly falling from the chair. Nurse catches her. Her father says, "Idiot. You nearly killed her."

At home, at night, the two men began their incantations of complaint. Everything that was wrong was caused by her. She cried alone in her closet with her dog.

Months later, when her mother returned home, she blamed the daughter for the stroke. Astonished, the girl went on a diet. She was very proud of herself. In weeks she lost a lot of weight. All the girls in her class were jealous. By winter she had a seventeen-inch waist and wore a size 4.

A year before my mother's death, I was to be photographed by a Jamaican musician for an album cover one afternoon. That morning I dreamed that a bumble bee was flying toward me. I put out my hand. It was not evident if I was trying to touch the bee or avoid its sting. I was stung. I told my mother about the dream and the photo session on the telephone. Although she was crippled, she sensed I was in danger and drove to the city. She could not walk up five flights and sent a policeman. I told him my mother was crazy. She was so upset, he believed me. She drove home. During the session I was brutally raped.

I did not include this story in the piece. I never told anyone this story. I told the story of the stroke in third person because I was disconnected from that pain. My sanity became more and more silent. Underground, I told stories, myths, fairy tales, enchanted tales in an attempt to rise up. But I could not tell my own story.

Myth: The first was a young shepherd, Eubouleus, a mortal who had wandered into the fields. He saw the gaping hole in the earth and stared down into the underworld. He saw the back of a god on a chariot with four black horses carrying a yellow-haired goddess into the dark. He stood transfixed. His pigs joyously leapt into the chasm to their death. The earth closed. He wandered back to the realm of mortals and became a teller of tales. He told everyone what he had seen. Most did not believe him. But no one could stop listening to the story.

The second was Helios, the sun. He heard and saw. The third was Hecate. She was accustomed to the futile cries of the dead and did not come to the field. And Demeter. She heard the sound of her child's voice and raced like a bird whose wings were torn from its back . . . like a cow whose udders were ripped from her belly. But there was no sign of violence. The daughters of Oceanus said nothing. They had been told not to speak.

Wretched Demeter searched for her daughter. She did not sleep. She did not eat or wash for nine days and nine nights. Only then, on the tenth day, Hecate, taking pity on her, came to her, pine torches lit, and told her that she had heard Persephone's scream but had not seen who took her away.

Static summer has ended. The hideous crime of usurpation of the Mother Goddess is unbearable for the earth. It attempts to awaken the source of life in order to rebalance her energy. This rape brings up the lifeless dry psyche. In ignorance, it breaks through consciousness, pulling down the feminine. And Demeter, angered, betrayed into numbness, now awakens with rage.

Narrator: I resented Demeter for her rage and her violence. She reminded me of my mother and a girlfriend who was jealous of my work. In a vengeful argument with my boyfriend, I discovered Demeter in myself. My first difficult task was befriending, not suppressing, my own rage.

I dreamed of carrying my front door, which kept falling off the frame, up a mountain. There, I saw a door frame, which became a stone ruin of an arch, with blue sky surrounding it. I found a photo of this same place. A temple of Aphrodite, built over an ancient mountain cave dedicated to Demeter.

I remembered that when Aphrodite, the goddess of love, saw the earth open and Hades rise up from the underworld she first grew angry. His dry, faceless body, tormented by ignorance, awoke her compassion. She ordered her son Eros to shoot an arrow. Eros pierced Death to the heart with Love.

Myth: And Hecate, silenced, hears Demeter's cry, and drawn out by the sorrow of the mother offers her knowledge and comfort.

Together they visit Helios. A modern man, polishing his chariot like a Cadillac, unaware of the relationship of his actions to nature. He is unaware of the symbolic meaning of his acts. He saw, he knew, but he accuses Demeter of being hysterical. "You should succumb to Zeus's wish. He gave his brother a wife. Your daughter will be a queen in the underworld." He cannot face the rage of Demeter and leaves. "I have to go."

In a fury, Demeter takes off her crown, which bound her to the gods, and flings it to the earth.

"I am thrice betrayed. Zeus placed his throne on my mountain. He raped me in the fields. He took away my daughter. I will not serve the earth until I see the face of my child again."

With that, she put up her cloak, covering her thick hair, and manifested as an old woman, not as a deity. She walked across the earth, and the grass grew cold and withered. It was autumn and the earth was folding into itself.

"Who else but human beings know the truth of suffering and the deceit of the gods!" So she chose to live among them.

Demeter wept, and the moisture of her grief awakened her lover Poseidon, whom she never denied. Not in the mood for sex, she disguised herself as a mare and hid among a herd of horses. Aroused by this deception, Poseidon turned himself into a stallion and mounted her. From their union were born a winged horse and a girl named Despair.

Demeter sat a long time at the edge of the bridge that passes between both worlds. She arose as the deity she had been. A goddess with a horse's head, hair of snakes, holding a dolphin in one hand and a dove in the other.

Demeter entered the city of Eleusis and sat at the well outside the city. The daughters of Queen Metanira, who had just given birth in her old age to a baby boy (Demophoon, "gates of the city"), went to the well to draw water. They saw the old woman. She was noble and beautiful.

"What is an old woman doing alone outside the city?" they asked. Demeter told a story that to us, who have heard the truth of the myth, appears to be a lie. But it is the outer story that can be heard by those listening only with outer ears.

She was the servant of a queen in Crete and escaped on a pirate boat, a prisoner of those who raped and pillaged. They had stopped nearby to feast, and she ran away. She was seeking work as a nursemaid.

The girls tell Metanira, who thinks an old woman might be suitable to serve her son.

As she entered the palace, Demeter's cloak caught on the lintel of the door. For a moment, the room was suffused with radiance. Unaccustomed to the presence of a goddess, or any deity for that matter, the queen did not know what had happened. But instinctively she climbed from her throne and offered it to the old woman.

The goddess quickly adjusted the cloak and refused. She was mourning. She would rather sit on a three-legged stool. The queen was distressed by her depression. The girls offered her wine, but she drank only pennyroyal tea. They could not cheer her up.

Then Baubo was called. Baubo, the laughing one, the wife of the shepherd, a storyteller in her own right. She cheered up the old woman with a lascivious dance in which she bared her breasts and her vulva. And she told stories. The sort that women tell.

Narrator: Because I do not know the stories that Baubo told, I will tell you one of my own.

I continued to dream that my mother was alive. This time I made my way to the sea. There was an apartment complex around an oval courtyard. I heard she was living on the first floor. Still alone and cripped. A man said that she was not home. She was sitting outside the archway on stone steps. I started toward her. I felt overjoyed. I saw a friend, Diane Wolkstein, walking with an eleven-year-old girl. I offered the daughter a red hair band from my pocket and told them I was going to see my mother at last.

My joy increased as I walked through the stone arch. I saw my mother's back. Her thick auburn curls. The flowered dress she loved to wear in the summer. Then two people passed her, and she turned, yelling at them, cursing in a wild, gruff, hideous voice.

Her face was ugly. I began to scream, I felt inconsolable sorrow, and awoke, still screaming.

At the time of this dream—1989—I was undergoing radiation treatment for breast cancer. Three years into the story.

A Tibetan rinpoche and his wife and baby were staying at my house. I asked for help. I was miserable from the dream. He said, "It was only a dream." I was furious at his callous behavior.

A half hour later he asked for tea. I was fuming. Not only did I not want to serve a man, but I felt that he had been uncompassionate. I made the tea reluctantly. As I served it, he said, "There are meditation students who spend years on retreat doing the six yogas of Naropa in order to realize that all of life is a dream." My anger dissolved. I concentrated on pouring tea. My pain was real. My sorrow was visceral. We smiled at one another.

To come to the myth with an open mind and heart is to bend down on all fours and drink from a fresh source between rocks in the earth, and to stand proudly joining heaven and earth through the channels of one's body. The language of myth speaks from and to the psyche. Its magical processes set the seasons in motion unabashedly. It simultaneously awakens the inner mind, the chambers of the heart, the soul, the channels of the body, and inherent awareness and calls forth the regenerative powers of the earth.

It is a fertility ritual. It is a description of the growth, decay, and rebirth of grain. It is a story about a mother and daughter. It is my story and it is your story. It is a myth that has lain too long inert—the victim of literal patriarchal logic—but has not lost its vigor.

Myth: During the day the goddess nursed the baby with her finger. He grew like a young god. The king and the queen were pleased. But at night, when the mortals slept, she placed the baby in the fire. She would burn away his obstacles and ignorance and make him and all the children of Eleusis immortal.

Demeter does what Zeus cannot do. She alone can give birth

and death. She alone can reconnect mortals with the divinity within them so they will not have to live under the delusion that it is Zeus who nurtures them.

The earth continues to grow cold. Autumn reigns. The leaves turn colors. The seeds fall underground to be held in the earth.

I picture Persephone pouting, angry, dismayed, rejected, and on a hunger strike. Her only companion, Hades, loved her ignorantly. She refused to be comforted. He showed her his kingdom, and she felt pity for the soulless dead who dwelled without spirit. But she refused to be queen. Above her she saw the earth freeze, and sometimes she caught green seeds that fell into her skirt. Hades was confused by her refusal to accept his love.

On Olympus, Zeus, back turned, was ignorant of all that occurred. He did not see. Even his own brother's, his dark inner brother's, entreaties were not heard. To avoid looking within, he made wars, sold guns, profited by rape and murder. Something was wrong, but he did not pay attention or listen to his inner needs.

The most curious part of the tale is what takes place in the palace of Eleusis.

The goddess, now nursemaid, burned the boy in the fire. The mother, awakened by the cries of her baby, mistook the work of the goddess for the work of a madwoman, a demoness, a criminal, and shrieked. The goddess, disturbed, revealed herself. The queen, overwhelmed, prostrated before her, leaving the baby for her daughters. Angered, Demeter said, "You stupid mortals. I would have made your child and all the children of Eleusis immortal. Now your sons will grow up as gods, but they will kill each other on the battlefield."

The daughters could not comfort the baby, for he had been nursed by the goddess. The male baby is left longing for the goddess. The newborn self longs for the mother.

The goddess called for the king and promised to teach her mysteries so that those in his life could connect with the profound energy of the mother. She alone promised agriculture, the secret knowledge of the growth, decay, and rebirth of the seed in the body of the world. Her mysteries awaken the psychic seed in the heart of the body.

She says, "Build me a temple." She went within. It is the hope of the king that the fields will begin to flourish. With the goddess gone, the autumn has left the fields barren, the women barren. It is a fallow time. But growth does not occur. Demeter remains inside the temple and grieves.

This time on earth is a darkness and death. It is the deepest of winters. It seems as if the entire world will die.

Narrator: My mother had open-heart surgery. During the surgery, which she dreaded, she had multiple strokes. She remained in a coma for days. On the eighth day the nurses sent her metal brace and shoe back home with me. "It was taking up too much space." I tried to phone the doctor to stop young interns from talking about her condition at her bedside. They were excited because she was the first case in which blood clots were known to go from the heart to the brain. I understood that although my mother was unconscious she could hear. Their words were inhuman and unkind.

The doctor was always either taking a shower or playing golf. He complained about my calls to my father. I was disturbing him. I was angry. His high-tech approach to her heart was devoid of wisdom and magic.

On the tenth day I went into the intensive care unit in the morning. Up until that time we were only allowed in for five minutes at a time. I was determined to keep the young interns away. I found a tube going into her neck that had come out, and, frightened, I replaced it.

I spoke to her and apologized for all that had happened in my childhood. I knew that she also forgave me. I said, "Mom, can you hear me?" She mouthed my name. I became hopeful. Then I said, "If you can really hear me, lift your hand." She lifted her left hand slightly. I ran out to get my father to tell him that she was going to live. I knew we had to call the doctor and have a specialist work with her again. She had consciousness.

In the hall, the doctor angrily grabbed me and forbade me to reenter the intensive care unit. I was disturbing "his patient." He sent me home. My father was annoyed with my disobedience. He went home with me.

I went to my room. I spoke out loud to my mother. "Let me know if you are going to live or die." I repeated it over and over. I incanted this mantra to my mother. I sank into the place I knew when I was little, where I heard voices and saw visions. My room became white. I saw the door to the intensive care unit open, and standing there was my mother. She smiled, threw away her cane, and waved at me.

I knew she was dead. I went downstairs when the phone rang. It was the doctor. "Miss Simms. Your mother is dead." I turned. My father's face was contorted. I nodded "yes" and held him in my arms as if he were my child. He wept and then walked to his office to be alone.

Myth: Beneath the earth Persephone walked alone. She did not speak. She surveyed the gardens of the dead. In an inner garden she saw a pomegranate, split, open, its seeds glaring in the dim light. Hungrily, stealthily, she tasted four seeds.

An old gardener saw her.

On earth the king and queen protected the temple of the goddess. She was among them, but there was still winter.

Baubo returned to the old cavernous shrines in the mountains. She placed stone statues and made offerings. She made love to her husband. She honored the old mother goddess for fear that she would be forsaken and all of life would end.

Narrator: On my mother's birthday, September 3, 1991, twenty-three years after her death, I left Salt Lake City with my dear friend Terry. "Let's get lost in the desert," says my friend. Not much conversation on the drive down. I never want to close my eyes. The landscape keeps changing. Suddenly we drive into a canyon. Grass gives way to sand, and the Colorado Range begins. The enormity swells the limits of my mind.

Three hours later we park on the side of a road beside stone mountains overlooking a construction site. "Let's take a walk," she says. We go, my feet in fancy sandals. Red mountains emerge out of the desert. Monolithic walls loom above us. I can't help asking, "Where the hell are we?" We climb on soft rock. No path. I am wearing blue linen clothes. My eyes are in my feet.

She stops. A wall of stone blocks our path. I look up. My heartbeats turn to lightning. Tears blur my vision. My entire body begins to quake. I am home. My ancestors welcome me. The spirit world is speaking. There is no logic to this journey. I beg to get lost and not understand. My identity vanishes. If I had corn I would offer it, singing.

My first Anasazi signs on the raw stones. Petroglyphs. Horned creatures from the other world. Antelope. Owl. Spirals and footprints. Strange deities. Golden brown paint, unfathomable language. Still dancing, a thousand years later. Even the ones we can no longer see are dancing.

We fall onto the stone and embrace. Two women drawn here by the death of our mothers. We lie in each other's arms and cry. My veins are throbbing. My skin is loosening. "Turn me to wind and bless me," we sing.

I am begging to be turned inside out so I can hear the language of all things. Silence is prayer.

Here on the great stones I can feel the heartbeat of the Mother in my bones.

I have spent so long on this journey. My body has been the cauldron, my heart breaking again and again. I reach up and let my girlfriend pull me forward. She gives me back my natural mother, and I am reborn.

We strip naked in mud and fall laughing into cold water. We bleed into dry sand. We sleep for a long time in a cave. One minute is silence, the next wind. A fly's wings make music. Everything that ever was or will ever be is here formed into dry stone. "All this is made by wind and water," she says, my guide up. Her heart lights pine torches and leads me out of darkness. She is my Hecate.

We walk and see it all: the great mother stones, turrets, minarets, serpents, stages, buildings, great pyramids of Egypt, double-headed Coatlique. I know now that everything in our minds is made of wind and water. There is nothing but the constant becoming of form and emptiness, sound and silence, out of empty space. My skin breathes for the first time.

I have the desire to leap into canyons and be turned to yellow bone, drying in sunlight, become stone. I want to crumble to dust and touch the very insides of existence. If I vanished, it would not matter.

A long time ago, a Maori elder told me that I tell stories to call my ancestors to me. I will tell this story in order to honor the place of dreams where ancestors speak to us.

We drove back to town and downed "gut bomb" tacos and cold beer. Shopped for books and earrings, confused.

If this is being lost, then I have found my way. It is not necessary to remember who we are. "One can't take oneself too seriously," she says.

Myth: At last, Zeus realizes that without the mother there is no life on earth and there will be nothing for him to rule. He sends the goddess Iris, in her dyed rainbow dress, to offer gifts of wealth and a special place in Olympus if Demeter will give up her grieving. Of course, she refuses. He sends gods and goddesses with gifts. She refuses them all. She will let the earth die.

At last, startled by defeat, he sends Hermes, the bringer of dreams, the spirit in the intellect, to Hades to request that Persephone return.

Hecate opens the doors to the underworld herself. But Persephone has eaten the seeds of the pomegranate and cannot return. She will rise up and return. Hades is moved. He weeps with the knowledge that she, whom he has loved, without whom he cannot live, will return. He loves his noble queen. She has been more than his equal. In his realization, he becomes more than a faceless man.

Narrator: I concentrated on stories of my mother and myself, but the myth is internal. It is rebalancing the separated parts. Outwardly, I had to come to terms with the story of my mother. But internally, I had to free the mother and the child, as well as my relationship to my shadows and the earth, in order to function.

After further research I found that Persephone and Hades have a working marriage. Each independent, bearing new life together, each a ruler.

Myth: Hermes went to the underworld. Hecate lit up the path with pine torches. The way that had been dark, obscured, impenetrable was illumined. She led the chariot back up to earth. She and Hermes, together with Hades, now with face, rode beside Queen Persephone. She who had tasted of the seeds of the earth returned to the earth in winter.

As Persephone rose up to the earth she wept. For the earth was barren, and the souls of the dead lingered helplessly by the gates of Hades. She promised she would take them through to the other side so they could be reborn.

When Demeter saw her daughter she raced from the temple like a young doe. They embraced. They wept and their sorrow was quelled at last.

Demeter, knowing the treachery of Zeus, asked, "Did you eat anything in the underworld?" Persephone told her about the four seeds. And Demeter declared that her daughter would return for one-third of the year to the dark, and on earth there would be winter. She would rise up and bring spring.

Persephone told her mother the entire story from the moment that she was taken away beneath the earth until the moment that she returned.

When the story was ended, Demeter saw that her child had become a woman. Persephone saw that her mother had changed. Hecate appeared, and hand in hand they walked across the earth. Beneath their feet the earth grew warm, flowers sprouted and bloomed. The rain fell and a spring of immense beauty flourished in the world. Creatures that had been barren gave birth, eyes that had been dry grew moist and wept, and all things blossomed outrageously with joy.

Demeter and her daughter on their own volition rose up to Olympus but did not stay long. There they were honored. Poseidon and Demeter rejoiced. Persephone returned to the underworld and ruled side by side with Hades. She was served by Hecate, who guided her path with light. The king, Triptolemus, learned agriculture; and Demeter taught her mysteries, and the earth was enlivened.

Only Baubo was cautious. She continued to serve the ancient Mother in the caves, for should the goddess be wholly forgotten, the winter would prevail.

Narrator: Last dream. I was climbing up a tall ladder to my parents' house. I entered my father's dental office and saw old women in transparent cocoons on shelves. I went through the kitchen and outside to a place enclosed in glass, sunlight streaming into the room. At a table sat two beautiful women, one black woman wearing African clothes and adornments, the other pale-skinned with light hair, wearing colored robes. I sat between them. The door opened and my mother entered in her flowered dress, as she was when she was young, in the summer. I stood up and took hands with the two women and said, "Ladies, this is my mother."

Here the story ends.

It is said that those who are initiated by this myth know bliss in this life and do not fear death. And those who do not hear the story live as ghosts in this world. May the telling of this tale benefit all sentient beings and the earth.

ABOUT THE CONTRIBUTORS

PATRICIA BERRY, a Jungian analyst who practices in Boston, is the author of *Echo's Subtle Body*.

VERA BUSHE, a graduate student in psychology, is active in the Vancouver Jung Society.

CAROL P. CHRIST is a free-lance scholar and writer who lives in Greece; her books include *Diving Deep and Surfacing* and *The Laughter of Aphrodite*.

H.D. (1886–1961) was a poet and novelist whose writings, in addition to the *Collected Poems*, include *HERmione* and *Palimpsest*.

JOHN DAUGHTERS, a doctoral student at Pacifica Graduate Institute, is a hypnotherapist with a practice in Kailua, Hawaii.

NAOMI R. GOLDENBERG, author of *Changing of the Gods* and *Resurrecting the Body*, is professor of religious studies and coordinator of women's studies at the University of Ottawa.

MERIDEL LE SUEUR, poet, journalist, and writer of fiction for both adults and children, was born in 1900 and has pursued an active career as a socialist and feminist for most of her long life. A selection of her work appears in *Ripening*.

BRUCE LINCOLN, professor of anthropology at the University of Minnesota, is the author of *Emerging from the Chrysalis, Myth, Cosmos, and Society,* and *Discourse and the Construction of Society.*

HELEN LUKE, founder of the Apple Farm Community in Michigan, is the author of *Woman: Earth and Spirit* and *Old Age.*

RIVER MALCOLM, a Jungian-oriented therapist with a practice near San Diego, has published several chapbooks of poetry, including *No Goddess Dances to a Mortal Tune* and *The Woman Who.*

ERICH NEUMANN (1905–1960) was a Jungian analyst who practiced in Tel Aviv; his books include *Amor and Psyche, The Great Mother,* and *The Origins and History of Consciousness.*

GLORIA FEMAN ORENSTEIN, a professor in the program for the study of women and men in society at the University of Southern California, is author of *The Theater of the Marvelous* and *The ReFlowering of the Goddess.*

ANNIS PRATT, who taught English and women's studies at the University of Wisconsin for twenty years, is the author of *Archetypal Patterns in Women's Fiction* and *Dancing with Goddesses: Archetypes, Poetry, and Empowerment.*

HERTA ROSENBLATT was born in Germany in 1903 and came to this country in 1935; a poet who writes in both German and English, she has published more than three thousand poems.

LAURA SIMMS is a professional storyteller who lives in New York City.

CHARLENE SPRETNAK, who teaches women's spirituality at the California Institute of Integral Studies, is author of *The Lost Goddesses of Ancient Greece* and editor of *The Politics of Women's Spirituality.*

ALMA LUZ VILLANUEVA writes both poetry and short fiction; she has published two volumes of poetry, *Bloodroot* and *Life Span*.

POLLY YOUNG-EISENDRATH, a Jungian analyst with a practice in Philadelphia, is author of *Hags and Heroes, You're Not What I Expected: Learning to Love the Opposite Sex,* and coauthor with Florence Widdemann of *Female Authority: Empowerment and Women's Psychology.*

FURTHER READING

CLASSICAL TEXTS

Athanassakis, Apostolos N. *The Orphic Hymns*. Missoula, Mont.: Scholars Press, 1977.

Boer, Charles, trans. *The Homeric Hymns*. Chicago: Swallow Press, 1970.

Brown, Norman O. *Hesiod's Theogony*. Indianapolis and New York: The Bobbs-Merrill Company, 1953.

Evelyn-White, Hugh G., trans. *Hesiod, The Homeric Hymns, and Homerica*. The Loeb Classical Library. Cambridge, Mass.: Harvard University Press, 1974.

Frazer, James George, trans. *Ovid: Fasti*. The Loeb Classical Library. Cambridge, Mass.: Harvard University Press, 1976.

Grene, David, and Richmond Lattimore, eds. *The Complete Greek Tragedies*. Chicago: University of Chicago Press, 1959.

Hinds, Stephen. *The Metamorphosis of Persephone: Ovid and the Self-conscious Muse*. New York: Cambridge University Press, 1987.

Hopkinson, N., ed. *Callimachus: The Hymn to Demeter*. New York: Cambridge University Press, 1984.

Miller, Frank Justus, trans. *Ovid: The Metamorphoses*. The Loeb Classical Library. Cambridge, Mass.: Harvard University Press, 1984.

Simpson, Michael, trans. *Gods and Heroes of the Greeks: The* Library *of Apollodorus.* Amherst: University of Massachusetts Press, 1976.

COMMENTARY AND INTERPRETATION

Bachofen, J. J. *Myth, Religion, and Mother Right.* Princeton: Princeton University Press, 1973.

Bolen, Jean Shinoda. *Goddesses in Everywoman.* San Francisco, Harper and Row, 1984.

Burkert, Walter. *Greek Religion.* Cambridge, Mass.: Harvard University Press, 1985.

Carlson, Kathie. *In Her Image.* Boston: Shambhala Publications, 1989.

Carrington, Karin Lofthus. "The Alchemy of Women Loving Women," *Psychological Perspectives,* no. 23: 64–82.

Chesler, Phyllis. "Demeter Revisited—An Introduction," *Women and Madness.* New York: Avon, 1972.

Farnell, Lewis Richard. *The Cults of the Greek States.* Vol. 3. Chicago: Aegean Press, [1906] 1971.

Friedrichs, Paul. "The Fifth Queen: The Meaning of Demeter," *The Meaning of Aphrodite.* Chicago: University of Chicago Press, 1978.

Gadon, Elinor W. "Demeter's Mysteries," *The Once and Future Goddess.* San Francisco: Harper and Row, 1988.

Gaster, Theodor, ed. *The New Golden Bough: A New Abridgment of the Classic Work by Sir James George Frazer.* Garden City, N.J.: Doubleday, 1961.

Goldenberg, Naomi R. *Resurrecting the Body.* New York: Crossroad, 1993.

Guthrie, W. K. C. *The Greeks and Their Gods.* Beacon Press: Boston, 1981.

Hall, Nor. *The Moon and the Virgin.* New York: Harper and Row, 1980.

Harrison, Jane Ellen. *Prolegomena to the Study of Greek Religion.* Cambridge: Cambridge University Press, 1903.

Harrison, Jane Ellen. *Themis: A Study of the Social Origins of Greek Religion.* Gloucester, Mass.: Peter Smith, 1974.

Johnston, Jill. *Lesbian Nation: The Feminist Solution*. New York: Simon and Schuster, 1973.

Jung, Carl. "The Psychological Aspects of the Kore." *Essays on a Science of Mythology*, C. G. Jung and C. Kerenyi. Princeton: Princeton University Press, 1969.

Keller, Catherine. *From a Broken Web*. Boston: Beacon Press, 1986.

Keller, Mara Lynn. "The Eleusinian Mysteries of Demeter and Persephone." *Journal of Feminist Studies in Religion* Vol. 4, no. 1 (Spring 1988): 27–54.

Kerenyi, Carl. *Eleusis: Archetypal Image of Mother and Daughter.* New York: Pantheon, 1967.

Kerenyi, Carl. *The Gods of the Greeks*. London: Thames and Hudson, 1979.

Kerenyi, Carl. "Kore." *Essays on a Science of Mythology*, C. G. Jung and C. Kerenyi. Princeton: Princeton University Press, 1969.

Meador, Betty DeShong. "The Thesmophoria: A Women's Ritual." In *Uncursing the Dark*. Wilmette, Ill.: Chiron Publications, 1992.

Mylonas, George E. *Eleusis and the Eleusinian Mysteries*. Princeton: Princeton University Press, 1961.

Otto, Walter F. "The Meaning of the Eleusinian Mysteries." In *The Mysteries: Papers from the Eranos Yearbooks*, edited by Joseph Campbell. New York: Pantheon, 1955.

Pauli-Haddon, Genia. *Uniting Sex, Self, and Spirit*. Scotland, Conn.: Plus Publications, 1993.

Rich, Adrienne. *Of Woman Born*. New York: Norton, 1976.

Rohde, Erwin. "The Eleusinian Mysteries." In vol. 1 of *Psyche: The Cult of Souls and Belief in Immorality among the Greeks*. New York: Harper and Row, 1966.

Scully, Vincent. *The Earth, the Temple, and the Gods*. New Haven: Yale University Press, 1979.

Wasson, R. Gordon. *The Road to Eleusis*. New York: Harcourt, Brace, Jovanovich, 1978.

Winkler, John J. "The Laughter of the Oppressed." In *The Constraints of Desire*. New York: Routledge, 1990.

Woolger, Jennifer Barker, and Roger J. Woogler. *The Goddess Within*. New York: Fawcett Columbine, 1987.

Zuntz, Gunther. *Persephone*. Oxford: Oxford University Press, 1971.

FICTION AND POETRY

Donovan, Josephine. *After the Fall: The Demeter-Persephone Myth in Wharton, Cather, and Glasgow*. University Park, Penn.: Pennsylvania State University Press, 1989.

Joseph, Jenny. *Persephone*. Newcastle-Upon-Tyne, England: Bloodaxe Books, 1986.

Orlock, Carol. *The Goddess Letters*. New York: St. Martin's Press, 1987.

Ritsos, Yannis. "Persephone," *Grand Street*, 6, no. 4 (Summer 1987): 143–56.

Tarn, Nathaniel. *The Persephones*. Santa Barbara: Christopher's Books, 1974.

Wilner, Elinor. "Eleusis." In *Shekhinah*. Chicago: University of Chicago Press, 1984.

CREDITS

"The Homeric 'Hymn to Demeter' " is from David G. Rice and John E. Stambaugh, *Sources for the Study of Greek Religion,* Missoula, Mont.: Scholars Press, 1879, 171–83. Used with the permission of Scholars Press.

Ovid's account of the myth is from Mary Innes, trans., *The Metamorphoses of Ovid,* London: Penguin Classics, 1955, 125–33. Used with the permission of Penguin Books, Ltd.

"The Woman's Experience of Herself and the Eleusinian Mysteries" is excerpted from Erich Neumann, *The Great Mother,* Princeton, Princeton University Press, 1955, 305–24. Reprinted by permission of Princeton University Press.

"Demeter" by H.D. is taken from H.D., *Collected Poems 1912–1944,* New York: New Directions, 1983, 111–15, 179–80. Copyright 1982 by the estate of Hilda Doolittle. Reprinted by permission of New Directions Publishing Corp.

"Persephone" is a story included in Meridel Le Sueur, *Ripening,* Old Westbury, N.Y.: The Feminist Press, 1982, 76–84. Used with permission of the author and her daughter Rachel Tilsen.

"The Myth of Demeter and Persphone" is excerpted from Charlene Spretnak, *Lost Goddesses of Ancient Greece,* Boston: Beacon Press, 1992, 105–18. Used with permission of the author per her agent, Frances Goldin.

"The Dance of Mother Woman," "A Last Game of Childhood," and "Were You Weeping?" are from Herta Rosenblatt, *The Goddess Poems,* Burnsville, N.C.: Celo Press, Inward Light Reprints, 1982, 20, 25, 26. Used with the permission of the author.

"The Crux" by Alma Luz Villanueva appeared in Janine Canon, *She Rises Like the Sun,* Freedom, Calif.: The Crossing Press, 1989, 181–82. Used with the permission of the author.

"Learning from My Mother Dying" by Carol P. Christ is an original essay written for this volume. Used with the permission of the author.

"The Return to the Mother" is excerpted from Christine Downing, *Myths and Mysteries of Same Sex Love,* New York: Continuum, 1989, 201–4. Used with the permission of the author.

"Demeter, Persephone, and the Pedagogy of Archetypal Empowerment" by Annis Pratt is an original essay written for this volume. Used with the permission of the author.

"The Two Goddesses" is from River Malcolm, *No Goddess Dances to a Mortal Tune,* self-published, Del Mar, Calif., 1992, 3–8. Used with the permission of the author.

"The Rape of Persephone" is excerpted from Bruce Lincoln, *Emerging from the Chrysalis: Studies of Rituals of Women's Initiation,* Cambridge, Mass.: Harvard University Press, 1981, 72–90. Copyright 1981 by the President and Fellows of Harvard College; reprinted by permission of the publishers.

"Cycles of Becoming" is an unpublished typescript essay by Vera Bushe. Used with the permission of the author.

"Mother and Daughter Mysteries" is excerpted from Helen Luke, *Woman, Earth and Spirit: The Feminine in Symbol and Myth,* New York: Crossroad, 1981, 55–68. Used with the permission of Crossroad/Continuum.

"The Rape of Demeter/Persephone and Neurosis" by Patricia Berry is excerpted from *Spring 1985,* 186–97. Used with the permission of the author.

"Persephone in Hades" is excerpted from Christine Downing, *The Goddess: Mythological Images of the Feminine,* New York: Crossroad, 1981, 30–50. Used with the permission of the author.

"Demeter's Folly: Experiencing Loss in Middle Life" by Polly Young-Eisendrath is excerpted from *Psychological Perspectives* 15, no. 1 (Spring 1984): 39–63. Used with the permission of the C. G. Jung Institute of Los Angeles and the author.

"Hekate, Rhea, and Baubo: Perspectives on Menopause" is excerpted from Christine Downing, *Journey through Menopause,* New York: Crossroad, 1987, 34–50. Used with the permission of the author.

"Sightings of Maternal Rage and Paternal Love in the Homeric 'Hymn to Demeter' " by Naomi R. Goldenberg is an original essay written for this volume. Used with the permission of the author.

"Hades Speaks" is an unpublished typescript paper by John Daughters. Used with permission of the author.

"An Ecofeminist Perspective on the Demeter-Persephone Myth" by Gloria Feman Orenstein is an original essay written for this volume. Used with the permission of the author.

"Long Journey Home" by Laura Simms is based on a performance piece and was expressly prepared in this written form for this volume. Used with the permission of the author.